Framing Public Memory

Framing Public Memory

Edited by
KENDALL R. PHILLIPS

THE UNIVERSITY OF ALABAMA PRESS
Tuscaloosa

Typeface: Perpetua

∞

The paper on which this book is printed meets the minimum requirements of American
National Standard for Information Science–Permanence of Paper for Printed Library
Materials, ANSI Z39.48—1984.

Library of Congress Cataloging-in-Publication Data

Framing public memory / edited by Kendall R. Phillips.
p. cm. — (Rhetoric, culture, and social critique)
ISBN 0-8173-1389-3 (cloth : alk. paper)
1. Public history. 2. Memory—Social aspects. 3. History—Psychological aspects.
4. Historiography. 5. Public history—United States. 6. Public history—Germany.
7. History—Philosophy. I. Phillips, Kendall R. II. Series.
D16.163.F73 2004 901′.9—dc22

2003022013

Dedicated to two men who were great
scholars, teachers, and my friends:
Richard B. Gregg and Harold L. Lawson

Contents

Framing Public Memory

Introduction

Kendall R. Phillips

"Public memory" has become a familiar key term in the humanities and social sciences. The last twenty years have seen a rapid proliferation of the term's use in such disciplines as architecture, communication studies, English, history, philosophy, political science, religion, rhetoric, and sociology. The rapid growth in the transdisciplinary study of public memory can also be seen in the number of published case studies and the amount of material encompassed within this rubric, from monuments to television programs and museums to city streets.[1]

Some sense of public memory is evident in human civilization as far back as we can reckon.[2] Recognition of the importance of collective remembrance is clearly part of the pyramids of ancient Egypt, for instance, or the eulogies of ancient Greece. In part the systematic study of collective memories can be traced to the work of French sociologist Maurice Halbwachs in the 1920s. Halbwachs, following Durkheim's notion of collective conscience, contends that all acts of memory are inherently social—literally that to remember is to act as part of the collective. In turn our collectivity is deeply intertwined with our capacity for and enactment of remembrance. Halbwachs's insights, however, were largely underappreciated until the rapid development of public memory studies in the 1980s and 1990s.[3]

The present volume is an intervention into the broad and rapidly expanding transdisciplinary study of public memory. By bringing together scholars from various disciplines, *Framing Public Memory* seeks to promote a broader reflection on the current state of public memory studies and a consideration of some of the pressing questions to which future students of public memory might profitably attend. To this end, the collected essays sketch the frameworks of public memory, frameworks I will consider in more detail presently.

Although the current volume does not focus on the development of public memory studies, a brief review of this development may be useful. The relatively sudden rise in the study of public memory had numerous causes. A thorough analysis of the conditions leading to its growth is beyond the scope of this introduction and, indeed, unnecessary as the task has been taken up by others. It is, however, worth noting at least one of the most pervasive contexts within which this recent interest in public memory has emerged—the increasing mistrust of "official History."[4]

A distinction between memory and history is evident as far back as Halbwachs, who saw history and memory as opposing ways of recalling the past. History, with its apparent claims to accuracy and objectivity, is— or at least had been—viewed as implying a singular and authentic account of the past.[5] Memory, on the other hand, is conceived in terms of multiple, diverse, mutable, and competing accounts of past events. As claims to a singular authoritative "History" became increasingly (and rightly) untenable in the face of compelling critiques leveled by poststructural and multicultural critics, scholars turned to the notion of memory, or perhaps more accurately "memories," as a way of understanding the complex interrelationships among past, present, and future.

Memory, thus, is conceived as fluid and dynamic or, as Pierre Nora puts it, "Memory is life, borne out of living societies founded in its name. It remains in permanent evolution, open to the dialectic of remembering and forgetting, unconscious of its successive deformations, vulnerable to manipulation and appropriation, susceptible to being long dormant and periodically revived."[6] This sense of "living" memory is in stark contrast to a sense of a fixed, singular history, suggesting that societies are both constituted by their memories and, in their daily interactions, rituals, and exchanges, constitute these memories. As well, this sense of memory highlights the extent to which these constituted and constituting memories are open to contest, revision, and rejection. Thus, in a very real sense, to speak of memory in this way is to speak of a highly rhetorical process.

Indeed, the study of memory is largely one of the rhetoric of memories. The ways memories attain meaning, compel others to accept them, and are themselves contested, subverted, and supplanted by other memories are essentially rhetorical. As an art interested in the ways symbols are employed to induce cooperation, achieve understanding, contest understanding, and offer dissent, rhetoric is deeply steeped in a concern for public memories.[7] These memories that both constitute our sense of collectivity and are constituted by our togetherness are thus deeply implicated in our persuasive activities and in the underlying assumptions and experiences upon which we build meanings and reasons.

The reader interested in either rhetoric or public memory will, therefore, find in this volume a wealth of resources for thinking about the interrelation of these concepts. Although many of the contributors to this volume are not rhetoricians per se, there is a consistent concern for the ways that memories attain meaning and become public—two concerns central to the study of rhetoric. Of course, it would be inappropriate to dismiss the various disciplinary approaches represented here. Indeed, one of the strengths of this collection is its interdisciplinary nature. Thus, a reader might approach this volume as a collection of essays from prominent scholars from different disciplinary frameworks all focused on the notion of public memory. Taken this way, the volume represents an effort to foster an interdisciplinary dialogue on the notion of public memory and an opportunity to survey the various ways public memories are manifested and the ways they might be interrogated and understood.

Frames of Public Memory

In collecting these essays, however, I have become convinced that there is a larger, more coherent theme underlying them, and I have organized the essays with this in mind. In my reading of the essays there are two different though not incompatible ways the notion of public memory is rendered. Or, more specifically, there is a different sense in which the terms *public* and *memory* are conjoined. These differences can be suggested by considering two ways of unpacking the phrase "public memory": "the memory of publics"; or "the publicness of memory."

The Memory of Publics

I have grouped the initial set of five essays under the heading "The Memory of Publics" and I mean by this title that each of these essays engages the way that memories affect and are effected by various publics. The important sense here is that some entity that can be labeled a public exists and, further, that these entities have memories. While each contributor inflects this sense of a public in his or her own way, there is an overarching sense that something like a public sphere, or counterpublic, is intended.[8] Thus, following the logic that the whole is greater than the sum of its parts, to speak of public memory as the memory of publics is to speak of more than many individuals remembering the same thing. It is to speak of a remembrance together, indeed, of remembrance together as a crucial aspect of our togetherness, our existence as a public. The essays in this section illuminate various aspects of this conception of a "public's memory."

Edward Casey's essay is an excellent general introduction to the broader study of public memory. Casey delineates "public memory" as memory that occurs in the open, in front of and with others, and as distinct from concepts like "collective memory" or "social memory." These public memories are those about which we can interact, deliberate, share. And, in turn, these public memories serve as a horizon within which a public finds itself, constitutes itself, and deliberates its own existence. The arena of public memory becomes a realm within which we act together.[9] This notion of action becomes important as Casey notes parallels between his conception of public and that of Hannah Arendt, who saw the public as a realm of action; an arena in which humans achieve immortality by inscribing themselves into public memory via their actions before others. Thus, the horizon of public memory both constitutes our sense of public and allows a space wherein individuals can become public beings.

Hannah Arendt's concern for remembrance reappears in the essay by Stephen Browne, which attends to the dark underside of public memory—erasure, silence, forgetting. If the existence of a healthy and functioning public is intertwined with its capacity for remembrance, then the gradual erosion by forgetting must represent a grave danger. Browne recovers this deeper concern within Arendt's critical writings and reads Arendt's controversial book *Eichmann in Jerusalem* as a provocative meditation on the failure of memory and of "the persistent and fatal capacity of human beings to forget."

Thus, one can read Casey and Browne together as establishing a broad sense of the importance of memories to publics—Casey notes how memories serve as a horizon within which publics emerge and constitute themselves, and Browne examines the potentially fatal consequences of the erasure of memory.

The struggles over remembering and forgetting, the question of whose memories are inscribed into the broader public horizon and whose are not, are taken up more concretely in the next two essays. Rosa Eberly explores her own work with students at the University of Texas at Austin to recall memories of the Texas Tower shootings, memories the officials of that community seemed intent on keeping submerged. Eberly's quest for the memories of this traumatic event lead her to the ephemeral public sphere of local talk radio and, ultimately, to the undergraduate classroom, which Eberly conceives as a "protopublic sphere," in an effort to see how other publics work outside and against the authorizing power of "official memory."

Charles Morris pursues a similar interest. His chapter examines reactions to Larry Kramer's declaration that Abraham Lincoln was homosexual. In reading these reactions, or overreactions, by the guardians of Lincoln's official memory, Morris illuminates the ways memories are suppressed and the rhetoric of erasure, which Morris labels *mnemonicide*.

Thus, the essays by Eberly and Morris can be read together as an exploration of the struggle of publics to assert their memories, the negative reaction of other publics to such assertions, and the rhetorical struggle involved in these contests. Within the broader horizons of remembrance and forgetting exist the dynamic relations of authority over public memories and the forces of resistance.

This theme of authority over memory, or who has the power to authorize a set of memories and the ways that authority is contested, is complemented by the final essay in this section. Implicit in the notion that publics have the capacity to authorize (or reject) certain memories is a sense that publics have a responsibility to remember certain things. The most poignant instances of this responsibility lie in the almost universal urge to remember shameful events and collectively express regret. Barry Schwartz and Horst-Alfred Heinrich remind us that although we may find expressions of regret in various cultures, the emergence of such regret is a product of culturally specific and complex relations of institutions of history and governance, and the cultural logic of the average person. Focusing on the cultural logic of average people, these authors suggest that feelings of responsibility for the past are bounded within cultural forms of reasoning about the past. Schwartz and Heinrich explore the differences in cultural senses of responsibility in their comparison of Americans and Germans and the ways each conceives their relations to past shameful events. These authors observe that responsibility may be part of public memory, but it is affected by the patterns of reasoning and norms of a given public.

Across these opening essays some sense of public memory emerges with a particular emphasis on publics. Publics, these essays suggest, must have memories, the capacity for remembrance being one of the defining aspects of a public. However, to say that publics have memories is not a simple statement, and the essays in this first section suggest that to engage public memory as "the memory of publics" is to encounter a complex set of factors: the oscillation between horizons of remembrance and forgetting; the contrast between the capacity of certain publics to authorize memories and the struggles of other publics to contest them; and the willingness of a public to accept responsibility for its remembrance or to absolve itself of responsibility. Thus, the scholar seeking to interrogate public memory within the frame of the "memory of publics" should at the very least be attentive to the three interrelated dimensions explored in these chapters: remembrance/forgetting; authority/resistance; responsibility/absolution.

The Publicness of Memory

One need not, however, necessarily conceive of public memories in relation to social entities known as publics. One might, rather, think of public memories as those that have been visible to many, that have appeared in view of others—the "publicness of memory." This conception is not mutually exclusive to the previous conception, since the memory of a public would necessarily manifest itself publicly. The essays in part 2, however, bring our attention to the importance of this other sense of public memories—their public appearance.

Charles Scott's provocative essay opens part 2 by elaborating the neglected complexities involved in saying that a memory appears publicly. Here Scott questions the subject-object relation between people and memories (that is, that people have memories) and notes that we appear in memory just as memories appear in us.[10] Scott's focus here is on the nonsubjective aspects of memory: the memorial dimensions enacted in our repeated practices, discourses, and languages, our every cultural action being laden with cultural memories that give these actions their meaning and purpose. This surplus of memory imbued in our activities is deeply intertwined with our very sense of culture—the memory of culture occurring within these practices—and it is in this sense that we stop talking about memories as things "had" but as things "happening" or, more appropriately, as things "appearing." Scott reminds us that to speak of appearance, however, is to also speak of loss—the loss of presence in appearance. Or, in other words, to speak of something appearing is not to grasp its totality but to experience within appearance the loss of that which appears. Thus, to speak of memory appearing publicly is to acknowledge the loss of memory in that appearance—its mutable and transitory nature—just as to speak of our appearing within memory is to acknowledge the loss of us. Thus, even within culture's repetitive return to memory we cannot speak of memory appearing as what "is," or even what "was," but the loss of presence that occurs in appearing means we more rightly speak of memory in the subjunctive: memory "might." Thus, to speak of the appearance of memory in public is to engage a fragmentary, mutable, and always fleeting phenomenon.

Scott's challenging view of a nonsubjective, repetitive, and subjunctive sense of memory appearing publicly is worth diligent reading as it casts public memory in another light, focusing on the appearance of memories in public. Interestingly, two of the aspects he attends to are also explored in the next two essays, albeit in slightly different contexts. Barbie Zelizer considers the publicness of memory in relation to visual images and what she conceives as the subjunctive voice of images in public memory.[11] Zelizer contends that these visual images that make our public memories visible should be thought of in terms of "voice," which she defines as "the relationship developed between the spectator and the image—involving state of mind, attitude, temporal and sequential positioning." Zelizer notes that the voice of the visual in memory is a subjunctive voice; images invoke in us the possibilities and uncertainties of these removed moments. The exemplar of this subjunctive visual voice is the "about to die" image, and Zelizer finds our collective memory filled with these images of individuals just before the moment of death, in that subjunctive moment of possibility. Thus the sense of loss in appearance is manifested here quite concretely: the seeming certainty of a photographic image of a historical event presented within the subjunctive voice of possibility, the loss of certainty.

The transitory and fragile nature of memory's appearance in public is also taken up by Bradford Vivian, who explores the repetitive nature of appearing public memories. The repetition of memories, Vivian notes, is not suggestive of their stability; each repetition of memory occurs (or appears) differently. Thus, to wander a landscape of repeated memories is to wander through an ever-shifting terrain or, as Vivian describes it, to live a nomadic existence. To attend to our nomadic wanderings through this landscape of remembrance and amnesia is to focus not on the content of public memory but on the unstable and changing ways these memories occur and to recall the political and ethical implications of these occurrences. As Vivian notes, "[R]egarding memory as a repetition of difference rather than a repetition of the same . . . enables one to value the productive capacities of forgetting and mutation elemental to even the most monumental forms of public memory."

Despite the inherently transitory and fragmentary nature of these appearing memories, or perhaps because of it, one can often identify cultural forces employed to stabilize and unify these memories as they emerge into public view. These hegemonic forces seek to craft the appearance of memories, to create in them a sense of permanence and normalcy. Such stabilizing efforts, then, can be thought of as acting in opposition to the subjunctive and mutable nature of memories elaborated in the opening three essays. These hegemonic forces and their capacity to influence the appearance of memories in public are the focus of the final two essays. Barbara Biesecker surveys the terrain of recent American memories of World War II, examining memorials, museums, books, and popular films. Across these varied manifestations, Biesecker observes a conservative agenda at work—a reconstruction of a traditional national unity built around the sacrifices made during World War II. What becomes important in Biesecker's analysis is the way these reemerging memories are being crafted—in films, books, monuments, museums, etc.—into a new, conservative notion of national identity.[12] Here, fifty years after the end of the war, the reemergence of the memory of World War II is being cast within a clear, unified, and singular framework of national identity.

Amos Kiewe frames his concern for the crafting of public memory within the classical rhetorical notion of the eulogy, a mode of public address designed not simply to memorialize an individual but to pass on cultural ethics by describing exemplary lives and deaths. Kiewe focuses on the final speeches of Ronald Reagan, contending that they represented his attempt to create his own eulogy and, in turn, to determine the social lesson of his public life. This exploration turns our attention again to the way that memory's appearance in public can be influenced and developed by those who wish to predetermine and stabilize what are inherently fluid and transitory memories.

Despite our best efforts, however, memories refuse to remain stable and immutable. Their appearance, often unbidden, within our cultural experience is like a mirage: vivid and poignant but impermanent and fluid. No matter their importance or revered place in our collective lives, we cannot grasp them fully nor fix them permanently. We can only envision a fixed stable memory, chiseled in stone or encased within museum walls, when we neglect—or better yet subvert—their nature as appearing. However, if we attend to the appearance of memories in public, then the illusion of their stability is dispelled and the transitory and fluid nature of memory in public is recovered.

The essays in part 2 remind us that to think of memories occurring publicly is to encounter a complex set of factors: the subjunctive nature of the loss of presence inherent in appearance; the mutative nature of repetition; and the efforts of cultural forces to combat this inherent instability through hegemonic practices. Thus, the scholar seeking to interrogate public memory within the frame of the "publicness of memory" should be attentive to these three interrelated factors: appearance/loss; repetition/mutation; and hegemony/instability.

In this way, part 2 opens an interesting dialogue with the perspective of part 1. Where part 1 operates within a general subject-object logic—where publics have memories, contest memories, etc.—part 2 opens up the nonsubjective aspects of memories appearing in public—the uncertainty of memories, their elusiveness, their mutability. Even in spite of cultural forces that work to fix these memories, as memories appear in public they are already escaping the hegemonic cultural forces that produced them. Thus, where part 1 suggests that publics have memories, part 2 reminds us that in the slippery relationship between us and our memories it is difficult to determine whether we have them, or they have us, or perhaps neither is sufficiently the case. What becomes important is that in speaking of or critiquing "public memory" we do not neglect the complexities involved in the appearance of memories publicly.

I do not mean to suggest that there is some inherent opposition between the essays in each part. To speak of public memory must be to simultaneously speak of certain groups of individuals remembering together (the memory of publics) and to speak of those memories appearing before or perhaps simultaneously with those groups (the publicness of memory).[13] What is important here is to recognize that these instructive essays explore the two interrelated but different frames and that each frame captures different elements of this complex social phenomenon. Thus, the factors raised in conceiving the memory of publics—remembrance/forgetting, authority/resistance, responsibility/absolution—are necessarily complicated by the factors raised by the publicness of memory—appearance/loss, repetition/mutation, hegemony/instability—and vice versa. As one attends to the horizon of remembrance and forgetfulness, one must be mindful that these remembrances are the appearances of memories, inherently transitory and receding.[14] As one examines the mutability of repeated memories one must also be mindful of the underlying struggles by various groups to maintain or resist memories. As we speak of cultural responsibility and/or absolution we should also be mindful of the hegemonic tendencies that want to inscribe memories—of triumphs or tragedies—in stone and fix them in seeming immutability.

These permutations could go on almost endlessly as the dimensions of each frame of public memory interact with the various other dimensions. What this volume does, then, is to play between these two broad frames of public memory and remind us that public memory exists simultaneously in both frames; to speak of memory in one frame is to encounter a host of complexities invoked by the other. Those wishing to engage public memory—to theorize it, critique it, or analyze its content or manifestations—should be mindful of which frame is being invoked and which neglected. Recognizing this slippery space in between the memory of publics and the publicness of memories may open productive lines of inquiry and critique, thereby making the study of public memory both more pressing and more complex.

The Frames of *Framing*

This book was generated during the kind of interdisciplinary dialogue it seeks to foster, and its origin underscores the importance of studies of public memory. An interdisciplinary conference was organized at Syracuse University in the fall of 2001 to discuss public memory. The event was scheduled for September 28 and 29. Seventeen days before the conference was to take place two planes were crashed into the World Trade Center in New York City, a third plane was crashed into the Pentagon, and a fourth plane crashed outside Pittsburgh. In a little less than an hour September 11 was marked deeply into the American psyche.

There was much that had to be done in the immediate aftermath for the families of the victims, and even those who were not immediately connected to the tragic events needed to grieve. When the immediacy of these activities receded, the question of the conference had to be raised. Should we go forward? Was it safe? Was it appropriate? After much thought and deliberation, the decision was made to go forward. Indeed, as some expressed it, the events of September 11 made the topic of the conference even more pressing. The spontaneous memorials erected across New York City and the country, the instantaneous framing of the event by the media in relation to other national tragedies (especially Pearl Harbor), and the overwhelming feeling that no one would ever forget the events of September 11 convinced us to go ahead with the conference. The memory of September 11 is evident in this volume. Some of the scholars who hoped to be part of the project were unable to do so in light of the tragedy. Some of the scholars who were able to participate refocused their work to take up the events. Barbie Zelizer's examination of press coverage in the immediate aftermath is an excellent example of a scholar adeptly reading current events through carefully crafted theoretical lenses. Ed Casey's recollections of the spontaneous memorials in Union Square Park and his visit to these memorials on September 17 bring a concrete poignancy to his deeper meditation on the experience of public memory. All of the contributors, whether they engage the events of September 11 explicitly or not, were deeply affected by them, as were the discussions during the conference—the discussions were both more difficult and more pressing as a result. While some of the explicit references to the conference and its historical circumstances have been removed in the development of this volume, others have been left, in part as a recognition that these scholarly contributions also emerged within broader frames of memory.

The interdisciplinary dialogue we began in Syracuse was made possible by a number of individuals and institutions. First and foremost, the conference and subsequent volume would have been impossible without the generous support of Syracuse University's College of Visual and Performing Arts and its dean, Carol Brzozowski. My colleagues in the Department of Speech Communication also provided kind support, and the Department of Political Science provided useful funds.

Numerous individuals were crucial to the success of this endeavor. My colleague Diane Grimes gave important and greatly appreciated aid. Six graduate students helped at the conference and are worthy of much praise: Paul Butler, Gabor Hardy, David Heineman, Jessica Reeher, Amy Robillard, and Virginia Rodino. I'd also like to acknowledge the continuing support and help of my wife, Catherine Thomas.

Finally, I would like to give a warm word of thanks to the excellent folks at the University of Alabama Press. John Lucaites, series editor, was also a great help.

Notes

1. There are a number of very useful reviews of public, collective, and/or social memory studies including: Stephen H. Browne, "Reading, Rhetoric and the Texture of Public Memory," *Quarterly Journal of Speech* 81 (1995): 237–65; Jeffrey K. Olick and Joyce Robbins, "Social Memory Studies: From 'Collective Memory' to the Historical Sociology of Mnemonic Practices," *Annual Review of Sociology* 24 (1998): 105–40; and Barbie Zelizer, "Reading the Past against the Grain: The Shape of Memory Studies," *Critical Studies in Mass Communication* 12 (1995): 214–39.

2. For an interesting discussion of the way memory has been conceived at

different points in history, see Jacques Le Goff, *History and Memory* (New York: Columbia University Press, 1992).

3. Maurice Halbwachs, *On Collective Memory* (Chicago: University of Chicago Press, 1992).

4. The notion that memory studies arose, in part, as a result of mistrust of official history is discussed by Barry Schwartz, "Introduction: The Expanding Past," *Qualitative Sociology* 61 (1996): 275–82. Others have suggested such causes as the growth of multiculturalism (see Michael Kammen, *Mystic Chords of Memory: The Transformation of American Culture* [New York: Knopf, 1991]), challenges to the nation-state (see John Bodnar, "Pierre Nora, National Memory and Democracy: A Review," *Journal of American History* 87 [2000]: 951–63 and David Cressy, *Bonfires and Bells: National Memory and the Protestant Calendar in Elizabethan and Stuart England* [Berkeley: University of California Press, 1989]), the development of poststructural thought (see Patrick Hutton, *History as an Art of Memory* [Hanover, NH: University Press of New England, 1993]), or as an attempt to reconcile American guilt for atrocities committed and reforge an American identity (see Efraim Sicher, "The Future of the Past: Countermemory and Postmemory in Contemporary American Post-Holocaust Narratives," *History and Memory* 12 [2000]: 56–91).

5. For an insightful account of the notion of objectivity in historiography, see Peter Novick, *That Noble Dream: The Objectivity Question and the American Historical Profession* (Cambridge: Cambridge University Press, 1990).

6. Pierre Nora, "Between Memory and History: *Les Lieux de Mémoire,*" *Representations* 26 (1989): 8.

7. Memory, or *memoria,* is one of the five classical canons of rhetoric, and its importance as a "treasury of things invented" is clearly articulated by, among others, Cicero. See *De Oratore,* trans. H. Rackman (Cambridge, MA: Harvard University Press, 1969). For more on the interrelation between rhetoric and memory in later periods, see two excellent works by Mary J. Carruthers: *The Book of Memory: A Study of Memory in Medieval Culture* (Cambridge: Cambridge University Press, 1993) and *The Craft of Thought: Meditation, Rhetoric and the Making of Images, 400–1200* (Cambridge: Cambridge University Press, 2000).

8. While not explicitly invoked by all the contributors to this first section, I think something like Jürgen Habermas's sense of a self-constituting and self-transforming public sphere is implicit in this conception of a public having

memories. See Jürgen Habermas, *The Structural Transformations of the Public Sphere* (Cambridge, MA: MIT Press, 1989). Of course, there is also a sense in some of these essays, especially Eberly and Morris, that various publics may be in competition for "memory resources," and this sense of competing publics and counterpublics seems similar to Nancy Fraser's influential corrective to Habermas. See Nancy Fraser, "Rethinking the Public Sphere: A Contribution to the Critique of Actually Existing Democracy," in *Habermas and the Public Sphere*, ed. Craig Calhoun (Cambridge, MA: MIT Press, 1992), 109–42.

9. Casey's sense that memories are "emplaced" is more fully considered in his book *Remembering: A Phenomenological Study* (Bloomington: University of Indiana Press, 2000).

10. Scott's notion of nonsubjective memories is explored more fully in his *Time of Memory* (Albany: State University of New York Press, 1999).

11. Zelizer's explorations of the relation between visual images and memory are also taken up in *Remembering to Forget: Holocaust Memory through a Camera's Eye* (Chicago: University of Chicago Press, 1998) and her edited volume *Visual Culture and the Holocaust* (New Brunswick: Rutgers University Press, 2001).

12. Biesecker's essay is an extended version of an essay previously appearing in the *Quarterly Journal of Speech* 88 (2002): 393–409.

13. Here it is worth at least noting my own longstanding skepticism of the notion of publics or public spheres. See my "Spaces of Public Dissension: Reconsidering the Public Sphere," *Communication Monographs* 63 (1996): 231–48. Though I do recognize the collective nature of memories and their importance, I am skeptical of the modernist logic imported by Habermasian notions of public spheres.

14. In a way, perhaps, this suggests that existing within the oscillating horizons of remembrance and forgetting means existing in a subjunctive mode.

I
The Memory of Publics

I

Public Memory
in Place and Time

Edward S. Casey

I

Despite its monolithic resonance, "public memory" is not just one kind of thing. Different itself from other basic forms of remembering, it occurs in several distinctive ways. Let me begin by mentioning some of these ways in relation to a single fundamental trait, proceed to discuss other kinds of memory, and then return to public memory for closer analysis.

The trait I have in mind is this: public memory is radically bivalent in its temporality. Where other modes of remembering deal primarily with the past—with the notable exceptions of recognition (focused on the ingression of the past into the immediate present) and reminding (which often projects us into a future event of which we wish to be reminded)—public memory is both attached to a past (typically an originating event of some sort) *and* acts to ensure a future of further remembering of that same event. Public monuments embody this Janusian trait: their very massiveness and solidity almost literally enforce this futurity, while inscriptions and certain easily identifiable features (for example, the giant seated Abraham Lincoln of the Lincoln Memorial) pull the same physical object toward the past it honors. In cases such as these, the perduringness of the construction itself acts to guarantee the intimate tie between past and future as if to say: just as the stone from which I'm made stems from time immemorial and will, as sheer material, last into the indefinite future, so the event here signified, though stemming from a quite particular past, will be remembered forever. Thus the monument does not merely embody or represent an event (or person, or group of persons), but it strives to preserve its memory in times to come—at the limit, times beyond measure. (Or at least this is so in the case of national monuments, the avowed purpose of which is to reflect and support the putative immortality of the state. In more modest instances, there is no such pretension to exist without temporal limit, for instance, in the memorials that mark the places where friends or family have been killed in highway accidents.)

This is not to say that public memory requires the density of stone to mark and re-mark it. At another extreme, a eulogy is certainly a form of public memory—it is pronounced before others and is meant to direct their attention to the character and accomplishments of the departed— but it is constructed entirely in words. Only rarely is the text preserved; it is discarded, even as the speaker hopes to have implanted in the minds of his or her listeners a *new* memory that will last—if not indefinitely then at least for the upcoming weeks or months when grief will be most acute. In certain cases a public speech, meant for the moment, gets preserved despite its author's intentions: several of Cicero's state eulogies, Lincoln's Gettysburg Address, FDR's speech on the occasion of the attack on Pearl Harbor.

What this points to is that public memory, though thriving on tenacious media such as stone or brick, is not dependent on them. A mere photograph, reproduced on cheap newsprint but (in the case of a major newspaper) reaching thousands of readers, is medium enough, as we know from poignant photographs of the devastated World Trade Towers. Sometimes a single photograph (for example, that of a Vietcong suspect being shot in the head at close quarters) itself becomes an icon of public memory: what began as the record of a transient moment gains its own permanence in the annals of public memory. Paradoxically, its very flimsiness is an asset: whereas we must travel to Washington to view the Lincoln Memorial, any copy of the Gettysburg Address or the Vietcong photo suffices to bring us immediately to its content. The crucial tie-line between past and future that is at the heart of public memory can be effected on the slenderest of reeds—so long as these reeds are at once easily reproducible and widely accessible.

This is not to say that the present is of no compelling interest in public memory. Often it is: the present in the making, the present that is *now*, is considered to be of central significance in the future. This is the situation we designate by saying: "This event will be forever etched upon our memory." We say this on the very day of its happening, as on that fateful Tuesday, September 11. No one doubted, and many said explicitly, "This day will not be forgotten"—echoing Kant's exclamation that the French Revolution is "a phenomenon that cannot be forgotten."[1] In the case of September 11, not forgotten not just by individuals but *not forgotten by virtually every American then alive* (and by many others around the globe). The power of the event in the present was so shattering—so obviously and massively destructive—that there could be no doubt of its perdurance in the public domain: its futurity was assured from the start. Not for a moment could that moment be forgotten, and this did not require speeches or monuments. Indeed, it generated its own kind of spontaneous memorial: photographs of those still missing that were pinned to windows and walls, or taped to enormous sheets of butcher paper, with the names and descriptions of those lost written underneath. Buckets swung from trees into which other photographs were placed. "People attached bouquets to the railings, and notes thick with pain. One note read: 'You are missed and loved and will never be forgotten.'"[2] At fire stations lists of "missing members" were bedecked with flowers: "[A]n impromptu memorial to the missing firefighters had sprung up outside the Rescue 1 station house at 450 W. 43rd St. Carnations, roses, daisies and lilies stretched half the width of the sidewalk and spilled toward the curb."[3] Although none of those memorialized in these various makeshift manners was a public figure, by the mere fact of being thus noted, however elliptically, those pictured became part of public memory, either by virtue of the fact that their image was being actually perceived by those on the scene (themselves standing in for a much larger public that could not be present) or because their image was published in the *New York Times* and other newspapers.[4]

What does it mean to become part of public memory? Only minimally to come to the attention of the (reading or viewing) public, to be observed by them. Much more pertinently, it means to be understood right away, without hesitation or interpretation, in its basic signification—a "victim of this disaster." A victim is a public person—if not yet explicitly so, then potentially so (that is, as someone who can be recognized as such, present a case in court, complain in public, etc.). Precisely because a victim cannot argue for himself—because he is dead or lacks the knowledge or resources to become a plaintiff—public testimonial is all the more requisite if that person (however unknown to the public initially, however much a stranger) is to reclaim recognition or vindication.[5] Without the testimonial, verbal and/or pictorial, the victim recedes into oblivion, remembered only by his or her family and friends—thus part of individual and social memory—but not belonging expressly to public memory, at most a cipher or empty number in that memory (that is, as just one among the many dead as currently counted).

In this last case, then, not only may the medium be less than permanent but the very value of permanency itself—still at stake in speeches or images that are meant to be indefinitely preserved—is no longer necessary for admission to public memory. Entry to the latter can occur in the form of something not destined to last, so fragile that it will be taken away from public view in a matter of days or even hours. Even a document that does not depict a given person but a mere transaction of that person—such as an application for a job, the record of a bank account, etc.—can be assimilated to public memory in the right circumstance, as when such documents were merely published in newspapers and journals several days after the disaster.[6]

But much more remains to be said about public memory. I shall do this after undertaking a brief comparative phenomenology of memory overall.

II

There are four major forms of human memory—beyond certain basic distinctions such as short-versus long-term memory, which apply to all forms of remembering. These are individual memory, social memory, collective memory, and public memory proper. Let me say some schematic things about each.

Individual Memory

This refers to the person who is engaged in memory on any given occasion. That person, the always unique rememberer, remembers in several particular ways, not just recollecting states of affairs (recalling *that* something happened) but also remembering-*how* (to do certain things), remembering-*as* (x as y), etc. And the same person remembers different kinds of things—not just *things* but whole environmental complexes, auras, and worlds (and how these are given). Moreover, we remember by way of being reminded, by recognizing something, and by reminiscing with others. The latter has proven more significant than I had first thought: it is a primary prop of social memory; and it introduces the crucial factor of language into memory, and thus narrative and history. When we also consider that there is a distinctive body memory and place memory and many acts of commemoration, we are already beyond any model of memory as confined to the individual mind and its representations.

I had spelled out most of this in my book *Remembering,* which appeared in the late 1980s, when I wrote a chapter titled "Collective Memory" and another called "Forgetting," neither which I saw fit to publish. But I would now say that it was a mistake to have imagined that I could keep the traits of individual remembering wholly apart from those of the remembering we do with and through others; they are distinguishable but not separable dimensions of the same basic activity. Every single act of remembering that I do comes saturated with social and collective aspects, as well as with cultural and public determinants. However idiosyncratic and personal a given act of remembering may be—whatever its individuated style and bearing—and despite the fact that all remembering takes place *in* an individual (I reject the idea of a "mémoire collectif" that all humans share), still each such act has certain formal dimensions that exceed any individual's contribution. More important, each such act is always as interpersonal as it is personal, as much *between* beings as locked inside my own being. The primary locus of memory is found not only in body or mind (or even brain, mind's physiological counterpart) but in an intersubjective nexus that is at once social and collective, cultural and public. My essay in this volume attempts to explore these extrapersonal dimensions of remembering, with special attention to public memory.

Social Memory

This is the memory held in common by those who are affiliated either by kinship ties, by geographical proximity in neighborhoods, cities, and other regions, or by engagement in a common project. In other words, it is memory shared by those who are *already* related to each other, whether by way of family or friendship or civic acquaintance or just "an alliance between people for a specific purpose."[7] In this case, memory both presupposes these preexisting relationships and is often concerned with aspects of the relationships themselves. (There can, however, be social memories of events that one did not experience oneself but that were undergone by consociates whom one does in fact know: for example, how my Uncle Ralph mismanaged the family business—something that happened before I was born.) Crucial here is that social memories are not necessarily public: families can harbor memories that are known only to themselves; such privacy is often itself prized as such, providing that intimacy and bonding that are so important to the maintenance of family life. Only when family (or other group) members become celebrated or notorious in certain ways does the sociality of many of their shared memories become "public property," that is to say, out of their immediate control regarding audience, interpretation, or use, as in the case of the Kennedys. (The same thing can happen to entire neighborhoods—when a person living in a given block is very prominent, this occasions media and other forms of attention to that place.)

What does "sharing memories" mean? I take this to signify the situation in which those who have had the same—I don't say precisely *identical*—history as a given group or who live in the same place remember what has happened to that group or in that place (and often both). This does not mean having the same *experience* of remembering—that will always be idiosyncratic in one measure or another—but instead remembering something (some event, some occasion, some physical thing, even some thought) that others in one's kin or place-group are also remembering at the time or could do so. When this is in fact happening, it is tantamount to "co-reminiscing," that is, remembering in quasi-narrative form when assembled in a particular place (the front porch in an earlier era, at dinner tables on holidays). But it can also happen when two or more group members are talking to each other on the telephone or communicating in real time in a chat room on the Internet. What matters is neither the exact technology nor the precise location but the fact (or its imminent possibility) of (a) having had the same history, at least via the proxy of another family member; (b) there having been a common place in which that history was enacted and experienced; and (c) being able to bring the history-in-that-place into words or other suitable means of communication and expression (one might have social memories through a comparison of paintings done during a particular period in a given place, say, abstract expressionists who worked in lower Manhattan in the 1960s).

Collective Memory

By this term, I mean the circumstance in which different persons, not necessarily known to each other at all, nevertheless recall the same event—again, each in her own way. This is a case of remembering neither individually in isolation from others nor in the company of others with whom one is acquainted but *severally.* "Severally" signifies plural remembering that has no basis in overlapping historicities or shared places but is brought together only in and by a conjoint remembrance of a certain event, no matter where those who remember are located or how otherwise unrelated they are to each other. Nor do they have to remember at the same time. All that matters is commonality of content. The most striking instance of collective remembering is the phenomenon of "flashbulb memories" that have been studied in the wake of John Kennedy's assassination—and that have doubtless happened again after September 11. In both cases, virtually every adult in the United States vividly recalls not just a catastrophic event but *just where he or she heard it,* for example, the actual circumstance of learning the bad news. I was in a barber's chair in Chicago in the first case, at home in Stony Brook in the second. Despite the vivacity of the local detail of first hearing—which differs greatly from person to person—I am linked to all others who also remember exactly where they were on hearing of these two emergencies. We are remembering it collectively, from our several stances. Not because there is anything called "collective memory" as Levy-Bruhl posited too rapidly as a deep faculty possessed by all human beings, but because our entire experiential and memorial focus is on one altogether stunning event. Not the experience but the focus—amounting to a monothetic obsession—is what is shared in collective memory.

Social memory derives from a basis in shared experience, shared history or place, or shared project. Collective memory, in contrast, has no such basis but is instead *distributed* over a given population or set of places. Instead of possessing a taproot from which all memory stems as in the case of social remembering, collective recollection is not effected by members of existing clans, or regions, or projects in common (or if it is, this membership is irrelevant to the collectivity). The grouping is not based on prior identity or particular placement. It is formed spontaneously and involuntarily, and its entire raison d'être is a convergent focus on a given topic: typically an event but also a thought, a person, a nation. The members of this momentary collectivity are linked solely by the cynosure on which their attention falls.

But this attention need not occur at the same time (I may have heard of Kennedy's assassination at a different time than you), and it comes from disparate directions—as disparate as are those brought together on the occasion. Thus they are in an essentially external relationship to each other and only loosely assembled, not unlike a *Versammlung* in Heidegger's sense of the term, though now strictly limited to a focus on a single *memorandum*.

Collective remembering is unremittingly plural—so plural that individual or group identities do not count; what is important is only the sheer fact that those remembering are remembering the same thing. This is quite different from social or individual remembering, where the singularity of the rememberer or group of co-rememberers is what counts. In the latter case, intimacy and bonding are important aspects of remembering—as we often observe in the case of intense co-reminiscing. But in the collective situation, all relations are so external that intimacy is not only irrelevant but intrusive. Students of collective life in cities have underlined this last feature: Richard Sennett refers to "the tyranny of intimacy" and (much influenced by Jane Jacobs's similar view) asserts that "the city must be a place where people can join with other people without compulsion to know them as persons."[8] When people in cities together remember a given event—whether awesome or trivial—they do so on just this condition of remaining comparatively anonymous in their very plurality, their extended severalness, their manyness in the midst of their oneness of attention. Only the *focus memorium* unites them; otherwise, they are rhizomatic in their dispersion, lacking any single shared basis in experience, history, or place.

Public Memory

The three kinds of memory we've identified so far contribute to public memory. Individual remembering remains indispensable at the level of the experiential and the idiosyncratic: however wide the swath of memory may become, in each case individuals effect it and undergo it. Remembering is always *je meines* ("in each case mine"). Social memory intensifies such personal recall by adding the outreach of group identities that go beyond personal experience to include (as it always does include) family history and other shared enterprises. Collective memory may be said to be a negative condition of public memory, insofar as it allows for co-remembering without co-reminiscing and for the massive convergence of those who remember the same thing without knowing each other personally. If individual and social memory are the two inner circles of public memory, collective memory is its outer perimeter, the loose net within which events and other items are recalled in comparative isolation and hence at the extreme opposite position from individual remembering, which necessarily happens with and for a given person in a given place.

But what, then, is public memory? To begin with, by saying "public" we mean to contrast such memory with anything that takes place privately—that is to say, offstage, in the *idios cosmos* of one's home or club, or indeed just by oneself (whether physically sequestered or not). "Public" signifies out in the open, in the *koinos cosmos* where discussion with others is possible—whether on the basis of chance encounters or planned meetings—but also where one is exposed and vulnerable, where one's limitations and fallibilities are all too apparent. In this open realm, wherever it may be—in town halls, public parks, or city streets—public memory serves as an encircling horizon. It is there as a basso profundo in the chorus of the body politic, its medley of voices. It is there, however, not just as presupposed but as an active resource on which current discussion and action draw: members of the public count on this historical *Hintergrund,* they speak in terms of it, and they take off from it. Indeed, they can revise it on the spot, but then they are revising *it.* The "it" is a continuant that serves to stabilize any given direction of public events. The intrinsic mutability of these latter, their unpredictable course, sometimes their turpitude and tumultuousness, call for something that stays constant, or at least more or less the same, throughout the vicissitudes. No wonder that every revolution, no matter how radically it questions the official public memory of the ancien régime, immediately establishes as if by mandated necessity a new version of such memory—meant to be just as perduring as the previous version and hopefully more lasting, a new calendar of events to be publicly remembered, etc. At the limit, one can speculate that traumatic public events such as the Trade Towers disaster require the almost instantaneous installation of a new public memory—this time, a public memory of the victims regarded en masse.

In this latter case, we are witnesses to the creation of a genuinely new horizon, an *inner* rather than *outer* horizon (in Husserl's distinction). An established and received public memory serves in untroubled times as an encircling presence—sanctioning and protecting, legitimating and supporting from afar (an afar of history and culture and typically geography, its primary location being in a federal capital or some other established place). It is a continual horizon out there around the public arena, underwriting it as it were. But in its origin a given public memory is constituted from within a particular historical circumstance, usually a crisis of some sort. Then it arises in the form of an inner horizon, that is, as closely surrounding a particular thing or event that forms a "hearth" for the emerging memory.

The vigil I attended on Sunday, September 17, 2001, in Union Square Park was a case in point. By then September 11 had been accepted as the catastrophe it was—any disbelief had vanished, and only some residual hope for survivors still remained (and that was quickly disappearing). For days the posted pictures and descriptions of the missing to which I have already alluded had appeared all over New York, not just near the site of the calamity but in Penn Station, on stray walls, everywhere. But until the Sunday night vigil there had been no attempt to draw together these fragmentary images and desperate messages. A "Mural of Hope" was created at one entrance to Union Square, displaying scores of these cries of despair. But throughout the park many other such displays were set up so that the public space as a whole became a mausoleum of sorts. But it was also something else—a public hearth. This was underscored by the innumerable votive candles that were lit in many places in the park, sometimes in a small cluster around images of several missing persons and sometimes in much larger groups that constituted an entire scene of fiery tribute.

Most people, including myself, moved quietly through the park, pausing to look at the faces of the departed, as if paying homage to people one never knew—but knew now in the context of disaster. Others sang peace

Figure 1.1. Candlelight memorial in Union Square Park, New York City, September 17, 2001 (courtesy of Edward S. Casey).

Figure 1.2. Patriotic memorials in Union Square Park, New York City, September 17, 2001 (courtesy of Edward S. Casey).

songs or played various musical instruments. The atmosphere was mourn-ful and sad but not morbid. There was a distinct sense of relief to find oneself in the presence of others—albeit strangers—with whom to share grief. But more than relief was at stake in this extraordinary circumstance: something constructive was in the air. What was this?

To start with, there was a palpable sense of coming to terms with a trauma instead of letting oneself be crushed by it. Incredulousness and numbness—not to mention outrage and despair—were ceding place to another phase of handling the trauma, one that refused to be buried under it. This was the experience of doing something in particular that would last beyond this given occasion—that would stay in place in years to come (when, doubtless, the full effects of the trauma will be felt, a trauma that will perhaps never be "overcome"). I refer to the building of a public hearth to which those present, and those who witnessed indirectly by word of mouth, could recur in times ahead—a *stabilitas loci,* a place for further and future remembering. This place is both actual—it is the very place of Union Square as animated that unforgettable Sunday evening—and memorial, not only looking back but also supporting later additions from subsequent experiences that fit into its horizonal structure and find room in an ever-expanding enclosure of conjoint recollection.

Over time the inner horizon of this hearth will gradually transform itself into an outer horizon of public memory that will be designated by constant deictic markers of exact date and place and by a consolidated memorial mass that retains the gist if not the detail of the occurrence I have described. This mass and these markers will move slowly into the perimeter of the public mind, eventually taking up a station in the Ameri-can public's sense of significant events in the early twenty-first century. It will be referred to as something like "the Union Square vigil in the wake of the World Trade Tower disaster." It will have become (in the future per-fect) part of the external horizon of public memory. This is not to imply that it merely recedes and pales in the future. It may remain a vivid pres-ence throughout, a major node in the horizonal structure, a "marker event" in the nation's history. Perhaps; we cannot tell. Just as the trauma itself came without warning, so its own futurity possesses no certain course.

Despite its high accessibility within a given culture—enhanced when technology stores memories several times over as image and word—public memory is not a sure thing. It has its own degrees of endurance and reliability. Being public does not guarantee constancy over time: to be public is to be subject to continual reassessment and revision. We like to think that public memory is always there to reassure us as to our national or regional identity, and as an external horizon it does in fact play just this role. It is there to be *invoked.* But invocation itself occurs in many guises and with many degrees of nuance. Often we cannot count on invoking anything like a constant public memory, despite its rhetorical appeal and despite the often urgent needs of citizens (and even more so, politicians) to refer to something like the same heritage or tradition and to be able to transmit this to oneself and others in a consistent and repeatable way.

In fact, a given event in public memory is subject to two forms of revision on the part of the public itself: first, a discovery of a glaringly false part of its content; second, a reassessment of its primary significance as a wider, or simply different, ethical or historical context arises. The public memory of the Vietnam War illustrates both points: the public was actively misled by the military and by at least two presidents as to what actually happened in this war, and, with time, it has become even more clear that our interests in pursuing it were much less than noble. At the present the war is certainly part of public memory but such a problematic part that no one, not even a politician, can invoke it unambiguously as if it were a stable event to be cited with pride or for any other single rhetorical purpose. The same is true, with important differences, for the Civil War, in this case a troubled part of the lingering horizon of our own self-inflicted aggression against ourselves. In another cultural setting, the legend of Trumpeldor, the one-armed early Israeli settler who died defending his home against marauding Palestinians, exhibits the same double disintegration. On the one hand, his famous "last words" ("It is good to die for your country") have been discredited since he did not know the Hebrew in which they have always been quoted and since in Russian (which he surely spoke) they probably meant "fuck your mother." On the other hand, complicating the impact of such discrediting stands the fact that this particular legend of self-sacrifice in war is no longer so poignant or moving now that so much grief has occurred in the ongoing struggle with Palestine: "[W]ithin the context of the post-1967 political reality," writes Yael

Zerubavel, "it is no longer possible to accept as given the message that Trumpeldor's [originally cited] statement conveys."[9]

My point is not that public memory is fragile and fickle, nor that its entropic tendency makes it subject to continual corruption. Instead, I am signaling the effects of what is a truly constituent feature of public memory, namely, its formation through ongoing interchange of ideas and thoughts, opinions and beliefs. It is just because public memory is so much in the arena of open discussion and debate that it is also subject to revision or, for that matter, resumption (for example, when a certain faded memory is revived and revalorized at a later time, such as John Brown's raids during the civil rights period).

Let me put this last point still more strongly: public memory is the very condition for all such interchange, which could not take place without it. When I posit it as the external horizon of the public domain, I do not mean that it is somehow *beyond* this domain, indifferent to it and distant from it. On the contrary: as is the case with any horizon (internal or external), it is a constituent feature of the phenomenon for which it is the horizon. We know this from the experience of ordinary visual perception, which would lose all coherence were it not to be set within a horizon that at once delimits and organizes any given "layout of surfaces" within the visual environment. The external horizon does not merely surround what is perceived within its compass; it gives to what resides in this compass its special character, its distinctive "style" (in Merleau-Ponty's generous sense). Most important, it allows the various contents of the perceived landscape to coexist in a viable way—to become parts of the overall configuration. By the same token (and allowing for understandable shifts in context), a memorial horizon not only engirdles its subject matter but actively subtends it, giving it its own identity and shape, its cast and character, its characteristic physiognomy. However subject to revision and even replacement a given public memory may be, some significant such memory will always persist: if Vietnam or the Civil War are controversial by their very nature, behind them remains the American Revolution as an ongoing legendary presence, just as behind the rapidly receding Trumpeldor legend there is still a comparatively unquestioned belief in "the days of milk and honey," that is, "the 'golden age' of Antiquity when the Hebrews lived as a nation on their own land, the Land of Israel."[10] Beyond the "invented traditions" that are always being posited in response to the challenge of new circumstances, there is a perduring past, legendary or historical, which is the persisting horizon of public memory.[11]

Most crucially, it is precisely because of this actively encompassing and intimately establishing role that the horizon of public memory makes possible the very dialogue that can call for its own redescription or even its own rejection. The *vita activa* underlined by Hannah Arendt as the indispensable core of the public sphere—an active life of talk, first enacted in the agora in the West—would not be possible were it not for the enabling presence of public memory at its fringes. This memory, not unlike the walls of the city, literally defines the terms of the agon, providing the conditions within which open dialogue can happen. In this respect, it is the equivalent of the habitual body, which acts as a second basic condition of all productive discourse—a form of inner horizon that is furnished by the interlocutors' own gesticulating and moving and perceiving bodies in the scene of discussion. This body has its own history and its own memory (this is why I like to speak of "habitual body memory"[12] in this context), but this memory is at once quite private (that is, just the history of the delights and insults experienced by my own body) and very much repressed (most notably in the case of women's bodies in social and public situations). Hence, it is rarely subject to discussion as such—at least not until recent times—but even so, it is a material condition of possibility for the open discussion that is part and parcel of public memory proper.

It follows as well that what I earlier identified as the temporal structure of such memory—its inherent bidirectionality with regard to past and future—is also made possible by the horizonal powers of public memory. Stemming from a deep, sometimes even immemorial past ("a past that was never a present," as Levinas says), it allows for and encourages recursion to it as remaining the same over time—hence as a fount of inspiration, or at least of reliability—while in its revisability it shows itself open to a future in which it may mutate. In that future, it may become other than it *was,* even if what it was remains requisite for the very constitution of the public realm itself. And the present? It is the forever eluded moment of happening, of the event which *will be* remembered (or forgotten) and then, in that future moment, assume its identity as what *has been the case* (whether recalled or not, whether historical or legendary): "Days will come and songs will be sung about [early Israeli heroes such as Trumpeldor] and legends will be formed about them."[13] The present, strung out between the no longer and the not yet (as Aristotle first put it in *Physics*), gestures to a future of things to come, even as it surely will become part of what has become. But what happens in it is crucial, as we can see from the events in Union Square or in any revolutionary moment. What occurs there, even if it commemorates another event, is itself an event of instituting public memory itself, or at least that part of it that will become available to others not now present as a public memory—occupying a significant stretch of its horizon, ingredient in its very structure.

III

Public memory is not a nebulous pursuit that can occur anywhere; it always occurs in some particular place. Let me bear out this basic but elusive fact in a series of five short observations[14]:

(i) *public place.* In contrast to other primary kinds of remembering—which can occur with people who are quite isolated from each other (individual memory or collective memory) or in already constituted groups (social memory), public memory occurs only when people meet and interact in a single scene of interaction. This means that place is not indifferent, as it is in flashbulb memories and many other instances of remembering wherever we happen to be. On the contrary, it is integral to public memory, which is not merely situated in a public arena or literal "common place" but *enacted* there. The place, in other words, lends itself to the remembering and facilitates it at the very least, but also in certain cases embodies the memory itself (as when people engage in conjoint remembrance in the presence of certain memorials, ranging from the Tomb of the Unknown Solider to the Vietnam Memorial to ordinary grave markers). It is not accidental that Memorial Day parades in the United States characteristically end up in cemeteries, where speeches are made and (sometimes) memories of the departed exchanged. This is more than a matter of setting; it is a question of an active material *inducement* by the place—its power of drawing out the appropriate memories *in that location.*

(ii) *public presence.* Place provides the vital substructure of public memory not only by virtue of certain of its features that enable, embody, and induce shared remembrances but also for the very practical reason that it offers a space in which human bodies can come into proximity. Such proximity is not for the sake of intimacy—something often sought in social memory—but for the sake of a public presence that can be accomplished only when people congregate for a common purpose. This presence is really a co-presence of each to the other, all within eyeshot and (usually) earshot. This is a specifically interhuman presence, a form of community however brief it may be.

(iii) *public discussion.* A place that nurtures (or at least allows) communal presence, intense *Gemeinschaft,* is a place that encourages direct communication between those who have come together around a shared *Sache.* Public discussion always takes place in quite specific locations: the agora, the forum, and (still at times) Hyde Park. All three of these are established places for promoting speech in common. But such common places also spring up spontaneously, as in the case of Union Square (once the scene of discussions concerning the fate of organized labor, then for many years merely a public park, most recently the place for the vigil I attended). The vagaries of a given public space correspond to its changing role in supporting (or failing to support) public discussion.

Given a supportive place (and given a political atmosphere that is not entirely repressive), such discussion arises in many forms—sometimes as overt debate (favored by the British), sometimes as philosophical dialogue (as reported by Plato), sometimes as exhortation on the part of a single speaker, sometimes as nostalgic recollections of events or people. What is most striking is the fact that each of these variant forms of common discussion in a suitable place occurs for the most part in words. The praxis of public memory is primarily discursive. Even when images figure prominently as at Union Square they are accompanied by verbal descriptions that act to pin down the image itself. Tawana Griffin, whose photograph was displayed at the park, was described as "30 years old, 140 pounds, 5′5″ in height" and having "four tattoos, one on the upper part of each arm, one on the left breast, and one on the center of the chest," along with a "torn right earlobe and [a] split right finger nail." The company for which she worked in the Trade Towers was identified, along with its location on the 101st floor of World Trade Center 1. Given the unlikelihood of her survival, these words practically constituted an epitaph. In their grim finality they are not subject to debate, but they contribute to the public discussion that was occurring in the park—the expressions of regret, of revenge, of what America should do next, etc. Already part of public memory, they were also part, however implicitly, of the discussion that was occurring in the place where they could be read by all who were present.

The role of language in this situation is to articulate what might have remained sequestered and undiscussed, held in private thought or emotion. In Hannah Arendt's celebrated interpretation, this began in the West with the agora, where issues of the polis were actively discussed everyday in the same political space: "In the experience of the polis, which not without justification has been called the most talkative of all bodies politic . . . the emphasis shifted from action to speech, and to speech as a means of persuasion. . . . To be political, to live in a *polis,* meant that everything was decided through words and persuasion and not through force and violence."[15] But to be in the public realm is not only a matter of persuading interlocutors. The discourse, spoken or written, that takes place in this realm brings topics that concern many into an arena of appearance that is tantamount to a shared reality. As Arendt continues:

> [E]verything that appears in public can be seen and heard by everybody and has the widest possible publicity. For us [that is, those in the West], appearance—something that is being seen and heard by others as well as by ourselves—constitutes reality. . . . Each time we talk about things that can be experienced only in privacy or intimacy, we bring them out into a sphere where they will assume a kind of reality which, their intensity notwithstanding, they never could have had before. The presence of others who see what we see and hear what we hear assures us of the reality of the world and ourselves.[16]

This casts a special light on the events at Union Square that memorable night. What had become insufferable when experienced alone or with close friends and family called for a wider scene of discursive praxis. In that scene, filled with images and words, with gestures and walking and other bodily movements, not only could private grief be shared but it was made articulate in the presence of others: it was brought to public appearance, made present and real for all who participated.

(iv) *common topic.* Not only private and collective grief, however, are articulated in a public space. So too is a common topic, a matter of deep concern to all who gather in a given place. Whether the topic is the next presidential candidate, environmental policy, the status of illegal immigrants, or a recent disaster, this topic bonds the participants, who converge on it even as they disagree about its status or implications. It is not a matter of coming to agreement, hence not of persuasion per se. The topic may be so divisive that no agreement is possible; the participants may be in a circumstance of a *differend* in Lyotard's sense of the term: a dispute for which there is no known mediation, much less resolution.[17] In the immediate aftermath of September 11, how were we to respond to the terrorist "attack"? By a retaliatory attack on the country "harboring" Osama bin Laden? Or by trying to capture him and bring him to justice in the World Court? I heard both views expressed in Union Square—and many others in between. It was not a time for figuring out what to do; what mattered most was that the topic linked everyone present in a common concern and that the imagistic, gesticulatory, and linguistic practices in which we engaged all addressed this concern in one way or another.

(v) *commemoration in place.* Coursing throughout a public place in which everyone is co-implicated is something else beyond the place itself, its presence, the discussions it engenders, and the topics thereby treated. This is the commemorating that any public, thus gathered, effects by virtue of the very fact of their congregation. This is commemoration in various guises. "Remembering together" as the word literally implies, *commemoration* signifies a conjoint recollection (or other mode of memory), not merely severally and disjointedly as in the case of collective memory or socially in the company of kin or other regular consociates but as *effected in one place.* Commemoration, which I have treated elsewhere,[18] ranges greatly—from explicit eulogies to tacit allusions to a past that is honored. Like public memory itself, it points both backward—to the vanished event or person—and forward (by means of the resolute wish to preserve the memory of the event or person, or even to act on it).

What is most striking is that in public commemorating one need not think explicitly of the *commemorandum:* one only has to enter a certain ritual in the right way, for example, by joining a Memorial Day parade even if one is not thinking expressly about any of the veterans or wars being honored. Moreover, one need not have known the action in order to commemorate it. When I look intently at the faces and descriptions of those lost in one of the Trade Towers, I may not recognize anyone, but I am already commemorating them—not in the detail of their personal lives but in the stark fact that they once existed and now no longer do because of an act of violence. Even in this ignorance, it is remarkable how engaged I can be in this form of commemoration—an engagement that is at once focused on missing individuals and on the entire group of those lost.

Even if no words are spoken, such silent commemoration is still a form of public memory. Much that is mute is nevertheless shared. Commemoration is effected in the presence of others in a place to which we have all come. This happens not just as a set of similar experiences: more important, everyone there is beginning to work through the difficult emotions and thoughts occasioned by a public trauma, a wound to the body politic. If words are coming only haltingly, this is due to the weight of the trauma, which acts to immobilize and paralyze those suffering from it. In fact, the silence of most of those present in Union Square spoke for itself; as Lyotard insists, silence is itself a fully signifying phenomenon.[19] But it exists only in the very space of discourse that is possible even if not actual at the moment. Possible in the place of commemoration itself, where, once actualized, it will contribute powerfully to a more complete working-through than can occur with feelings and thoughts alone.

IV

Place subtends such memory, being the ground and resource, the location and scene of the remembering we do in common. In that place, feelings and thoughts rise from within as responses to events and persons without: the publicity of place shelters the privacy of emotion and idea but only insofar as these latter are themselves always on the way to becoming public—on the way to language, to the speech and writing that articulate these closely held items. The topics to which language brings us draw together from above as it were what is otherwise only disparate and idiosyncratic within the minds of individual rememberers. Public memory in turn gathers place, people, and topics in its encompassing embrace by acting as the external horizon that encircles the situation—the human situation, the human condition, the place we are always at when we are not merely standing by others or with family and friends.

Regarding this situation—*our* situation, never just mine or yours—place acts from below, feeling and thought from within, topics from above, and public memory from around. What Heidegger termed "the around-ness of the environment" (as the German phrase "das Um-uns-herum der Umwelt" is sometimes translated[20]) is here shared out by place and public memory, acting as epicenters between which the privacy of feeling and thought and the overtness of shared subject matters lie linked by language. Throughout, bodily actions render at once dense and effective the relationships between the primary terms of this schematic model of life in the public domain.

What difference does such a model, admittedly mainly descriptive, make in our understanding of this always problematic, always promising domain? What conclusions if any can we draw for the fate of public memory today? These questions are all the more pressing in view of the impression that I seem to have subordinated public memory by making it into the external horizon of the *vita activa*.[21] But is this tantamount to marginalizing public memory itself?

I think not. Let me say why not—why the topic is not just alive but burning—in five concluding remarks.

1. Whatever its position vis-à-vis other parameters of the public realm, public memory is constitutive of identities of many kinds: national and regional for certain but also (by way of encroachment) social and personal. There is little in our lives that is untouched by public memory, even if we do not focus on it except on ceremonial occasions or in massive emergencies. Thematized or not, however, it remains an abiding presence: like any horizon, it is at once encompassing and only tacitly present until singled out as such. A large part of the very power of public memory resides in its capacity to be for the most part located at the edge of our lives, hovering, ready to be invoked or revised, acted upon or merely contemplated, inspiring us or boring us: in every case, public memory is integral to what I have called "public presence."

2. The stakes of public memory are therefore high. Just because it is such an implicit presence, it is all the more formative of public life and public thought. In this regard, it is analogous to habitual body memory, which guides our corporeal lives from within by embedding cultural and somatic schemata in our very flesh; and it is like the psychical incorporation of others by way of introjection in the aftermath of missing and losing them. Both soma and psyche are in effect memorials to diverse influences, past and present; and they carry these literal influences into a future of personal and interpersonal action. So, too, with public memory: fixated without in monuments and texts, it is carried on within in our individual and shared sense of public identity. This identity specifies what kind of citizens we are, indeed what sort of human beings we are, as "citizens of the world," not just in a cosmopolitan or Enlightenment sense but as feeling and thinking members of the species. In its very horizonality, public memory encircles our lives; but it also enters into our most intimate redoubts—as we learn in a time of trauma, such as September 11, which brought out such a powerful sense of American identity (or more exactly, American *identities,* ranging from super-patriotic to super-skeptical, but all within the open horizon of publicly remembering that we are Americans in such a situation).

3. For two very good reasons, public memory needs a place of enactment, a scene of instantiation. First, public memories are continually subject to revision, as we have seen most strikingly in the case of Trumpeldor (but as we could also trace in many of our own national legends such as Paul Bunyon or Wild Bill Hickok). Second, their temporality is such that (as Merleau-Ponty said of paintings) they have "almost all their life still before them."[22] In that life much can change, not just in their conception or interpretation but in their very content and force as they are retold slightly differently from generation to generation and as they are transmitted and received with important changes over time. Far from being defects, these two forms of mutability demonstrate the capacity of public memories to speak to each era, not so much in this era's own given language (perfect translatability is an idle ideal) as in terms of its changing needs and perceptions. Without this elasticity, public memories could not survive as the effective presences they are: just as a perceptual horizon cannot be reduced to a single "horizon-line," public memories do not possess a hard edge. Their content is not altogether malleable—if it was, they

would lack the force to last over generational and historical change—but it is subject to alteration at any moment.

In view of this intrinsic mutability, public memory requires what the Romans called *stabilitas loci,* "stability of place," in which to arise and last. Places harbor and hold memories of many kinds, both personal (as we know from Proust's descriptions of the talismanic places of his childhood) and interpersonal (as in the case of a family home that becomes the seat of a reunion). They ground and collect social as well as collective memories. Maurice Halbwachs, the French sociologist and student of collective memory, emphasized precisely that "space is a reality that endures. . . . The collective thought of the group of believers has the best chance of immobilizing itself and enduring when it concentrates on places, sealing itself within their confines and molding its character to theirs."[23] Places are especially effective in the case of public memories, which are even more desperately in need of spatial anchorage than other kinds of shared remembering. Think only of military cemeteries that are built on or next to the battlefields where the buried soldiers once fought: being anchored there, at that place, brings the public memory of a given battle or war back to mind with special poignancy. The same holds true for the Vietnam Memorial wall, which tethers public memory to one place of recognition and mourning even if it is far from the original scenes of military action. Without such concrete implacements, memories would have "no referent in reality; or, rather, they [would be] their own referent: pure, exclusively self-referential signs."[24] These words of Pierre Nora speak for the necessity of place in the very heart of public memory.

Not that places themselves are immune from reinterpretation and even physical restructing. Claudia Koonz has shown this at work in the struggle over whether, and how, to preserve Nazi extermination camps, and James Young has written eloquently about this process in his classic *Writing and Rewriting the Holocaust: Narrative and the Consequences of Interpretation.* Koonz details the transformation of Buchenwald into a major tourist site—in contrast with Dachau, whose administration buildings and barracks were leveled by the local community, leaving only ruins near the crematoria.[25] Nevertheless, despite being subject to major physical or hermeneutical transformations, places with some lastingness will always be called for in the constitution and continuation of public memory.

4. One striking sign of this becomes evident in the case of public

trauma—disasters that affect the lives of all too many. Here place functions in two essential ways. First, it serves as a *place-of-sanctuary* to which to flee or retreat from the scene of trauma itself. The schoolchildren who fled from the public school that was only blocks from the World Trade Center made their way, through dust and smoke, to another school in mid-Manhattan—another place, a safe place.[26] My friend Parviz, who witnessed the collapse of the buildings from the proximity of Battery Park Plaza where he was working at the time, eventually found his way home to the West Village, leaving his van stranded and returning on a motorized scooter. Perhaps each of us, even if not in the city, returned to some sanctuary at the end of the day—if only to our own bedrooms or studies within the same house in which we were otherwise mesmerized by televised accounts. But then what of the place itself, the *place-of-trauma,* here that of the Trade Towers themselves?

This is a wounded place—a deeply injured, in this case obliterated, public place, a workplace in which work will never happen again as it did before. The wound inflicted on it was both to the physical buildings and to the American body politic for which they stood as such exemplary even if egregious presences—indeed, the two together, indissociable. It was striking that at Union Square that Sunday night there were many images—photographs, drawings and paintings, even woven rugs—of the towers. They, too, were missing and already missed. Mourning was beginning not only for the human victims but for the buildings themselves. And not just for the buildings as such but for their real and symbolic place in people's lives. The wound, we might say, was to *the body of the place of the polis.* The trauma inflicted was on place as well as people, as is testified by the pain many were having in looking at the New York skyline in the absence of the towers: "It hurts even to look in that direction," as one person said.[27] I have maintained for a long time that mourning (and not just nostalgia) can be of place, lost place, and if so we are in for a massive public mourning for the loss of this archetypal New York place. The mourning will be for the very place itself (here, the place provided by the buildings as well as the place on which they stood—now, tragically, all that remains), for all that the place made possible in the aspirations of others, and for all that would have happened there had the place not been destroyed.

5. Notice how time has crept back into this last line of thought, as if to underline the rightness of this essay's title: "Public Memory in Place *and*

Time." The Trade Towers are mourned for what had been there before the day of destruction, for what happened on that same day, and for a future that will now never take place. Their entry into public memory is temporally triplex: past and future as well as present. So we are back to where this paper began: the special two-indeed three-sidedness of public memory: Janus plus the present. The very idea of "memory," of course, lends itself to temporal analysis, as we know from James and Husserl and Bergson (and already from St. Augustine), all of whom in differing ways regarded memory as the consciousness of the past. But from this altogether natural starting point—part of what Husserl would call the "natural attitude" of time, or what I am tempted to call "chronocentrism"—we have been led, ineluctably as it were, to recognize the role of place in any full assessment of public memory. We started with an initial temporal analysis, moved to a description of such memory as external horizon (itself always both spatial and temporal), then plunged into place, and at the end touched on the temporal one last time. Strange course—strange phenomenon. We thereby reach a different bivalency, that of time and place themselves.

The fact is that the placial parameters of public memory are not secondary to temporal ones (as chronocentrism would have us believe) but altogether central, if not primary. In the end, we *must* acknowledge them as integral to the phenomenon of public memory in all its amplitude. For the more we pursue the time of such memory, the more we land in place as sine qua non for time, above all the time of our lives: our public lives, our lives with one another as part of the public domain. As "domain" itself implies (or "arena," "sphere"—all of the Arendtian terms apply in this context), this time always happens in some very particular place in which events can exfoliate or expire and people live or die.

The truth is that place subtends every kind of time, thus every kind of memory—individual and social, cultural and public. It underlies each of these memorial modes differently—too differently to encompass in any single formula. But in the case of public memory it does so in two basic ways which I have attempted to retrace in the central portion of this paper. On the one hand, place is part of public memory in the making, as we witnessed in the hearth event of the Union Square vigil, where a new form of public memory was beginning to emerge in that very place, both reflecting and requiring it. On the other hand, place remains central to a more fully consolidated public memory that has become a horizon for the future remembering of many others, not only those present at the moment of making. This horizon will have its own implacements, more stable than those in Union Square; it will be embodied and supported by more enduring memorials than the photographs and other images (accompanied by cursory words) strung up on walls and fences throughout lower Manhattan during that fateful time. But if the horizon in its very externality will be more perduring, its formative phase was more poignant. Each is needed—the hearth as well as the horizon—for a fully effective public memory to arise.

The Germans distinguish among a *Denkmal,* a monument meant to memorialize a person or event, a *Mahnmal* (a public reminder that acts as a warning), and a *Gedenkstätte* (a place in which a momentous event can be meditated).[28] Here time and place conjoin in the very language of public memory: if the *Denkmal* looks back to what has already occurred, the *Gedenkstätte* calls for thought in the present, while the *Mahnmal* asks us to take care in the future. All three temporal modes not only call for concrete implacement; each is already implaced in a particular scene, a given site—a scene or site in which we can truly say that public memory *takes the time to take place.*

Notes

1. Cited by Reiner Schürmann, ed., *The Public Realm: Essays on Discursive Types in Political Philosophy* (Albany: SUNY Press, 1989), 5.

2. Amy Waldman, "Grief, Lessened by Sharing and Solace from Strangers," *New York Times,* September 14, 2001, p. A8. "There are plastic pails tied to trees all over the site with handwritten signs marked 'photos' which are for any pictures we may find in the debris" (eyewitness report of Christina Maile, September 12, 2001).

3. Richard Lezin Jones, "A Growing Realization of an Unspeakable Loss," *New York Times,* September 15, 2001, p. A20.

4. See the photographs attached to Waldman, "Grief," A8.

5. On the victim, see Jean-François Lyotard, *The Differend* (Minneapolis: University of Minnesota Press, 1988).

6. See the account given in "A Paper Trail Leads to Sorrow and Some Hope," *New York Times,* September 14, 2001, p. A10: photographs of a credit union statement, a résumé, and a blank check.

7. Hannah Arendt, *The Human Condition* (Chicago: University of Chicago Press, 1958), 23. Arendt elaborates on the centrality of the family for the social realm in contrast with public space: "According to Greek thought, the human capacity for political organization is not only different from but stands in direct opposition to that natural association whose center is the home (*oikia*) and the family. . . . It was not just an opinion or theory of Aristotle but a simple historical fact that the foundation of the *polis* was preceded by the destruction of all organized units resting on kinship, such as the *phratria* and the *phylé*" (24).

8. Richard Sennett, *The Fall of Public Man: On the Social Psychology of Capitalism* (New York: Vintage, 1977), 338–39.

9. Yael Zerubavel, "Invented Tradition and Memory," in *Commemorations:The Politics of National Identity,* ed. John R. Gillis (Princeton: Princeton University Press, 1994), 113. Zerubavel details both the relatively recent (post-1921) origin of this legend and its current retreat as a national legend. She shows how its secularity allowed it to replace or at least supplement much earlier religious legends, while being replaced by still others as it became "the major target of doubts." At the same time, she demonstrates the intricate implication of history and legend in the Trumpeldor case (cf. 114ff.).

10. Zerubavel, "Invented Tradition and Memory," 107.

11. The phrase "invented traditions" is from *The Invention of Tradition,* ed. Eric Hobsbawm and T. Ranger (Cambridge: Cambridge University Press, 1983). Concerning this topic Zerubavel comments that "when a society undergoes rapid developments that shatter its social and political order, its need to restructure the past is as great as its desire to set its future agenda . . . such periods often stimulate the creation of new cultural forms that replace the weakening older traditions. These 'invented traditions' are particularly significant for the legitimation of the emergent social and political order, and their success depends, to a large measure, on their ability to reconstruct an acceptable view of the past" ("Invented Tradition and Memory," 105–6).

12. See my *Remembering:A Phenomenological Study* (Bloomington: Indiana University Press, 2000).

13. Yosef Klausner, "Al Kedushat ha-Aretz," *ha-Aretz,* March 21, 1921, p. 2, as cited by Zerubavel, "Invented Tradition and Memory," 107.

14. I have pursued further the role of place in relation to the political in "Powers of Place," unpublished manuscript, August 2001.

15. Arendt, *The Human Condition,* 26.

16. Ibid., 50.

17. Lyotard, *The Differend.*

18. See Casey, *Remembering,* chapter 10.

19. "Silence is a phrase. There is no last phrase" (Lyotard, *The Differend,* xii).

20. Martin Heidegger, *Being and Time,* trans. J. Macquarrie and E. Robinson (New York: Harper and Row, 1962), 136.

21. Indeed, is this not to marginalize the very topic of this volume and what we the contributors came together to discuss in a conference at a place whose name, "Syracuse," is redolent with the ancient Greek world?

22. M. Merleau-Ponty, "Eye and Mind," trans. C. Dallery in *Primacy of Perception,* ed. J. Edie (Evanston: Northwestern University Press, 1964), 190.

23. Maurice Halbwachs, *The Collective Memory,* trans. F. J. Ditter Jr. and V. Y. Ditter (New York: Harper, 1980), 156. Halbwachs adds: "Since our impressions rush by . . . we can . . . recapture the past only by understanding how it is, in effect, preserved by our physical surrounds" (140). Both cited in Claudia Koonz, "Between Memory and Oblivion," in *Commemorations: The Politics of National Identity,* ed. John R. Gillis (Princeton: Princeton University Press, 1994), 258–59.

24. Pierre Nora, "Between Memory and History: *Les lieux de mémoire,*" *Representations* 26 (spring 1989): 23–24, cited by Koonz, "Between Memory and Oblivion," 276n.

25. See Koonz, "Between Memory and Oblivion," 265–67. The case of Buchenwald is quite complex: cf. Koonz, "Between Memory and Oblivion," 271–73. See also James Young, *Writing and Rewriting the Holocaust: Narrative and the Uses of Interpretation* (Bloomington: Indiana University Press, 1990), passim.

26. A family center for relatives of the missing was opened at Pier 94 on the West Side Highway, offering child care, meals, telephones, Internet, etc.— another kind of sanctuary. See Jane Gross, "Relatives of Missing Find a Place for Their Comfort," *New York Times,* September 18, 2001, p. B6.

27. Bernadette Artus, cited in Nichole M. Christian, "On the Free Boat Ride, 'It Hurts to Even Look,'" *New York Times,* September 18, 2001, p. B6.

28. For these terms, see Koonz, "Between Memory and Oblivion," 259, 275.

2

Arendt, Eichmann, and the Politics of Remembrance

Stephen Howard Browne

On May 11, 1960, Karl Adolph Eichmann, former traveling salesman and chief executioner of the Final Solution, was seized by special forces in a suburb of Buenos Aires. From there he was flown under cover to Israel to face fifteen counts of "crimes against the Jewish people, crimes against humanity, and war crimes during the whole period of the Nazi regime and especially during the period of the second world war." The ensuing trial lasted eight months, and on December 5, 1961, he was sentenced to death by a special three-judge panel in the District Court of Jerusalem. In the words of the judges, "[T]he idea of the Final Solution would never have assumed the infernal forms of the flayed skin and tortured flesh of millions of Jews without the fanatical zeal and the unquenchable blood thirst of the appellant and his accomplices." On May 31 of the following year he was hanged and his ashes spread over the Mediterranean.[1]

From beginning to end the entire episode had been fraught with controversy. The arrest itself was of dubious legal standing—a kidnapping, really—and jurisdictional issues plagued the proceedings throughout. Indeed it was unclear on just what basis an individual could be tried in a country that had not yet existed when his crimes against it were committed. And David Ben-Gurion, who had ordered the capture and prosecution in the first place, declared that he did "not care what verdict is delivered against Eichmann," thus making clear his intention to bring the accused to a distinctive and some would say theatrical brand of political justice. Nothing about the trial, however, was to prove so provocative as the role played by a Jewish-American intellectual, refugee, and political theorist who had taken it upon herself to report its proceedings in the pages of the *New Yorker*. The author of *Totalitarianism* and *The Human Condition*, Hannah Arendt was at the time widely regarded as a thinker of stunning originality and insight, and these qualities she unquestionably brought to her task.

Once in Jerusalem, Arendt, in the words of Michael Denneny, "received a jolt whose impact was to set the course of her thinking for the next fifteen years, for she realized that this trial 'touched upon one of the central moral questions of all time, namely the nature and function of human judgment.'" At the same time, nothing could have prepared her for the onslaught of criticism that followed in the wake of her reports, published shortly thereafter in 1963 as *Eichmann in Jerusalem: A Report on the Banality of Evil*.[2]

The reactions were not all negative. Arendt's friend and correspondent Mary McCarthy thought it "morally exhilarating," indeed "a paean of transcendence, heavenly music, like that of the final chorus of Figaro or the Messiah." The poet James Lowell judged it "a masterpiece in rendering the almost unreadably repellent." Lowell insisted that contrary to her critics, he "never felt she was condescending, or hard, or driven by a perverse theory, or by any motive except a heroic desire for truth." Dwight McDonald concluded that the book was "a masterpiece of historical journalism that explained the real horror of Nazi genocide" and admitted that whatever the faults of her analysis, Arendt "tried to learn something from history" and so took "heart in a book like *Eichmann in Jerusalem*." While disapproving of both the book's "tone and formulation" and its more polemical critics, William Phillips concluded that *Eichmann in Jerusalem* was a "powerful account of Eichmann's contribution to the final solution."[3]

Others, to put it mildly, proved rather less impressed by the work. A review in *The Nation* claimed that it was little more than a "thin trickle of assertion through a flooded swampland of redundancies," a book, wrote Klaus Epstein in the *Modern Age*, "marred by prejudices, special pleading, and attachment to fixed ideas." Even her friend Gershom Scholem sadly insisted that it was the "heartless, frequently almost sneering and malicious tone with which these matters, touching the very quick of our life, are treated in your book to which I take exception." Lionel Abel, one of her most vociferous critics, publicly condemned the book for its misapplied "aesthetic" categories, found its argument "strange and shocking," "perverse and arbitrary," and finally dismissed the theory underlying it as wholly "invalidated." Indeed, to this day, even such sympathetic readers as Seyla Benhabib concede that *Eichmann in Jerusalem* "exhibited at times an astonishing lack of perspective, balance of judgment, and judicious expression."[4]

That Arendt's "report on the banality of evil" should provoke such disparate, heated, and enduring reactions is noteworthy, certainly, but to those familiar with her work not especially surprising. Virtually every one of her major publications through a career spanning much of the mid-twentieth century similarly prompted both criticism and praise, confusion and relief. To acknowledge this fact is to appreciate first that Arendt represents, among other things, a problem in interpretation: even her most astute students confess to struggling to decipher just what she means. Bernard Crick notes that readers of *Totalitarianism* are often "awed, bewildered, and enthralled all at once"; Bikhu Parekh judges the philosophical assumptions at work in *The Human Condition* "brilliant and valid in some areas but pedestrian and even invalid in others"; while Peter Fuss finds it "[r]ichly textured, astonishingly erudite, and difficult to read." James Miller observes that *On Revolution* is "a book of paradoxes," "marked by violent jolts, startling vistas. Shock mingles with surprise," he writes, "doubt with assent, in a tangled web of response that eludes any comfortable characterization." On receiving the 2000 Hannah Arendt Award Elena Bonner said: "Reading Arendt is frightening even today."[5]

At least two reasons may account for the challenges Arendt poses to the contemporary reader. One has to do with her resolute but often trying refusal to apply conventional categories and methods derived from disciplinary conventions. As many have observed, Arendt thought in spaces between traditional modes of inquiry, notably political science and political economy. In the words of Melvyn Hill, Arendt "took as her point of departure and her method as a political thinker not the sophistications of behavioral science nor of Marxist dialectics, but simply the perspective of the citizen who views the political world as the realm of freedom needed in order to act with others in matters of common concern." Similarly, Margaret Canovan explains that Arendt's thinking "cannot be categorized according to the accepted labels of 'political science,' 'conceptual analysis,' 'history of ideas,' or 'ideological manifesto.' " "[I]nstead," writes

Canovan, "it evidently purports, in the manner of the classics, to arrive at an understanding of politics which will be true to men's experience of political activity, and which will elucidate the place of politics within human life and the criteria appropriate for making judgments about it."[6]

A second explanation refers not so much to the singularity of Arendt's approach as to the ways in which she is frequently read, that is, to the habits of reception and interpretation that have shaped our understanding of her thought. So distinctive and formidable have been her major works that they have tended to be taken up as discrete texts; this much is understandable, perhaps, given the labor required to unpack the elusive and unique meaning inhering in each. Recently this tendency has been checked by those who are inclined to see in any given text the imprints and prefigurations of others in her works. In any case, some headway may be made against the frustrations of reading Arendt by refusing to interpret her key texts in isolation and assembling, so to speak, companion texts and letting them shed hermeneutic light on each other. Such will be the aim and approach of this essay.[7]

We are now in the midst of a renaissance in Arendt studies, and that is a very good thing indeed. At the same time it may obscure the fact that with the publication of *Eichmann in Jerusalem* her claim to intellectual preeminence was very nearly extinguished; we need only recollect how quiet was her passing in 1975 to see the apparent damage that work had inflicted on her reputation. In returning to the book, I have no wish to rehabilitate that reputation—beyond my abilities in one case, and not necessary in the other—nor to bury it again—equally foolhardy. I want rather to revisit the text because I think it offers us a fresh way to think through the politics of memory. To do so we need to position *Eichmann in Jerusalem* strategically between her previous work and the chorus of criticism following its publication. More specifically, I hope to show that by placing *Eichmann* intermediate to *The Human Condition* and the public reactions it prompted, we arrive at the most illuminating representation of her thought on memory. Read together, these texts lead us to the heart of Arendt's insight about the work of remembrance: that far from being merely nostalgic or retrospective, such work is always and at once new, discursive, and unpredictable. More generally, I suggest that the criticism provoked by *Eichmann in Jerusalem* may be usefully seen as a dramatic affirmation, however unintended, of Arendt's more theoretical statements on the sources, functions, and ends of memory. To that end, I remind us of Arendt's treatment of memory in *The Human Condition,* then examine her portrait of Eichmann as an anti-type in the drama of memory, and turn finally to her critics. These last, I shall argue, instantiate Arendt's view as to the work required to sustain the conditions requisite to human polity. First, however, we must consider the status and function of remembrance in Arendt's thought generally. On that basis, we may then be in a position to integrate her insights into a more satisfying account of her most notorious work.

Arendt on Remembrance

As a student of both Martin Heidegger and Karl Jaspers, Arendt could scarcely have avoided the philosophical problem of the relation between time and being. Her achievement, more positively, was to assert into her analysis the question of the political in ways not taken up by her mentors. In one form or another, the major Arendt texts evince a fundamental preoccupation with time generally and, more specifically, the role of remembrance in the constitution and reconstitution of human polity. We cannot detail this role at any length here, but a brief and selective survey of several texts will provide us with at least a working sense of what this category does for Arendt and what its status was in her thinking about the viability of political life in our time. Prior to and after *Eichmann in Jerusalem,* Arendt invoked the concept of remembrance and features it in subtle but decisive ways. This is especially the case in *The Human Condition,* the analysis of which will be deferred for more fulsome examination later. It is enough to suggest at this point that in *Totalitarianism, Between Past and Future,* and *On Revolution* we can see suggestive hints of the importance Arendt accords to remembrance as a political category. Three main lines of thought are then made evident.

First, remembrance is conceived as ballast against the intrinsic frailty and transience of human life as it is given. This conviction runs as a leitmotif throughout much of Arendt's thought, and it is central to her thinking about the prospects of being-with-others in the world. Indeed, she argues, without this capacity for remembrance, no such life would be possible—at least as it is lived in the manner appropriate to humanity as such. It is a point she presses to great effect in *The Human Condition,* as we shall see, but it is also given forceful expression in "The Concept of History," an essay with which she introduces *Between Past and Future*. The following passage is worth quoting in full:

> All things that owe their existence to men, such as works, deeds, and words, are perishable, infected, as it were, by the mortality of their authors. However, if mortals succeeded in endowing their works, deeds, and words with some permanence and in arresting their perishability, then these things would, to a degree at least, enter and be at home in the world of everlastingness, and the mortals themselves would find their place in the cosmos, where everything is immortal except man. The human capacity to achieve this was remembrance, Mnemosyne, who was therefore regarded as the mother of all other muses.[8]

For Arendt, the impermanence of all human productions was at once undeniable and subject to qualification; it was the task of memory to acknowledge, confront, and beat back the forces of forgetting—not, it is important to stress, by way of living through the past and certainly not out of any sense of lingering nostalgia for antiquity, but because, without the trust that memory bestows, all hope for meaningful action would dissipate into the winds of time. Accordingly, Arendt writes, "what goes on between mortals directly [their experience of being together in the world] . . . would never outlast the moment of their realization, would never leave any trace without the help of remembrance."[9]

As we can see even in these brief passages, the other side of the equation of remembrance is forgetfulness, the source and subject of considerable anxiety in Arendt's thought. Thus a second theme underwriting the argument: the persistent and fatal capacity of human beings to forget. Seldom latent, always potential, this capacity is marked most conspicuously by a failure of judgment, the tendency to forget that we exist in the world with and through others. Political judgment, more specifically, operates under conditions of plurality; in the words of Margaret Canovan, "Although each sees this world from a slightly different standpoint, sound judgments are nevertheless not limited by this standpoint but take into account also the positions of others and therefore shares by them." Forgetting, by contrast, collapses the space of judgment by eliminating the presence of others. To Arendt, this ever-present danger haunts the human condition, especially under conditions of genuine revolution when the possibilities of freedom and action are made startling clear. It was, for example, the basis for the tragic quality of the French Resistance, which seemed to forget the revolutionary tradition out of which it sprung almost as soon as its success had been secured. Without this tradition, she writes, "which selects and names, which hands down and preserves, which indicates where the treasures are and what their worth is—there seems to be no willed continuity in time and hence, humanly speaking, neither past nor future, only sempiternal change of the world and the biological cycle of living creatures in it." Such a loss, she concludes, "was consummated by oblivion, by a failure of memory, which befell not only the heirs but, as it were, the actors, the witnesses, those who for a fleeting moment had held the treasure in the palms of their hands, in short, the living themselves." At its extreme this forgetfulness will express itself as typical of the totalitarian state and the "startling swiftness" with which its leaders are forgotten; for "if there is such a thing as a totalitarian personality or mentality, this extraordinary adaptability and absence of continuity are no doubt its outstanding characteristics."[10]

Hence the imperative to remember: that through the recollection and embrace of political greatness, which is to say acting together in freedom to secure the conditions of freedom, the prospects of life in polity are enhanced if not guaranteed. The modalities through which this freedom and its remembrance are played out specifies the third dimension of Arendt's thinking on the subject. It is, she writes, through speech and action, words and deeds, that humans enact and affirm their collective identity as political creatures. Here Arendt draws heavily, as is her wont, from Greek antiquity, for there she discovered the essential role of the poets, whose genius "consisted in the immortal fame which the poets could bestow upon word and deed to make them outlast not only the futile moment of speech and action but even the mortal life of their agent." In this sense, remembrance functions to confirm the reality of those who, no longer physically present, had acted freely as political beings; it assures us that such things are possible, real, and thus may, against the odds, appear again. This interplay of freedom, speech and action, the political, and remembrance is efficiently captured in *On Revolution:* "[T]hese activities could appear and be real only when others saw them, judged them, remembered them. The life of a free man needed the presence of others. Freedom itself needed therefore a place where people could come together—the agora, the market place, or the polis, the political space proper."[11]

Taken together, Arendt's reflections on the protection remembrance affords against the waves of time and transience; the perils of forgetting and its consequent destruction of hope, meaning, and motive for political life; and the disclosure of that life through speech and action represent three tightly braided themes with which the fabric of her thought is given its distinctive texture. As we move now to take up the role of remembrance in *The Human Condition, Eichmann in Jerusalem,* and the critical responses to the latter, it will become clear, I hope, that the concept retains significant explanatory force and gives us a basis upon which these texts might be productively read.

Remembrance and *The Human Condition*

Upon its publication in 1958, *The Human Condition* was thought to contain "insights into history and politics" that seemed to Mary McCarthy, among others, "both amazing and obvious." In fact it is this very combination of the strange and the self-evident that continues to provoke Arendt's champions and critics, and I must confess that it troubles my analysis as well. At the same time, the work is marked, like many of her other texts, by a conspicuous tendency to strike conceptual distinctions that remain for many of her critics baffling or at best inconclusive: labor, work, and action; *vita contemplativa-vita activa;* freedom and necessity; politics and philosophy; thought and action. She has moreover been challenged in turn for being elitist, antifeminist, nostalgic, and excessively beholden to antique and antiquated political models; for lacking normative standards; and for being philosophically opportunistic. And then there is her curious habit of generating extensive lines of inquiry by philologically—and rather selectively—unpacking the meaning of certain words. But there can be no mistaking that the work, for all its eccentricities, presents us with the most promising avenue into her thinking about memory. Arendt does not dwell at great length on the matter, nor does she expend much effort to link the concept to the many, many others that constitute the text as a whole. Still, there is reason aplenty to revisit *The Human Condition* as our starting point, specifically her treatment of action and its constituent features—the public realm, natality, plurality, and speech. Here we will find if not a full-blown theory of memory then the operative assumptions on which such an account might be developed.[12]

The conditions of our humanity, Arendt contends, are three. Labor is that activity which corresponds to maintaining the life process itself; its realm is private and thus excluded by definition from the political. "Labor power," Arendt explains, "produces objects only incidentally and is primarily concerned with the means of its own reproduction; since its power is not exhausted when its own reproduction has been secured, it can be used for the reproduction of more than one life process, but it never 'produces' anything but life." Importantly for our purposes, Arendt recognizes the centrality of labor to the human condition even as she stresses its insufficiency: labor by its very nature is caught up in the recurrent cycles of the biological process; it leaves nothing lasting behind and therefore passes from memory. Work, by distinction, corresponds to the fabrication of a world worth living in. Here Arendt refers to humans as *homo faber,* creatures who create from the endless variety of things in the world the instruments and objects that make that world habitable. "Their proper use," writes Arendt, "does not cause them to disappear and they give to human artifice the stability and solidity without which it could not be relied upon to house the unstable and mortal creature which is man." Although not subject to the same forces as labor, the production of such instruments and objects promises at least a provisional respite from the demands of life biologically considered; in short, it gives to the human condition a certain durability, which in turn "gives the things of the world their relative independence from men who produce and use them, their 'objectivity' which makes them withstand, 'stand against,' and endure, at least for a time, the voracious needs and wants of their living makers and users."[13]

Action, finally, denotes that which actualizes our shared capacity for living freely in a world inhabited by others. Of the three, Arendt accords pride of place to the latter, for in action she discovers that condition which humans alone share and is therefore definitively human. Arendt, who once described political theory as the art of making distinctions, can be exasperating in this as in other such schemata; but it is clear that in the category of action she seeks to identify that which is decisive, essential to the prospects of our being-in-the-world:

> If the *animal laborans* needs the help of *homo faber* to ease his labor and remove his pain, and if mortals need his help to erect a home on earth, acting and speaking men need the help of *homo faber* in his highest capacity, that is, the help of the artist, of poets and historiographers, of monument-builders or writers, because without them the only product of their activity, the story they enact or tell, would not survive at all. In order to be what the world is always meant to be, a home for men during their life on earth, the human artifice must be a place fit for action and speech, for activities not only entirely useless for the necessities of life but of an entirely different nature from the manifold activities of fabrication by which the world itself and all things in it are produced.[14]

As near as I can tell, the category has no specific propositional content: it is rather a modality, a force that "always establishes relationships and therefore has an inherent tendency to force open all limitations and cut across all boundaries." As elusive as it is conceptually, action may be defined with reference to its place, that is in the space of appearance, where we see and are seen by others, and to the object against which that force is directed, that is to the creation of something new in the world. In the first case, action is always to be understood as that which is undertaken among others, in the public realm, the polis, needing, she wrote, "for its full appearance the shining brightness we once called glory, and which is possible only in the public world." Action thus takes on its aspect only under conditions of plurality, in a world of others at once similar as specie are similar and unique as autonomous agents are unique. In the second case, action marks that enduring capacity of human beings to begin anew. To act, she writes, is to "assert ourselves into the human world, and this assertion is like a second birth." Linking action with natality is absolutely basic to her argument: it is definitive of action that it starts something, that it literally activates the world by acting in the world; it is thus constitutive of ourselves as humans and of the freedom necessary to be fully human.

"With the creation of man," Arendt observes, "the principle of beginning came into the world, which of course, is only another way of saying that the principle of freedom was created when man was created but not before."[15]

Several entailments from this position bear directly on our subject. Action may be said to effect beginnings because the world in which they take place is unfixed, contingent, and ultimately frail. Under such conditions, action always carries with it the element of surprise; that which it creates can never be predicted or predetermined. Indeed, writes Arendt, "It is in the nature of beginning that something new is started which cannot be expected from whatever may have happened before. This character of startling unexpectedness is inherent in all beginnings and in all origins. . . . The fact that man is capable of action means that the unexpected can be expected from him, that he is able to perform what is infinitely improbable. And this again is possible only because each man is unique, so that with each birth something uniquely new comes into the world." In a fragile and impermanent world, that which is created by action is thus not only unexpected but constantly in danger of being forgotten. That it not be forgotten, and that it must not be if the world is to regenerate itself, is a charge imposed upon all those who would sustain the conditions of public life. By direct implication, action thus conceived is essentially, profoundly political; indeed it represents the very possibility of political life generally and specifically the prospects of democratic polity. As D'entreves stresses, Arendt's "theory of action articulates the historical experience and normative presuppositions of participatory democracy . . . and such a theory remains essential for the reactivation of public life in the modern world."[16]

Here we encounter the specific function of speech assigned by Arendt, that is, its capacity to disclose the meaning of action and to enter that meaning into the collective memory. Speech reveals action for what it is and the actor for who he or she is: "Without the accompaniment of speech," notes Arendt, "action would not only lose its revelatory character, but, by the same token, it would lose its subject." Through action and speech, she writes, "men show who they are, reveal actively their unique personal identities and thus make their appearance in the world." But it is just because that world is so intangible, so fleeting and relentlessly novel, that speech is required to not only disclose meaning but to give it permanence, to give it a reality and a history that it would otherwise lose. We see now, perhaps, the relationship posed by Arendt between action and remembrance. She summarizes the point as follows: "The whole factual world of human affairs depends for its reality and its continued existence, first, upon the presence of others who have seen and will remember, and, second, on the transformation of the intangible into the tangibility of things. Without remembrance and without the reification which remembrance needs for its own fulfillment . . . the living activities of action, speech, and thought would lose their reality at the end of each process and disappear as though they never had been."[17] The disclosive function of speech is accordingly instrumental as well: it reveals the meaning of action, and it heralds that meaning into the "web of human relationships" that Arendt takes to be definitive of human community. To the extent that that web underlies the conditions of polity, its power and purpose is to sustain the conditions of life itself. Indeed, she writes, "A life without speech and without action . . . is literally dead to the world; it has ceased to be human life because it is no longer lived among men." Arendt can thus conclude, "The organization of the *polis* . . . is a kind of organized remembrance. It assures the moral actor that his passing existence and fleeting greatness will never lack the reality that comes from being seen, being heard, and, generally, appearing before an audience of fellow men."[18]

Eichmann, Forgetting, and the Memory of Politics

Even so brief a review of *The Human Condition* suggests that we have in it the means to read *Eichmann in Jerusalem* in new and productive ways. In turning to the latter, I have no wish to resolve or even address directly the many perplexities that still haunt the text. *The Human Condition,* rather, may be viewed as a template for making sense of both works; more precisely, *Eichmann in Jerusalem* may be seen as instantiating in practice the theoretical claims summarized above. In this context, Eichmann functions as a kind of illustrative anti-type to the Periclean model figured in *The Human Condition;* it is a character study as well as a narrative, a dramatic rendering of a man rendered unreal in an unreal world—indeed a non-world where force is mistaken for action, superfluousness for plurality, and cliché for speech. Eichmann is thus made to stand as a kind of morality lesson for what happens when the space of appearance, action, renewal, and plurality disappears into the holes of oblivion. His is rather the space, if it may be called that, of erasure, of silence and the thoughtlessness that always attends forgetting. Eichmann, we shall see, cannot act because he occupies no space within which to act, cannot speak because there is no *who* there that speech might disclose, and cannot remember because under such conditions there is literally nothing to remember. Those familiar with the Penguin edition of *Eichmann in Jerusalem* will note in this sense how perfectly its cover photo captures the Eichmann ethos: there he sits in the courtroom, sealed off from the world in a glass booth, mutely staring ahead as if in disbelief at his own fate and the fate of those for whom he was responsible.

By way of approaching Arendt's portrait, we might begin with what she takes to be the primal fact of Eichmann's character: his essential thoughtlessness. This is, of course, the basis of her final claim about the banality of his evil, and it gave her much trouble as a result. It has been suggested that some of that trouble was due to her struggle to put into words a phenomenon heretofore unknown to the world. Thus Seyla Benhabib observes that "Arendt was punished by the Jewish community precisely because she, like so many others who were Holocaust survivors, had not found the right public language, the right discourse, through which to narrate past sorrow, suffering, and loss." If we read *Eichmann in Jerusalem* as a study in the consequences of forgetting, however, it becomes apparent that Arendt had found a powerful language with which to describe and condemn the evil that had beset the world.[19]

At the very least, Arendt gives us a means to comprehend just what it is that makes forgetting on such a scale possible in the first place. "The longer one listened to him," Arendt writes, "the more obvious it became that his inability to speak was closely connected with an inability to think, namely, to think from the standpoint of someone else. No communication was possible with him, not because he lied but because he was surrounded by the most reliable of all safeguards against the words and presence of others, and hence against reality as such." This failure is in the end a failure to exercise the human capacity for judgment, that is, to assess good from evil without recourse to convention, self-interest, or language rules. As Jerome Kohn succinctly writes, "Eichmann was not a dog but a man, but no more than a conditioned animal did he exercise free choice. Arendt is intent to show throughout her 'report' that Eichmann did not act spontaneously or take initiative, that he avoided responsibility and did not judge. He did as he was bid." Here was the ultimate source and ground of Eichmann's evil—his "almost total inability to look at anything from the other's point of view." Such a character flaw—I think Arendt is saying this flaw is descriptive beyond the man himself—thus is made to stand in the starkest of contrasts to the plurality marking the human condition. This thoughtlessness, this incapacity to imagine any perspective but one's own, is the surest evidence that his was a life without world, without, that is, the web of relations constitutive of our shared humanity. He was, as Arendt brilliantly puts it, "a leaf in the whirlwind of time."[20]

From this fact of Eichmann's character Arendt builds her case. It is a complex, striking, and painful rendering, but through it we begin to discern the outlines of what might be called the inhuman condition. Two deeply interconnected features of that condition are treated with reference to Eichmann's habits of speech and then to his memory—or lack thereof. Arendt was in the first instance clearly struck by Eichmann's unfailing ability to render complicated historical or moral questions into a cliché. Indeed, the accused seemed incapable of saying anything that was not at once transparent and empty—the precise opposite, that is, of the power she accords speech in her earlier work. From beginning to end, the trial displayed the spectacle of a man for whom language was literally meaningless—except as a kind of self-protection against authentic disclosure or communication. "Eichmann's retreat from reality into the clichés of ideological thinking or postwar reconciliation," notes Dana Villa, "signaled not a peculiar mendacity, but a bizarre and unsettling form of honesty: the honesty of the other-directed conformist who literally 'never realized what he was doing.'"[21]

Unable to think from the standpoint of others, he filled the vacuum of his mind with stock phrases and "had at his disposal," Arendt observes, "a different elating cliché for each period of his life and each of his activities." In this respect, the banality of his evil corresponded to the banality of his speech. His final words, Arendt reports in her chilling conclusion, were of a piece with this habit: "After a short while, gentlemen, we shall meet again. Such is the fate of all men. Long live Germany, long live Argentina, long live Austria. I shall not forget them." Arendt then notes: "Nothing could have demonstrated this more convincingly than the grotesque silliness of his last words . . . in the face of death, he had found the cliché used in funeral oratory. Under the gallows, his memory played him the last trick; he was elated, and forgot that this was his own funeral. It was as though in those last minutes he was summing up the lesson that this long course in human wickedness had taught us—the lesson of the fearsome, word-and-thought-defying banality of evil."[22]

By direct extension, Eichmann's capacity for remembrance may be readily glimpsed. Recalling Arendt's point in *The Human Condition*—that "each individual in his unique distinctness, appears and confirms himself in speech and action, and that these activities, despite their material futility, possess an enduring quality of their own because they create their own remembrance"—we see in Eichmann's portrait the image of someone for whom genuine remembrance was impossible. And this failure of memory in turn explained Eichmann's incapacity for judgment; unable to remember, he could not judge—could not, that is, incorporate into his "thought" the fact of others being in the world. Having been blown by the winds into history, he was possessed, Arendt writes, of an "extraordinarily faulty memory," ignorant of "everything that was not directly, technically and bureaucratically, connected with his job," functioning "only in respect to things that had a direct bearing upon his career." The past was to Eichmann what the cliché was to speech: a repository of self-gratifying fictions ready at hand, stories, as Arendt explains, that "ran along a different tape in his memory, and it was this taped memory that showed itself to be proof against reason and argument and information and insight of any kind."[23]

Like the cliché, such taped memories bore no more relation to the world than did the stock phrase; to invoke them was not to act in remembrance but to deny such action at all. Thus, I presume, the animus behind Arendt's seemingly cold assessment of what she believed were the fraudulent rituals of her own day. "Those young German men and women who every once in a while—on the occasion of all the Diary of Anne Frank hubbub and of the Eichmann trial—treat us to hysterical outbreaks of guilt feelings are not staggering under the burden of the past, their fathers' guilt; rather they are trying to escape from the pressure of very present and actual problems into a cheap sentimentality."[24]

Criticism and the Work of Memory

A decade after the Eichmann trial Hannah Arendt found herself still preoccupied with her experience there and, more pointedly, with what the accused "meant." The mind to which she bore witness in that Israeli courtroom had at once repulsed and fascinated her, for in it she had discovered something about the nature of evil itself—it was not deep as love is deep, nor heroic as the spirit is heroic; it was not radical but "banal." She discovered also that Eichmann negatively exemplified something fundamental about the nature and function of human judgment—hence she returned to the trial by way of accounting for her last major work, a projected three-volume study of thinking, willing, and judging under the title *The Life of the Mind*. Here she reflects again: "Clichés, stock phrases, adherence to conventional, standardized codes of expression and conduct have the socially recognized function of protecting us against reality, that is, against the claim on our thinking attention that all events and facts make by virtue of their existence. If we were responsive to this claim all the time, we would soon be exhausted; Eichmann differed from the rest of us only in that he clearly knew of no such claim at all."[25] As we have seen, one of the chief markers of such language is that it protects against memory itself; it is a peculiarly insidious form of amnesia, a kind of mental cliché that has a devastating effect on individuals and cultures. Eichmann, like those "young German men and women" given to "cheap sentimentality," was guilty in the first place of failing to think, hence to remember. This failure is perforce a failure to engage the world, to think and act in a world in a way that acknowledges the existence and the claims of other human beings. Remembrance, to recall our earlier discussion, is for Arendt a specific type of thinking, definitively political to the extent that it holds in trust the acts and deeds of those who have come before; it functions as a bulwark against the tides of time that otherwise erode our sense of hope and purpose. To remember is thus not simply to turn backward; it is itself a type of action that steadies us in the face of an unknown and unpredictable future; it allows us, as the poet Alan Dugan put it, "to walk out bravely into the daily accident."[26]

These considerations, I believe, provide us with a way to reconceive the critical responses to *Eichmann in Jerusalem*. Some speculation is unavoidable here, but we might begin by noting Arendt's notorious refusal to defend herself, concede the argument, or apologize for so offending her Jewish (and other) readers. Perhaps—and here is the speculation—she understood and appreciated at some level that the debate swirling around her "report" was, however discomfiting, precisely the kind of action she had envisioned in *The Human Condition* and precisely what was missing in Eichmann's Germany. For however just or unjust her critics, however personal, insulting, aggrandizing, and "right" or "wrong" their interpretations, the fact was that they were debating issues of general concern in public, risking their reputations and convictions, acting freely in a realm created by speech and deeds. Was this not glorious?

Make no mistake: the criticism was intense. Arendt's examination of the Eichmann trial called down the wrath of Jewish intellectuals in the United States and abroad, and that wrath has yet to fully dissipate even in this, her moment of rebirth in American political theory. As I have noted, much of the criticism had to do with her alleged anti-Zionism, her identification of the Jewish leaders with complicity in the Final Solution, and her reference to the banality of Eichmann's evil. Arendt's critics did not stop there, of course. Among the primary charges against her were several particularly telling complaints. The first, leveled most pointedly by Marie Syrkin, concerned the quality of scholarship Arendt brought to bear on her study. Here we are told that Arendt's "astonishing indifference to charges of gross inaccuracy and omissions of pertinent data" is explicable only because "Miss Arendt is considered exempt from the criteria reliability usually applied to any work which pretends to be objective scholarship rather than tendentious exposition." Lionel Abel similarly despaired of the book's "faults of omission" and "frequent misstatement of fact," and like many others he complained that she limited "herself to the description of the sensational facts, which, while they add to our nausea, add nothing to our clarity about what happened in Nazi Europe and why the Jewish leaders behaved as they did." To these charges Arendt was maddeningly indifferent.[27]

A second line of criticism proved equally vehement and perhaps more telling, more lasting. It concerns what her friend William Phillips refers to as the "snide, slightly hostile tone" that pervades the work, and it was this tone "of irony, of insinuation, of moral Olympianism that makes the treatment of the Jews in *Eichmann in Jerusalem* seem so cold and harsh." Gershom Scholem asked rhetorically how it was that her "version of the events so often seems to come between us and the events." Whatever her intentions, her critics concluded, whatever her brilliance or learning, Hannah Arendt lacked that love of the Jewish people, that Ahabath Israel, and for this they could not forgive her.[28]

Such criticism could be extended considerably. For our purposes, however, the point is not to mount the case against Arendt but to first acknowledge the controversy she sparked and then to ask what it might tell us about the work of memory. I would like to suggest that in the very fact of that criticism, in its animation, seriousness, and public character, can be found a kind of redemption for the ideas professed in *The Human Condition* and the praxis that was *Eichmann in Jerusalem.* Perhaps the most succinct way to the point is to invoke Arendt's own response to her friend Gershom Scholem: "What confuses you," she writes, "is that my arguments and my approach are different from what you are used to; in other words, the trouble is that I am independent."[29]

And it was this independence of mind—a mind that was not therefore abstracted from but deeply engaged in the world—that created from the circumstances of Eichmann's trial precisely those conditions articulated in her earlier thought. She had acted and said something new; what she said could not have been predicted, nor could she have predicted the consequences of her words. But in their very expression, in the debate she provoked and ideas she loosed upon the world, she provided a kind of antidote to the thoughtlessness and the cliché-ridden idiocy of Eichmann's speech. In the process she had helped reconstitute the conditions of remembrance essential to democratic polity. Hannah Arendt, in other words, had started an argument.

Notes

1. Quoted in Hannah Arendt, *Eichmann in Jerusalem: A Report on the Banality of Evil* (New York: Penguin, 1992), 20, 249.

2. Quoted in *Eichmann in Jerusalem,* 20; Michael Denneny, "The Privilege of

Ourselves: Hannah Arendt on Judgment," in *Hannah Arendt: The Recovery of the Public World,* ed. Melvyn A. Hill (New York: St. Martin's, 1979), 253–54.

3. Mary McCarthy, "The Hue and Cry," *Partisan Review* 31 (1964): 91; Robert Lowell, "More on Eichmann," *Partisan Review* 31 (1964): 261; Dwight McDonald, "More on Eichmann," *Partisan Review* 31 (1964): 262; William Phillips, "Arguments," *Partisan Review* 31 (1964): 283.

4. D. J. Goodspeed, "Violence in the Abstract," *Nation* 196 (1963): 379; Klaus Epstein, "The Eichmann Affair," *Modern Age* 8 (1963–64): 110; Gershom Scholem, "*Eichmann in Jerusalem:* An Exchange of Letters between Gershom Scholem and Hannah Arendt," in *The Jew as Pariah: Jewish Identity and Politics in the Modern Age,* ed. Ron Feldman (New York: Grove Press, 1978), 241; Lionel Abel, "The Aesthetics of Evil: Hannah Arendt on Eichmann and the Jews," *Partisan Review* 30 (1963): 219, 224, 230; Seyla Benhabib, "Arendt's *Eichmann in Jerusalem,*" in *The Cambridge Companion to Hannah Arendt,* ed. Dana Villa (Cambridge: Cambridge University Press, 2000), 65.

5. Bernard Crick, "On Rereading the Origins of *Totalitarianism,*" in *Hannah Arendt: The Recovery of the Public World,* ed. Melvyn A. Hill (New York: St. Martin's, 1979), 41; Bikhu Parekh, "Hannah Arendt's Critique of Marx," in *Hannah Arendt: The Recovery of the Public World,* ed. Melvyn A. Hill (New York: St. Martin's, 1979), 99; Peter Fuss, "Hannah Arendt's Conception of Political Community," in *Hannah Arendt: The Recovery of the Public World,* ed. Melvyn A. Hill (New York: St. Martin's, 1979), 158; James Miller, "The Pathos of Novelty: Hannah Arendt's Image of Freedom in the Modern World," in *Hannah Arendt: The Recovery of the Public World,* ed. Melvyn A. Hill (New York: St. Martin's, 1979), 177; Elena Bonner, "The Remains of Totalitarianism," *New York Review of Books* 58 (2001): 4.

6. Melvyn A. Hill, "The Fictions of Mankind and the Stories of Men," in *Hannah Arendt: The Recovery of the Public World,* ed. Melvyn A. Hill (New York: St. Martin's, 1979), 277; Margaret Canovan, *The Political Thought of Hannah Arendt* (New York: Harcourt Brace Jovanovich, 1974), 1.

7. For exemplary syntheses, see especially Seyla Benhabib, *The Reluctant Modernism of Hannah Arendt* (Thousand Oaks, CA: Sage, 1996); Richard J. Bernstein, *Hannah Arendt and the Jewish Question* (Cambridge, MA: MIT Press, 1996); Margaret Canovan, *Hannah Arendt: A Reinterpretation of Her Political Thought* (Cambridge: Cambridge University Press, 1992); and Maurizio Passerin D'entreves, *The Political Philosophy of Hannah Arendt* (New York: Routledge, 1994).

8. Hannah Arendt, *Between Past and Future: Six Exercises in Political Thought* (New York: Meridian, 1963), 43.

9. Arendt, *Past and Future,* 44.

10. Canovan, *Political Thought,* 111. See also Ronald Beiner, *Political Judgment* (Chicago: University of Chicago Press, 1983); Arendt, *Past and Future,* 5, 6; Hannah Arendt, *Totalitarianism* (New York: Harcourt, Brace, 1968), 3, 4.

11. Hannah Arendt, *On Revolution* (New York: Penguin, 1965), 31.

12. Mary McCarthy, quoted on back cover of Hannah Arendt, *The Human Condition* (Chicago: University of Chicago Press, 1958). For further assessments of these tensions, see the essays in Hill, *Hannah Arendt.*

13. Hannah Arendt, *The Human Condition* (Chicago: University of Chicago Press, 1998), 136, 137.

14. Ibid., 173.

15. Ibid., 176, 177, 180, 190.

16. Ibid., 178; D'entreves, *Political Philosophy,* 65.

17. Arendt, *Human Condition,* 95, 178, 179.

18. Ibid., 176, 198.

19. Benhabib, "Arendt's Eichmann in Jerusalem," 65.

20. Arendt, *Eichmann,* 49; Jerome Kohn, "Evil and Plurality: Hannah Arendt's Way to *The Life of the Mind,* I," in *Hannah Arendt: Twenty Years Later,* ed. Larry May and Jerome Kohn (Cambridge, MA: MIT Press, 1996), 153; Arendt, *Eichmann,* 32, 47–48.

21. Dana R. Villa, "The Banality of Philosophy: Arendt on Heidegger and Eichmann," in *Hannah Arendt: Twenty Years Later,* ed. Larry May and Jerome Kohn (Cambridge, MA: MIT Press, 1996), 184.

22. Arendt, *Eichmann,* 53, 252.

23. Ibid., 34, 78.

24. Ibid., 251.

25. Hannah Arendt, *The Life of the Mind* (New York: Harcourt Brace Jovanovich), 4.

26. Alan Dugan, "Morning Song," *Poems Seven: New and Complete Poetry* (New York: Seven Stories Press, 2001), 43.

27. Marie Syrkin, "The Clothes of the Empress," *Dissent* 4 (1963): 344; Abel, "Aesthetics of Evil," 211.

28. Phillips, "Arguments," 281; Scholem, "Exchange of Letters," 241.

29. Scholem, "Exchange of Letters," 250.

3

"Everywhere You Go, It's There"

Forgetting and Remembering
the University of Texas Tower Shootings

Rosa A. Eberly

Meyer: "Can you look at that Tower and not think of Whitman?"
Pryor: "No. You just can't do it."
> Interview of Richard "Cactus" Pryor, Austin native, long-time radio host, and author, by Chuck Meyer, host of *Good Morning Austin*, KLBJ-AM, August 1, 1996

John Sayles chose to end *Lone Star,* his epic film about Texas, with the command "Forget the Alamo."[1] However contested memories of the Alamo have been, the Alamo most certainly has been remembered.[2] Forget the Alamo? Why? How? Sayles has said of his film:

> A lot of what this movie is about is history and what we do with it. Do we use it to hit each other? Is it something that drags us down? Is it something that makes us feel good? You can get six different people to look at the Alamo and they have six different stories about what actually happened and what its significance was. The same goes for your personal history. At what point do you say about your parents, "that was them, this is me. I take responsibility for myself from this day on." That's also what this movie is about.[3]

Sayles's claim that certain memories should be forgotten as well as his distinction between individual and collective memories provide a regional context for understanding some of the different ways the 1966 shootings at the University of Texas at Austin have been remembered and why, arguably, some people and institutions might prefer that they be forgotten.

Herein I review some of the discursive artifacts that perpetuate different memories of what happened on August 1, 1966, when Charles Whitman, a former Marine enrolled as an undergraduate engineering major at the University of Texas at Austin, killed fourteen and injured thirty-one by sharpshooting randomly for over an hour from the observation deck atop the UT Tower.[4] In addition this chapter will suggest how public discourses about these artifacts most often blur distinctions among individual, cultural, institutional, and public memories. Because this study was conducted largely through my undergraduate rhetoric course titled "The UT Tower and Public Memory," this chapter will also recount some anecdotal evidence about interactions between and among various publics, institutions, and special interests regarding memories of the shootings and the status of the Tower itself as a topos.[5] This essay thus serves as an active reminder—not merely a nostalgic recollection—of rhetoric's productive and practical as well as critical or hermeneutic powers to use and shape memory through discourse.

That the events of August 1, 1966, are remembered—at least by individuals—first became clear to me as I listened to local talk radio on August 1, 1995, the twenty-ninth anniversary of the shootings. What I heard on KLBJ-AM's *Paul Pryor Show* that day ultimately convinced me that the events of August 1, 1966—and how those events are remembered by individuals, publics, and institutions—deserved study, deliberation, and perhaps intervention. After an initial one-hour segment with guests, Paul Pryor, son of "Cactus" Pryor (mentioned above), opened the phone lines to callers who had memories of the day. Paul Pryor had promoted the show by saying it would focus on the anniversary of the Tower shootings and several other topics, but calls recounting individual memories continued throughout the afternoon, extending Pryor's three-hour show. In addition to the many individuals who apparently needed to tell where they were and what they remembered of the day twenty-nine years before, Pryor's studio guests offered a provocative gloss on the status of individual, institutional, and public memories of the shootings.

Pryor's guests for the opener were Neal Spelce, a UT alumnus who was

news director of Austin's KTBC radio and television in 1966 and whose
voice is often associated with coverage of the shootings,[6] as well as Phil
Miller and Les Reedy, both KTBC reporters in 1966. As Miller recounted
his memory of seeing Austin policeman Billy Speed fatally shot by Whitman through a six-inch gap in a concrete baluster—what is often described as Whitman's "best shot"—Pryor asked Miller if he still thought
of what happened that day. "Does that still affect you today, Phil? Do you
think about that?"

Miller: "Yes."

Pryor: "I bet you do. You never forget that."

Miller: "I was going to say, uh, you know, that, um, this might be
one of the things that we all need to put behind us at some stage of
the game."

Spelce: "You know, it should, but I tell you what: uh, it made, so
many people it made such an impression on, who were there. And
the university campus is so much a part of this city, and it's awfully
hard to walk across that campus, even this long afterward, and
not all of a sudden———. I was out at the University of Texas commencement in May. Wonderful evening. Pageantry like you wouldn't
believe; not like when we graduated out there. It was festive; there
was music; there were colors. It was an unbelievable evening. And
then the Tower lit up orange. And, for a moment there, even though
I was wrapped up in the events of the commencement, for a moment there, all of a sudden, it just comes back."

Pryor: "And it's forever with all of us that were around then. And
I think what you say's true, Phil, that at some point you've got to
deal with the pain of it. Because it was a very painful experience.
But I think it's important, too, that, for example, the students there
now know about this. Because it is history and it was a very tragic,
unbelievable thing that happened here, in what we thought was the
safest city in the world."

Miller's turn from saying he still thinks of the day to saying "this might
be one of the things that we all need to put behind us at some stage of the
game" suggests the difficulty Texans and Austinites have had coming to

terms with their memories of the Tower shootings and perhaps of other tragic regional events. Texans have certainly had their share. As I had coffee and talked with a friend one day about whether to risk, as an assistant professor, offering a course on the Tower shootings, I noticed what was carved deeply into the table where I was sitting: "Texas is the reason JFK is dead."[7]

At its best, local talk radio once provided and some believe still can provide a means of forming or regenerating ephemeral local publics.[8] The discourses of individuals about the Tower shootings on the twenty-ninth anniversary and afterward were nearly univocal in their lack of any sense of publicness; even differences of opinion about whether the shootings should be remembered were supported by individual psychological warrants rather than by any awareness that the event and its resonances might warrant public judgment and conjoint action.[9] In Austin the relationship between public and institutional forgetting and individual remembering regarding the Tower shootings is clear: the memories of individuals had and have no place to go other than local talk radio—or coffeehouse tables and graffiti at the top of the Tower stairs.[10] Put differently, because neither the city of Austin nor the University of Texas at Austin nor any group of individual citizens engaging in conjoint action had or has yet offered a public place—a topos—for storing and inventing memories of the events of August 1, 1966, and their consequences, individual memory has been reenacted every year on local talk radio.[11]

That local radio has provided the only public topos for inventions of individual and public memories of the Tower shootings was confirmed through unsolicited calls to another KLBJ-AM news and talk radio show, *Good Morning Austin* with Chuck Meyer, on August 1, 1996. Meyer, who has worked in several major markets doing various combinations of news and talk, interviewed Tower shooting perennials "Cactus" Pryor, who worked for KTBC in 1966 and is now a senior vice-president of the LBJ Company, which owns KLBJ radio, and Robert Heard, an Associated Press reporter who was shot by Whitman and filed a report (his byline consequently was on stories about the shootings in newspapers around the globe).[12] Meyer, who had been in Austin only four months when his interviews with "Cactus" Pryor and Heard aired, did not intend to take any calls on the shootings.[13] Indeed, when the calls came in several minutes after the first interview was over, Meyer and his on-air cohorts were in the midst of a continuing gag they titled "Trousers for Todd," which consisted of asking listeners to bring large pants to the station to fit KLBJ's morning newsperson, Todd Jeffries. The show's banter made for discursive ground as unfurrowed and infertile as possible for expressions of individual mourning and memory to sprout and grow. Nonetheless, the calls came in—insistent and compelling enough for Meyer and his producer to decide to air them, even in the context of "Trousers for Todd":

> Meyer: "Well, the 'Trousers for Todd' campaign continues. Three more pairs of pants came in yesterday for you, Todd."
>
> Jeffries: "All right!"
>
> Meyer: "This is a wonderful thing. These are nice, too."
>
> Jeffries: "Let me see one of those, there."
>
> Meyer: "Well, and, whoever—-I wish they would have dropped a note off and let us know who this was. It's a nice, tasteful gray, 40 waistline, incidentally, Todd. This could fit you."
>
> Jeffries: "Want me to try these on?"
>
> Meyer: "Yeah! Try 'em on on the air."
>
> Jeffries: "Right now?"
>
> Meyer: "Go ahead. I've seen, uh, men in their skivvies before."
>
> John Midani (sportsperson): "You've *paid* to see men in their skivvies before."
>
> Meyer: "I didn't want to get into that, John. But, now that you mention it, you know."
>
> Jeffries: "God, I hope I have clean underwear on."
>
> Midani: "I hope you have any underwear on."
>
> Meyer: "This is one of those days that Mom warned you about: 'Always wear clean underwear.'"
>
> Jeffries (feigning a woman's voice): "Todd, you never know. You might have to take your pants off on the air."
>
> Midani: "How about that? I figured you for a boxers kinda guy."
>
> Meyer: "No, he's strictly briefs."
>
> Jeffries: "I enjoy the support. Uh, these are a little snug."
>
> Meyer: "Too bad we don't have a bed for you to lie down on so you could get these things on."

Midani: "Fasten them under your stomach."

Jeffries: "Give me some disco music."

Meyer: "Do you know there's a female intern in the next room?"

The music faded and Meyer said a caller named Jeannie was on the line and wanted to talk about the Tower shootings. She began, "I want you to know that this is one of the hardest calls I've ever had to make. But I wanted to let you know (pause) I appreciate your show."

Meyer: "Yes."

Caller: "My husband was the police officer who was killed at the university." (Caller hesitates and voice breaks.) "And, I'm sorry—"

Meyer: "That's ok. What was your husband's name?"

Caller: "Billy Speed."

Meyer: "Billy Speed was killed that day at the UT Tower."

Caller: "Yes, sir. He was a police officer."

Meyer: "Tell—tell our listeners for those who don't recall or are unsure just what the circumstances, uh, were there, uh, what the timeline was. Where was Billy?"

Caller: "Well, he was at work. At his job. And he was at the Tower, aiming to shoot the sniper there. I really don't know too much about it. All I can say is that he was there at the Tower, that was his district, and, to my understanding, the way the police department explained to me, the first shot missed him, and the second shot—he never knew what hit him. He was killed instantly."

Dead air.

Meyer: "Did you see him off to work that morning?"

Caller: "Yes sir, I did. We had an eighteen-month-old baby."

Meyer: "No."

Caller: "And she's thirty-one years old now."

Meyer: "Well, bless her heart. What is her name?"

Caller: "Her name's Becky. Rebecca Davis. She's a wonderful mother. She's got two small children. She teaches school out at Dripping Springs."

Brief dead air.

Meyer: "Well, Jeannie, how are you going to be today? Are you going to be all right?"

Caller: "Well, it's a little sad. But, you know, to be honest with you Chuck, I wish they would quit showing all this on television and bringing all this up. Because people would like to forget all this."

Meyer: "There are a lot of horrible memories for people."

Caller: "We want it to lie and die down. But how can it? If the media keeps bringing it up and the press keeps bringing it up? And, you know, this is something that we're trying to get over. I mean, I want to forget it, but every time I turn around—it's showing on the television right now. Everywhere you go, it's there."

Meyer: "Well, Jeannie, try to just shut that away today and maybe it will go away for the day. I do appreciate your calling. And our thoughts are with you today."

Caller: "I appreciate that."

Meyer: "You take care. And thanks for holding on."[14]

As with Phil Miller on Paul Pryor's radio show, Jeannie Speed's comments belie a complex attitude toward individual and public memories. While the radio makes discourse public, it does not necessarily make public discourse. That is, radio gives public access, but it does not necessarily lead to public discourse—to private people discoursing together in public about shared consequences, collective judgment, and conjoint action. Radio cannot teach publicness. Yet it was in large part these two radio shows that persuaded me that a study of the Tower shootings and memory was warranted in a rhetoric class, where students at the university would speak and write in common about whether and how they thought the Tower shootings were and ought to be remembered. In other words, seeking and not finding a topos from which to judge the state of public memory of the Tower shootings, I decided to head to the undergraduate rhetoric classroom, a place I consider a protopublic space.[15]

Over the past few decades, accounts of speaking and writing and of listening and reading have moved away from emphasizing the individual and static and toward focusing on the social, transactional, and processual. In criticism this move away from the individual created a space for theories of reader response and, in their wake, a host of other nominally reader-centered approaches to interpreting texts. Even when critics claimed to focus solely on texts or on how "the reader" understands, however, criticism has tended to reify the production and interpretation of texts not as social actions by real people and concerning real-life effects but as acts of individual expert auditors and ideal authors in response to ideal texts with ahistorical human concerns. Similarly, in writing classrooms the move away from the individual encouraged inquiries into social and collaborative writing among writers at all levels, from elementary school children to senior engineers and scientists. But this move away from the individual and static and toward the social and processual has not gone as far as it might because the very language critics and teachers use to talk about speaking and writing and listening and reading reifies the product-oriented assumptions many want to dispel.

Realizing the classroom as a protopublic space and encouraging students to see themselves as having rhetorical agency in different and overlapping empirical publics might help them—and us—come to terms with the particularity and situatedness of rhetoric and the need for effective communication to respond to the particular needs of particular and complex publics at particular times. Ultimately rhetoricians, through their teaching as well as their criticism and other scholarship—public as well as academic—could play a more active role in helping to shape what different publics remember and how the artifacts of cultural memory are understood. Thus, another representative anecdote for this chapter comes from Cicero's *De Oratore:* Early on the second day of conversation at Crassus's villa, Antonius, dissertating about invention and imitation, complains that his countrymen have not yet begun serious writing of history. "Do you see how far the study of history is the business of the orator?" he asks. "By what other voice than that of the orator is history—the evidence of time, the light of truth, the life of memory, the directress of life, the herald of antiquity—committed to immortality?"[16]

In the case of the 1966 University of Texas Tower shootings, a plethora of cultural texts over more than thirty years answers Antonius's rhetorical question with a litany of responses other than "the orator." The vast majority of cultural texts that allude to the shootings emphasize not the victims but the shooter, Charles Whitman. Besides the 1975 made-for-TV movie *Deadly Tower,* starring Kurt Russell, which airs regularly on TNT, references to Whitman occur in films from Stanley Kubrick's *Full Metal Jacket,* where a drill sergeant says Whitman "showed what one motivated Marine and his rifle can do"; to Richard Linklater's *Slackers,* in which an anarchist philosophy professor says the Tower shootings were Austin's "fin-est hour"; to Oliver Stone's *Natural Born Killers,* wherein Whitman serves as one of the celebrity "American Maniacs"; to, more recently, *The Delicate Art of the Rifle,* a North Carolina–made independent film that renames Charles Whitman "Walt Whitman" and concludes that "a Whitman's got to do what a Whitman's got to do." Film references to Charles Whitman con-sistently have a smirky ethos: the juxtaposition of Whitman's horrific deeds with the college photo of him distributed by news services around the globe in 1966—smiling former Eagle Scout and Marine sharpshooter, the proverbial all-American boy—sells coolness, detachment, the threat of furious and random violence, revenge.

T-shirts with that same photo of Whitman's smiling, crew-cut visage and a picture of the Tower over the legend "Be True to Your School" are for sale in many college towns. Another t-shirt, sold by a company called Burning Church Enterprises and advertised on the Web, features Whitman surrounded by images of his weapons.[17] Burning Church Enterprises, ac-cording to its web site, is "dedicated to destroying the human race" and sells shirts featuring the Unabomber, Charles Manson, and, again in the words of the site, "Shirts to shock and offend one and all. Guaranteed attention-getters!" The text selling the Whitman shirt offers memory as aesthetic commodity through its narrative sales pitch:

> August 1, 1966, a clear and cloudless day, was beautiful in more ways than one. From atop the Observation TOWER at the University of Austin [*sic*], it took Charles Whitman just over 90 minutes to kill 13 [*sic*] people and maim 31 more. Add to that the murders of his wife and mother the night previous, a nice upper/downer habit, and a Marine Sharpshooter Award and you have a feat truly fit for recog-nition. Buy the fucking shirt. Available in Ash, Black, White.

This memory of the Tower shootings as commodified in the image of Whit-man's smiling face and the icon of the Tower is also articulated through Whitman's place in the Mass Murderer Trading Cards canon,[18] and his handwriting was formatted for sale as a font for word processors through "Killer Fonts," another site on the Web.[19] "Tired of the same old love notes?" the text of the site asks. "Promise someone you're really Helter-

Skelter for them [sic] in the script of Charles Manson himself. Nibble on someone's ear with Dahmerbits."

In the text that probably contributed most to disseminating the "cruel" coolness of Whitman as hero, singer-songwriter and UT Plan II honors alumnus Kinky Friedman wondered in song how different Whitman really was from the rest of humanity: "Who are we to say the boy's insane?" he asks in his "Ballad of Charles Whitman."[20] An autopsy showed no necessary connection between a "pecan-sized" glioblastoma multiforme tumor and Whitman's behavior.[21] Whitman and his actions have thus also come to symbolize indeterminacy and fear: the Ron Howard movie *Parenthood,* starring Steve Martin, features a scene in which a father worries in an internal monologue over the image of a campus tower whether his son will become a "bell tower boy" because he was pressured into playing second base in a Little League game. Just as the 1991 post office shootings in Edmond, Oklahoma, are remembered through the phrase "go postal," Charles Whitman, archetypal "bell tower boy," has become a part of the vernacular of a violent culture's collective fears.

Perhaps the most chilling of this kind of manifestation of the commodified mass cultural memory of Whitman is Gregory Combs's "Charles Whitman Fan Club" web site. Combs's site was best known for its clickable campus map showing where each of the victims fell. Besides the "fan club" tone of the site, most integral to the study of memory was the site's response form. Combs received several thousand responses to the site during the first year it was up, and the site was "honored" as "Cruel Site of the Day" in the fall of 1996 and as one of the "Worst of the Web!" in 1997. The majority of the responses congratulate Combs on his inventiveness and laud the site as informative.[22]

These cultural artifacts in film, in clothing, on television, and on the Web are examples of what George Lipsitz has denominated "popular texts" because they are neither folkloric nor high culture. Still, because of the way they commodify a nearly univocal perception of Whitman's actions and his ethos, they raise the question of what distinguishes countermemory from memory—and for whom—in the very specific case of the UT Tower shootings. These artifacts, in the language of Lipsitz, both "draw on an oppositional cultural practice deeply rooted in art, in history, and in popular collective consciousness" and participate in "a commodified mass culture industry [that] covers the globe," part of "a symbolic order conducive to the interests of corporate America."[23]

Kenneth Burke told us more than half a century ago that language functions in culture in this complex a manner; what is counter and what is not—what is poison and what is cure, and for whom—is never easy to unknot. Perhaps not surprisingly, "Sniper," a song by Burke's grandson Harry Chapin that attempts to explain the cause of the Tower shootings, proved to be one of the more troubling cultural texts the students and I discussed in the Tower course.[24] The song's emphases on communication and memory make it a productive cultural text for a course on rhetoric and public memory. While nothing in the liner notes or elsewhere suggests Chapin intended the song to portray the events of August 1, 1966, accurately, Chapin's conjectures have absolutely nothing to do with what was discovered about Whitman's relationship with his parents and his possible reasons for doing what he did. Most troubling, perhaps, is Chapin's directing blame toward the sniper's mother and wife—one could say at women in general—when news reports and Whitman's diaries clearly indicate that Whitman's father, C. A. Whitman, motivated much of his eldest son's anger and self-loathing.[25]

The rhetorical complexity of producing and understanding symbolic action is a central reason why cultural texts demand individual and collective judgment and action; such judgments are, some of the students in the Tower class and I would argue, our critical refuge against the structural determinism of mass culture, whether in film, news reporting, popular music and television, political rhetoric, radio, advertising, or any other suasive text or medium. The students and I learned this together over several intense semesters, in classrooms that I defined as and that they came to some extent to understand as protopublic spaces: Rhetoric 330E, The UT Tower Shootings and Public Memory, an undergraduate rhetoric course that was also a substantial writing component course.[26] Among the less examined venues for studying how publics form, define themselves, act, and perhaps disintegrate are the sites of struggle over public memory. The Tower course offers an example of how rhetoric conceived as a productive and practical art allowed students not only to study the artifacts of cultural memory but to deliberate whether to intervene publicly in how a particular incident of common concern might be remembered by various publics and institutions.[27]

At first amused by the "fan club" spin of the vast majority of cultural products that mention Whitman, the students began to express their dissatisfaction with that cultural univocality soon after they heard the individual memories of people whose loved ones were killed or who were themselves wounded by Whitman. After we had spoken and written together about various distinctions between public and individual memory, and after we had studied and written evaluations of the cultural products created in response to Whitman and the Tower shootings, the students discussed at length the influence the university's institutional actions—and its failure to act—might have had on cultural memory of the shootings. Again and again the students and I deliberated whether and how to attempt to intervene in the way various institutions and publics remember the shootings and to make public judgments about the various cultural products that sustain memory of the incident and its perpetrator. Our central question in the fall 1996 section of the class became: Given the cultural products we had studied, would any memorial to the victims of the Tower shootings end up being a shrine to Whitman?

Unlike Kent State, which has real and virtual memorials to the victims of the campus shootings there in 1970, the University of Texas seems to have gone out of its way to erase the Tower shootings from memory. The UT police department captain told *Texas Monthly* in 1996, "The University wishes the whole thing would go away."[28] Official institutional history of the shootings is represented in a three-paragraph account in Dr. Margaret Catherine Berry's official history of the university.[29] Even more remarkable than the lack of an official history of the event is the active repression evident on the university's web site. I first observed this in April 1996, after the Tower course had been approved, when the university launched "Scenes from the Top." To attempt to compensate for keeping the Tower closed to students, alumni, and the public, the university added to its web page "Scenes from the Top," a series of still photos and video clips of the view from the top of the Tower in eight directions. I was amazed and students were later incredulous to find that in the texts of "Scenes from the Top" the university's chronology of the Tower began in 1974.[30] After plans for the course and my observation about the university's home page were published in local and state news reports, the university added Berry's three-paragraph account of the Tower shootings and suicides to its web page.[31] During the last weeks of fall semester 1996, however, one of the students discovered that at least one manifestation of the university's repression regarding the Tower had come to border on the absurd: upon going to the University of Texas admissions web site, the student was shocked to read the following opening sentence under a picture of the Tower: "This is the jumping off place for information about how to gain admission to The University of Texas."[32]

It was the students, in fact, who first articulated and persuaded me that the university's strategy, intentional or structural, to repress memories of the Tower shootings had been extremely successful: fewer and fewer students know about the shootings every year, and within two or three decades few people will be alive with individual memories of the events. Another student conducted an email survey of 1,500 randomly selected UT students to find out how they first heard about the Tower shootings and what kind of information they had. On the whole, information about the Tower shootings is spread by rumor and word of mouth, and information about Whitman comes mainly from cultural texts such as *Deadly Tower* and Kinky Friedman's "Ballad."

In each of the two semesters that I taught the course, students wanted to gain access to the top of the Tower, a desire I had not anticipated. During the fall semester of the course, the students persuaded me that we should write to then-president Robert Berdahl, now chancellor at the University of California, Berkeley, to attempt to gain access to the observation deck of the Tower. Through class discussion, a message forum on our course web site, and email, we drafted a joint letter to Berdahl, explaining the nature of the course and offering our reasons for believing access to the observation deck made at least as much sense for a course devoted to studying the Tower as it did for football recruits and visiting dignitaries. After several weeks we received a three-sentence written response from Charles Franklin, the university's vice-president for business affairs, denying us access to the Tower because the regents had closed it to the public in 1975.

It was the grail aspect of the Tower that first helped distinguish the classroom as a protopublic space for learning and deliberation from the classroom as a space for special interests to achieve their own specific ends. Although the course was overenrolled both semesters, it was required for no major, so most students who could not get into the course were willing to wait until it might be offered again. Before the fall semester section of the course began, I was contacted by a student who asked me to add him to the course list even though I told him that I was not able to override the twenty-two-student cap on enrollments in substantial writing component courses. The student, at the time a sophomore, told me he had been active in attempts to re-open the observation deck as part of an attempt to win election to a student government post; these activities, he argued, made him more suited than other students to take the course. I told him that he could attend class with other students on the waiting list and would be able to enroll if someone dropped the course.

This student distinguished himself from the rest of the class by asking the same question of every class visitor: "Do you think the Tower observation deck should be reopened?" What was even more striking was that he intervened in three class activities in a way that marked him as operating differently from the rest of the class—what the students and I, after long discussions, agreed was similar to a special interest. First, during the nearly two-week-long process of drafting the letter to Berdahl, the student ran into the president at a meeting in the Main Building. He gleefully came to class the next day and said he told Berdahl that he "would have to let us up in the Tower now, because our class was writing him a letter." The rest of the class groaned after hearing this, and we spent part of the session defining and evaluating his actions. (He told me later this was one of his favorite classes. He remained unconvinced of the class's judgment that his actions lacked propriety, given the goal of the letter and the interests of the class as a whole.)

Another incident that set him apart from the rest of the class involved his inviting a reporter from the *Daily Texan* to class on the day that Lana Holloway, one of Whitman's victims, was coming to class to discuss her memories of the shootings and their effects on her life. The reporter came and covered the event, but once again we took class time to discuss whether and how the presence of a reporter changed what happened in our class and whether the student should have asked the class to discuss with him whether to invite a reporter. Finally, the student brought a tape recorder to class on the day another visitor was among us. Readily admitting he wanted to record the comments of the visitor, Vice President for Student Services James Vick, for use in his student government work, he decided not to tape the class session after other members of the class persuaded him that doing so would change the nature of the discussion with Vick. I did my best to stay out of these discussions; that the class deliberations about definitional distinctions among privacy, publicity, and special interests continued on the class message forum suggests that the discussions were prompted as much by the students' concerns as by my own.

When it came to "getting to the top," however, my spring semester students seemed generally more comfortable with certain kinds of special interest. After I told this second group of students about how the fall semester class had collaboratively drafted a letter to Berdahl, several of the students told me how naive I was and that such is not how the University of Texas works. They cited example after example of how privilege rather than discourse cuts through the considerable red tape at the institution they knew better than I did. These were, after all, mainly fourth- and fifth-year seniors; this was my third year at UT. Two students, Stuart Vogt and Allison Chambers, took matters into their own hands, trying, through a loophole we discovered in the university's regulations, to gain admittance to the observation deck by writing a letter to Vice President for Business Affairs Franklin. Vogt was quite successful; he scored a meeting with Franklin's assistant and won tentative approval to go to the observation deck "in order to complete a writing assignment." Sharing his good fortune with the class, Vogt encouraged another student, Allison Chambers, to make the same argument to Franklin. When she did, Franklin's office discovered that the students were from the Tower course, and both were denied access to the observation deck; Franklin's office told them that only students with "unique" writing assignments could have access to the observation deck, thus de facto allowing students from any course but the Tower course access to the observation deck. Late in the spring semester another student in the Tower class, Jim Dedman, wrote as a class assignment and as an op-ed in the *Daily Texan* a column encouraging UT to clarify its policy on access to the observation deck.

For their final paper most students chose to write an editorial column about whether and how the university should memorialize the Tower shootings. Most supported a memorial, but they were deeply divided about the type of memorial; a few students argued vehemently that any memorial to the Tower shootings would become a memorial to Whitman, but others argued that the design of the memorial, as with the Vietnam Veterans Memorial, the Holocaust Museum, or the Kent State Memorial, could affect how people experience and use it, again allowing for active rather than determined response to cultural texts that attempt to shape memory. Several students concluded that a Web memorial to the victims would be most appropriate for the short term. This would counter the "fan club" ethos of cultural memory and the repression of institutional memory with a list of Whitman's victims and details of their lives, information about all the possible causes of Whitman's actions, and a clear sense of the consequences of violence, whatever its causes.[33] I was surprised that several students in the spring 1997 section of the course wrote for their final papers proposal arguments suggesting that I continue offering the course as a living educational memorial to the victims. By making public arguments in local and wider fora, students in the Tower course took an active part in whether and how Charles Whitman, his many, many victims, and the causes of his actions will be remembered.

These students are orators, much in the same way that a San Antonio Chicano singer-songwriter named Jose Morante was. Morante's *corrido*, "El Policia del Austin: Acion Heróica de Ramiro Martinez," written a few weeks after the Tower shootings, offers a version of the events of August 1, 1966, that is very different from how Whitman is remembered nationally and how the tragedy is repressed institutionally.[34] The *corrido* narrates the events of August 1, 1966, in classic *norteño corrido* tradition, for a particular public forming to counter perceptions of Mexican-Americans as criminals, to praise Ramiro Martinez, the "Tejano-Mexicano" who was one of two policemen to end Whitman's siege by shooting him on the observation deck of the Tower. "In Austin, Texas, this happened, and I must not exaggerate," the *corrido* begins; it argues that destiny marked Ramiro Martinez to "kill a criminal" that day. Among the other issues important to the contours of public memory in the *corrido*, the lyrics echo a common description of how people learned about what was happening at the Tower that day: "The radio announced the horrible massacre." It also describes the relation of the Tower to the university as well as the city—"The Tower in its majesty dominated the plaza"—and describes a common moral outrage over Whitman's actions: "The criminal died / The one who had outraged his country / By wounding thirty-one and killing sixteen people." Martinez, described in the *corrido* as "a good policeman," one who "lived according to the law," is celebrated as a hero to his community—his people and his town (*su pueblo*): "Monday, the first of August—I must not exaggerate / A Mexicano-Tejano knew how to raffle his life. / In Austin, Texas, it happened, that which I finish singing about. / Ramiro demonstrated that he knew how to love *su pueblo*." The lyrics of the *corrido* show how epideictic rhetoric can be directed at a local public to encourage remembrance of an event in an act of countermemory.[35] Further, the *corrido* exhibits a sense of publicness that none of the individual memories recounted each year on local radio was willing or able to express.

But of course memory is never that simple. Both policemen who shot Whitman sued MGM after the made-for-TV movie was released. Martinez received a settlement; the other policeman, Houston McCoy, whose name was not used in the film, received nothing, even though the film portrays him standing by passively as the actor playing Martinez fires the fatal shot. Whitman's autopsy showed that it was McCoy's bullet that killed the sniper. Why did Martinez sue the makers of a movie that portrayed him, rightly or wrongly, as a hero? In his words, "They portrayed my wife as a Hispanic woman who is pregnant and barefoot, the usual stereotype," he told a reporter for the Austin *American-Statesman*. Martinez's wife is German-American. "They had her arguing with me about going to the Tower, which didn't happen. And they portrayed the Austin Police Department as being racist against me. Just the opposite from the truth."[36]

Reading the UT Tower shootings as a case study in the connections among individual, cultural, institutional, and public memory suggests that rhetoric's productive and practical as well as its analytical powers are central to memory work. Furthermore, remembering rhetoric's productive and practical powers suggests that we and our students can choose to play a greater role in making individual and public judgments about artifacts of cultural memory, about institutional repression, and about the process of history-in-the-making. Imagining classrooms as protopublic spaces might move us closer to the evocative vision offered by John Gillis at the close of his introduction to *Commemorations:*

> Democratic societies need to publicize rather than privatize the memories and identities of all groups, so that each may know and respect the other's versions of the past, thereby understanding better what divides as well as unites us. . . . [W]e need civil times and civil spaces more than ever, for these are essential to the democratic processes by which individuals and groups come together to discuss, debate, and negotiate the past and, through this process, define the future.[37]

It has become a commonplace in public and private discourses that we live in an age "when people across the political spectrum decry the decline of 'civic life' [and when] government, politicians, and even politics itself have become objects of indifference and contempt."[38] But such sentiments are hardly new; indeed, in some forms they date as far back as the origins of public discourse itself. Those who hold rhetoric as a productive and practical as well as analytical or hermeneutic art need to keep searching for ways to reconceive and reenergize the practices of public discourse. Classrooms imagined as protopublic spaces—as evidenced by the experiences and actions of students in the first two sections of the Tower class—allow teachers and students to engage in rhetorical education as training for public life, widely defined.

Notes

Jeannie Speed's statement "Everywhere you go, it's there" refers to memories of the Tower shootings (her husband, Billy Speed, was killed by Charles Whitman), but her statement could refer as well to the Tower itself—both its physical presence on campus and throughout Austin and its looming place in the cultural imaginary of the university, the city, and arguably the state of Texas in 1966 and, for some, to this day. I am indebted to Daniel Barrera of the University of Texas Undergraduate Library for his immense help in conducting research for my undergraduate substantial writing component rhetoric course The UT Tower Shootings and Public Memory. I also want to thank the students in each of the several sections of that course for taking me up on my claims that classrooms can be protopublic spaces. I shall tell a fuller story of that course and those students in a book project. Finally, I want to thank Stephen H. Browne for encouraging me in this interdisciplinary endeavor; Sanford Levinson and Edward Linenthal for conversations about public memory; and Lester Faigley for showing me the bullet holes. Earlier drafts of this chapter were presented as papers at the 1996 Speech Communication Association annual meeting in San Diego and the 1996 Modern Language Association annual meeting in Washington, D.C.

1. I am grateful to Madison Searle, administrative associate in the University of Texas at Austin's Division of Rhetoric and Composition, for bringing this to my attention just after the film's release in autumn 1996.

2. See, for instance, Edward Tabor Linenthal, *Sacred Ground: Americans and Their Battlefields* (Urbana: University of Illinois Press, 1991).

3. John Sayles, "A Statement from John Sayles," http://lonestar-movie.com, November 4, 1996.

4. Whitman killed his spouse, Kathy Whitman, and his mother, Margaret Whitman, before he went to campus. See Gary Lavergne, *A Sniper in the Tower: The Charles Whitman Murders* (Denton: University of North Texas Press, 1997), the first book-length study of the shootings. In yet another commentary on how the shootings are remembered, Lavergne's book, re-released as a mass-market trade paperback book, is most often found under "True Crime" in bookstores.

5. See Rosa A. Eberly, *Citizen Critics: Literary Public Spheres* (Urbana: University of Illinois Press, 2000), 4–8, for my understanding of topos as literal and inventional. The presence on the campus and in the city of the Tower, a 1930s-style skyscraper, is considerable even today when the city is several times larger and more populated than it was in 1966. UT Professor Lynn C. Miller describes the presence of the Tower and its synechdochal function this way in *The Fool's Journey: A Romance* (Houston: Winedale Publishing, 2002), her first novel: "The Tower was shorthand for the University's main administrative building, which did indeed soar in phallic remove over the entire campus (42). The observation deck on the twenty-eighth floor of the Tower long served as a mandatory tourist stop and favorite destination for campus dates. The university temporarily closed the observation deck after each of at least five suicides and after the Whitman shootings. In 1975 the university's board of regents closed the Tower "permanently" after yet another suicide. Guests of the university and journalists regularly gained admittance to the observation deck, while student groups regularly

held petition drives to reopen it. (The "permanent" closing of the observation deck ended in 1999, due at least in part to the efforts of several students in the Tower class. I tell that story in an upcoming book project; if you scour the Web and Lexis/Nexus, you can find shards of the story.)

James Michener gets less than a page into his 1985 historical novel *Texas* (New York: Fawcett, 1985) before describing the Tower:

> I left my guest office in the shadow of the main building. When I got outside I glanced up at its tower; the sight of it always set me thinking about the conflicting messages that it sent. After any football university major sports victory, and they came frequently at Texas, it was illuminated gaudily in the school color, burnt orange, but on gray and misty mornings, which came less frequently, I knew that people recalled that horrible August day in 1966 when Charles Whitman, an Eagle Scout, gained a gruesome immortality. After murdering his wife and mother, he filled a footlocker with guns, ammunition and knives and drove to the university. Slaying the receptionist, he took the elevator to the top of the tower, where he unlimbered his arsenal and began shooting at random any students or casual passers-by. In all, he killed sixteen persons before sharpshooters gunned him down. Saluting the handsome tower, I crossed the bustling campus which had so excited me when I first reported there in 1959.

6. Spelce's live coverage of the shootings for KTBC-AM and KTBC-TV, the first live coverage of any news event in Austin, is probably the most often recalled local cultural text that refers to the shootings—other than the Tower itself—for those who were in Austin that day. Spelce generously provided me with audio and video from August 1, 1966, for my course and visited my classes to answer students' questions about his own memories of the day as well as his subsequent anniversary coverage of the shootings.

7. For a discussion of the peculiar relationship among Texas, Texans, and history, see Jeff Mandell, "Remember the Alamo . . . and Nothing Else," *Texas Observer*, August 1, 1997, pp. 12–15.

8. Ralph Engleman, *Public Radio and Television in America: A Political History* (London: Sage, 1996).

9. Gerard A. Hauser, "Constituting Publics and Reconstructing Public Spheres: The Meese Commission's Report on Pornography," in *WarrantingAssent:*

Case Studies in Argument Evaluation (Albany: State University of New York Press, 1995); Gerard A. Hauser and Carole Blair, "Rhetorical Antecedents to the Public," *PRE/TEXT* 3 (1982): 139–67.

10. Wesley Forni, a student in the Tower course, wrote a paper in 1996 describing, defining, and evaluating the graffiti at the top of the steps on the twenty-seventh floor of the Tower. The graffiti were painted over in the process of reopening the Tower observation deck for tours in 1999.

11. Paul Pryor hosted the anniversary radio shows for several years. It is not clear whether anniversary shows will continue. Spelce said he expects anniversary coverage in print, radio, and television to diminish until the fiftieth anniversary of the shootings.

On August 1, 1996, the University of Texas rang the carillon bells in the Tower once for each of Whitman's victims. This event, announced after plans for a prayer service at University Baptist Church across the street from the university were published, is by all accounts the closest to a public memorial the university has held specifically for the victims of the Tower shootings until plans for reopening the observation deck were announced in May 1999. The church's pastor, Reverend Larry Bethune, asked me to read the names of Whitman's victims for the university memorial, part of the local ministerium's Prayers for Healing from Violence.

12. Heard is now with *Inside Texas* magazine. Though he is adamant that too much is made of Whitman and that he does not want to be remembered as a victim of the shootings, he grants interviews fairly often. He told Meyer, "I think we make much too much out of Whitman. I think it deserves to be remembered. I don't think it deserves three pages in the newspaper with pictures and stuff. [Heard is referring to Hank Stuever, "99 Minutes, 30 Years Later," *Austin American-Statesman,* July 29, 1996, p. A1+.] I think the *New Handbook of Texas* did it about right: they wrote about five inches of just straightforward account of what happened, and they didn't get into a bunch of psycho-cultural crap about the meaning to world history. In my case, in a very minor way, I've been working for thirty years to get Charles Whitman out of the lead paragraph of my obituary" (KLBJ-AM, August 1, 1996).

13. Conversation with Meyer, October 16, 1996. Meyer attended the Tower class and answered students' questions about his reactions to the calls he aired August 1, 1996.

14. Audio excerpts of calls to Meyer from Jeannie (Beverly Jean) Speed and

someone who identified himself only as "John" are part of a web page composed by Wesley Forni and Star Gebser, two students in the Tower course: "Memorial to the Victims of the University of Texas Tower Shootings," http://www.cwrl. utexas.edu/~eberly/330e/memorial/documents/memorial.html.

15. Eberly, *Citizen Critics,* 161–74; Rosa Eberly, "From Readers and Audiences to Publics: Rhetoric Classrooms as Proto-Public Spaces," *Rhetoric Review* 18 (1999): 165–78.

16. *Cicero on Oratory and Orators* (Carbondale: Southern Illinois University Press, 1970), 2:xv.

17. Burning Church Enterprises, http://wymple.gs.net/~bce/catalog.html, November 10, 1996. Matthew Dunlap, a student in the fall 1996 section of the Tower course, brought this site to my attention.

18. Lisa Brown, a student in the fall 1996 section of the Tower course, brought these cards back to my attention and wrote a paper on Whitman's inclusion in the series.

19. See Killer Fonts, http://www.killerfonts.com. Josh Baker, a student in the Tower class, wrote a paper evaluating Killer Fonts based on Barry Brummett's lexicon for cultural texts in *Rhetoric in Popular Culture* (New York: St. Martin's Press, 1994).

20. Kinky Friedman, "The Ballad of Charles Whitman," Glaser Publications, Inc./BMI, 1973. This brief excerpt from the lyrics suggests the "cruel, cool" ethos of the song:

> Got up that morning calm and cool
> He picked up his guns and walked to school.
> All the while he smiled so sweetly
> And it blew their minds completely
> They'd never seen an Eagle Scout so cruel.

> Now don't you think for the shame and degradation,
> For the school's administration,
> He put on such a bold and brassy show?
> The chance looked right, it's adolescent
> And of course it's most unpleasant
> But I got to admit it was a lovely way to go.

There was a rumor of a tumor
Nestled at the base of his brain.
He was sitting up there with his .36 Magnum
Laughing wildly as he bagged 'em
Who are we to say the boy's insane?

21. See Lavergne, *Sniper in the Tower,* 238–71, for a discussion of questions about Whitman's autopsy and other records.

22. Gregory Combs, "Charles Whitman Memorial," http://www.io.com/ ~combs/htmls/charles.html, February 10, 1997. In a visit to the spring 1997 section of the Tower course, Combs told us that he changed the title of the web site from "Charles Whitman Fan Club" to "Charles Whitman Memorial" after "a few threats." Combs's surprise that anyone would react to his site as anything other than humor prompted a long and productive class discussion about Web ethos. There are of course many other cultural texts we studied in the Tower course that deal directly with or allude to Charles Whitman and the shootings. I regret that there is not space here to discuss *The Impossible Tree,* a memoir by Frances Gabour Lamport, or *The Simpsons* episode that alludes to the shootings. Steven Phenix's unpublished play *Texans and Their Guns: A Tragedy for the End of the Millennium* (Austin Circle of Theatres and Vortex Repertory Company, 1994, photocopied) and the collaboratively written and produced *Tower Massacre Musical* (1999) deserve critical attention and will be discussed in my book project.

23. George Lipsitz, *Time Passages: Collective Memory and American Popular Culture* (Minneapolis: University of Minnesota Press, 1990), 230–31, 233, 259.

24. Harry Chapin, *Sniper and Other Love Songs* (Elektra, 1972). It was through Chapin's song that I first learned about the shootings when I was in junior high in Dallastown, Pennsylvania. At the Burke Centenary in Pittsburgh in May 1996, I asked Harry Chapin's brother Tom whether he had ever talked to Harry about what inspired "Sniper." Tom said Harry wrote the song after reading a poem by James Dickey, but he could not remember which one. I asked him whether the poem was about a stewardess falling from an airplane ("Falling"), and Tom Chapin said yes, he was quite sure that was the poem. He said his brother was fascinated by Dickey's attempt to make poetry about the processes of a mind and body in extremis.

25. Lavergne, *Sniper in the Tower,* 53–55, 255–56.

26. While offered through the Division of Rhetoric and Composition (DRC), the course was for its first several offerings listed as English 330E; after the DRC voted to change its course prefix to RHE, the course was listed as RHE 330E.

27. This chapter encompasses the first two times I taught the Tower course.

28. Joe Holley, "A Whitman Sampler," *Texas Monthly,* August 1996, p. 30+.

29. Margaret C. Berry, *The University of Texas: A Pictorial Account of Its First Century* (Austin: University of Texas Press, 1980), 326.

30. "Scenes from the Top," http://www.utexas.edu/tours/top/, September 20, 1996.

31. "Why the Observation Deck Is Closed to Visitors," http://www.utexas.edu/tours/top/closed.html, September 20, 1996. In addition to Berry's three-paragraph account, the text of this page is as follows: "In response to requests from several visitors, TeamWeb has added this page to explain why the observation deck is closed."

32. Stephanie McDowell, a student in the fall 1996 Tower course, brought this text to my attention. After I published an op-ed about the Tower in the Austin *American-Statesman,* the site was changed.

33. Forni and Gebser, "Memorial," August 9, 2003.

34. Jose Morante, "El Policia de Austin: Acion Heróica de Ramiro Martinez," performed by Los Reyos del Alamo, Sombrero S02275-B (1966). The lyric excerpts were compiled from translations by John Slate, Dan Barrera, and Susan and Roberto Romano.

35. Dan Barrera's discussion about the *corridos* with the fall 1996 section of the Tower class was extremely helpful. In addition, Susan and Roberto Romano were of great help in thinking through the implications of the *corridos.* For an introduction to *corridos* as well as readings of other political *corridos,* see Dan William Dickey, "The Kennedy *Corridos:* A Study of the Ballads of a Mexican American Hero," master's thesis, University of Texas at Austin, 1978.

36. Bob Banta, "The Heroes: Ending Whitman's Life Changed Theirs; From Different Backgrounds, Two Police Officers Came Together Once, and Then Diverged Again," *American-Statesman,* July 29, 1996, p. A7. See also Lavergne, *Sniper in the Tower,* 167–80.

37. John Gillis, ed., *Commemorations: The Politics of National Identity* (Princeton: Princeton University Press, 1994), 20.

38. Alan Brinkley, "Unceremony: The Conventions Will Come to Order," *New Yorker,* August 12, 1996, pp. 4–5.

4

My Old Kentucky Homo
Lincoln and the Politics
of Queer Public Memory
Charles E. Morris III

O Memory! Thou midway world 'Twixt earth and paradise, Where
things decayed and loved ones lost In dreamy shadows rise, And, freed
from all that's earthly vile, Seem hallowed, pure, and bright, Like scenes
in some enchanted isle, All bathed in liquid light.

Abraham Lincoln (1846)

The sacred thing is *par excellence* that which the profane should not
touch, and cannot touch with impunity.

Emile Durkheim (1915)

Nearly vanquished by the ravages of AIDS, National Book Award winner
Paul Monette somehow mustered the requisite fortitude for his last so-
journ to the nation's capital, so that he might join his brethren in April
1993 for their March on Washington. Too debilitated to participate fully,
he garnered energy enough to fulfill those personal and political obligations he deemed most significant to the symbolic advancement of the
cause. And so he stood at the feet of Lincoln. His reflections on this occasion bear mentioning in full:

There is nothing to match the Lincoln, in America anyway, for noble
proportion and spiritual lift. On the wall to the left is the Gettysburg

Address; on the right the Second Inaugural. *With malice toward none, with charity for all.* I suddenly needed to stand in the spot where Marian Anderson sang her Easter concert, barred from Independence Hall by the D.A.R. . . . All under the eyes of Lincoln, eighty years after the Emancipation Proclamation. Another quarter century later, and the tempered gaze of Lincoln—warrior and wise man—bore witness to the passion of Dr. King. I didn't think the Lincoln of my understanding would have any trouble equating the Civil Rights struggle of people of color with the latter-day dreams of the gay and lesbian movement. There's too much compelling evidence in his own life—the bed he shared for four years with Joshua Speed above the general store in Springfield; the breakdown he suffered when family duties sent them apart—of the "dear love of comrades." In any case, I was choked with tears and in awe to be there. . . . And oh, how we needed a Lincoln to stand for equal justice and bind us all together again.[1]

In Monette's memoir we find the meaning of public memory itself: a purposeful engagement of the past, forged symbolically, profoundly constitutive of identity, community, and moral vision, inherently consequential in its ideological implications, and very often the fodder of political conflagration. That he would find both universal and particular value in the remembrance of this American icon is not surprising; as his recuperation of Anderson and King suggests, much of our history is, in a sense, a chronicle of those who have found solace and inspiration in Lincoln's rather malleable legacy. What is noteworthy, however, is the revolutionary mettle potentially derived from such mnemonic encounters. As David Blight has written of Frederick Douglass's appropriation of Lincoln and the Civil War: "Historical memory . . . was the prize in a struggle between rival versions of the past, a question of will, of power, of persuasion. The historical memory of any transforming or controversial event emerges from cultural and political competition, from the choice to confront the past and to debate and manipulate its meaning."[2]

While a dying Monette could only articulate a fleeting if hopeful vision for Lincoln's memory as an animating force that might bind gays and lesbians to each other and to the national inheritance, his comrade Larry

Kramer, whom he once described as "more than a witness, more than a leader, in his own way like the Elie Wiesel who stood on the heath tearing his hair,"[3] would do more. In February 1999, Kramer would unwittingly transform that vision into the struggle Blight describes. Those familiar with Kramer's penchant for political theater might have expected his "outing" of Lincoln in a speech at the University of Wisconsin to be quickly dismissed as merely the latest manifestation of his creative propagandistic imagination. For residents of Springfield, Illinois, and Lincoln scholars, however, Kramer's queer public memory of the Great Emancipator constituted a salvo that incited homosexual panic, one that has persisted into the new millennium, exposing a cultural fault line implicating rhetoric, history, public memory, and queer politics. The revolution of memory commenced by Kramer illustrates the complex dynamics initiated when public memory and (homo)sexuality collide, allowing us to examine these explosive components as they are marshaled in a symbolic contest for the communal meaning of historical identity.

I use the word "revolution" carefully and deliberately, not primarily for its hyperbolic force or polemical charge, but more for what it suggests about memory and gay American culture and the rather dramatic stakes for a queer present and future. In a rudimentary sense, what is described here is a deliberate *turn toward* memory in a culture for which public memory itself is defined more by absence than presence. Fragmented as a community, wasted by disease, and haunted still and in multifarious ways by the legacy of the closet, gays and lesbians find that public memory's typical infrastructure is largely missing or disabled. In writing of Stonewall, for instance, which is arguably the anchor of contemporary gay and lesbian public memory, Martin Duberman writes, "The decades preceding Stonewall . . . continue to be regarded by most gays and lesbians as some vast Neolithic wasteland—and this, despite the efforts of pioneering historians . . . to fill the landscape of those years with vivid, politically astute personalities."[4]

Nonacademic memory work, moreover, often more potent because of its vibrant narrative and fewer evidentiary constraints, has been hindered in profound ways by AIDS. The AIDS Quilt, perhaps the most public, most powerfully symbolic memory text, nonetheless represents a memory void, a lost generation of memory agents who serve as poignant markers of queer community but speak as eloquently of their incapacity to convey and preserve their past.[5] Among the living, motive may stand as firm an impediment as means. In San Francisco, with its rich ties to a queer past visible in numerous memory sites and commemorative practices, especially those associated with Harvey Milk, public memory falters nonetheless. Historian John D'Emilio observes, "The memory in this community doesn't last more than a few years."[6] Kramer himself offers a potential explanation: "To write a history composed mostly of events like this is a depressing undertaking. I suspect there is much less joy than sorrow buried in our graves."[7]

But in those graves Kramer saw the very bonds of gay community, a vital past that, although ignored by straight historians and queer theorists alike, must be remembered if that community is to prosper in the future. Thus the embodiment of Lincoln in public memory emerged viscerally in Kramer's lecture, "Our Gay President," at the University of Wisconsin's Midwest GLBT College Conference in February 1999. For the edification and inspiration of a relatively small crowd, Kramer boldly claimed to have new documentary evidence that clarified the nuances of a long-standing and fragmentary narrative regarding the nearly four years that twenty-eight-year-old Abraham Lincoln and twenty-four-year-old Kentucky merchant Joshua Speed spent as bedfellows in Springfield, Illinois.

In order to appreciate Kramer's fulgurous contribution to this tale, its general contours and controversial elements must be briefly recounted.[8] An aspiring lawyer and politician, Lincoln nonetheless arrived in Springfield penniless in April 1837. Already deeply in debt, Lincoln seemed crestfallen over the cost of seventeen-dollar bedding in Joshua Speed's general store, which touched the proprietor:

> The tone of his voice was so melancholy that I felt for him. I looked up at him, and I thought then as I think now, that I never saw so gloomy a face. I said to him: "The contraction of so small a debt, seems to affect you so deeply, I think I can suggest a plan by which you will be able to attain your end, without incurring any debt. I have a very large room, and a very large double bed in it; which you are perfectly welcome to share if you choose." Lincoln's decision was swift. After immediately climbing the stairs to the bedroom, he re-

turned, "a face beaming with pleasure and smiles," exclaiming, "Well Speed I'm moved."[9]

The two bachelors slept in the same bed through December 1840. Such an arrangement was quite common at the time, as historians are quick to observe, but it is not too fanciful to suggest that that bed might be read as a metonymy for their intense emotional bond, which could not be equaled, even by their betrothed, during their years together.[10] They were, even by conservative estimate, "something like soul mates."[11] Lincoln's friend and future bodyguard Ward Lamon called Speed "the most intimate friend Mr. Lincoln ever had."[12] William Herndon, roommate, friend, and Lincoln biographer, balked jealously at Nicolay and Hay's claim in their biography that Speed was Lincoln's *only intimate friend,* but nonetheless conceded that "Lincoln loved this man more than any one dead or living."[13] On the eve of Speed's marriage, an event that marked the final emotional juncture in their friendship, Lincoln wrote, "You know my desire to befriend you is everlasting—that I will never cease, while I know how to do any thing."[14]

Their friendship seemingly derived not only from generosity but also a shared interest in law and politics, which they discussed (along with bawdy tales) at great length on many evenings with male friends, and, especially, their mutual anxieties regarding women. Both men, inexperienced despite their numerous attractions and courtships, seemed to struggle intensely with the idea of physical intimacy with women.[15] Lincoln apparently fell in love twice (if not three times) during the late 1830s, only to thwart engagement plans with Mary Owens and Mary Todd. Charles Strozier argues that in the face of this romantic tension, these friends found in each other succor if not a resolution to their troubles: "It would appear, therefore, that Lincoln and Speed's close relationship centered on their similar and reinforcing conflicts. . . . It is probable that such close male contact during the years of Lincoln's greatest heterosexual tension heightened the difficulty he found in securing intimacy with a woman. . . . Speed provided an alternative relationship that neither threatened nor provoked Lincoln. Each of the two men found solace in discussing their intimate maleness substituted for the tantalizing but frightening closeness of women."[16] Most prominent Lincoln scholars share Strozier's account of Lincoln's angst regarding the opposite sex, but they minimize or ignore its centrality to his friendship with Speed, particularly its emotional implications for both.

Lincoln's feelings for Speed are evident most explicitly, and mysteriously, in the closing year of their intimate friendship. In December 1840 Speed disclosed to Lincoln his intention to sell the store, which fell short of his financial aspirations, and his plans to return to his family in Kentucky in the wake of his father's death. Dashed hopes for love with Matilda Edwards, whom Lincoln may also have been courting, also likely influenced his decision. "There is nothing here," he wrote his sister, "but some of the cleverest fellows that God ever made—the truest friends and warmest hearts—that is worth living in this country for."[17] Lincoln's reaction remains a contested issue, one that emanates from conflicting interpretations of what he called "that fatal first of Jany. '41."[18] On that day the sales notice for Speed's store appeared in the local paper, and Lincoln broke off his engagement to Mary Todd. Whether he lost his nerve, as some thought, loved Matilda Edwards too much, as others surmised, or was despondent over Speed's imminent departure, which few are willing to entertain, is uncertain. That he fell into a terrible depression during the early weeks of January is certain, documented by those who thought him "crazy as a loon" and suicidal.[19] In his own estimate: "I am the most miserable man living. If what I feel were equally distributed to the whole human family, there would not be a cheerful face on earth."[20]

Lincoln recovered quickly, if not fully, perhaps in part because Speed did not actually leave Springfield until May 1841. In August Lincoln paid an extended visit to the Speed family home in Louisville, during which his friend experienced a budding romance with Fanny Henning. They almost immediately became engaged. Between September and the end of the same year the men were again in Springfield together, likely discussing Speed's intense, escalating doubts about his relationship with Henning. As many have observed, Lincoln served well in the role of trusted and patient confidant and counselor, returning the cherished favor he had enjoyed during his own failed engagements.[21] His flurry of passionate correspondence to Speed in January and February 1842 bespeaks the depth of their friendship, even as it raises questions about its nature.

Lincoln's version of a pep talk is, to say the least, peculiar, though lack of interpersonal context makes reading the only extant (one-sided version of) exchange between the men rather difficult. Articulating his "deepest solicitude for the success of the enterprize you are engaged in," Lincoln claims in his first letter to "adopt this as the last method I can invent to aid you, in case (which God forbid) you shall need any aid." Evidently Lincoln expected that the case would, in fact, present itself, for he outlines "*three special causes*" and "*one general one*" to explain his "reasonable" belief that Speed "would feel verry [*sic*] badly some time between this and the final consummation of your purpose." This latter point in time, they both knew from years of anxiety, represented sexual intercourse, the nadir of hetero-sexual relations as it was constituted in their imaginations. In addition, generally, to his "*naturally . . . nervous temperament,*" Lincoln explained, Speed would be vulnerable to bad weather, a lack of conversation with friends, and "*the rapid and near approach of that crisis on which all your thoughts and feelings concentrate.*" In response to that crisis, namely the "apprehension that you do not love her as you should," Lincoln reassured Speed that it was not because she expected it or because she was wealthy. No, he had not "*reasoned* [himself] *into* it," for he did not then know her to be "moral, amiable, sensible, or even of good character." In truth he had found himself "unable to *reason* himself *out* of it" because her "*personal appearance and deportment*" had impressed "the *heart* and not the head." It was those "heavenly black eyes." As a final measure of comfort, Lincoln urged that he not worry about Fanny "scouting and despising you, and giving herself up to another" since he had no such apprehension in the first place and therefore could not "bring it home to your feelings."[22] Consensus has not been achieved regarding Lincoln's use of *praeteritio* here, but all are clear that as before, the trials of love were weathered and romance endured because of their friendship.

A month later, and just weeks before the wedding, Fanny Henning nearly died, or so Speed feared. Again Lincoln wrote with words of solace. "I hope and believe, that your present anxiety and distress about *her* health and *her* life, must and will forever banish those horrid doubts, which I know you sometimes felt, as to the truth of your affection for her." Those doubts, Lincoln observed, could not be matched in "their immeasurable measure of misery," even by the prospect of Fanny's death. "The death scenes of those we love, are surely painful enough; but these we are prepared to, and expect to see. They happen to all, and all know they must happen." If, perhaps, Speed could not fully appreciate Lincoln's insight, further consolation followed. "Should she, as you fear, be destined to an early grave," Lincoln reminds Speed, she has prepared well through the religion "he once disliked so much." He expressed his hope that Speed's "melancholly [*sic*] bodings" were unfounded but optimistically concluded that whatever happened, his worry provided "indubitable evidence of your undying affection [and love] for her."[23] David Donald's interpretation of these letters, like Lincoln's advice, is clinical and presumably salubrious: "In effect, Lincoln and Speed were acting out a game of doctor and patient; in the winter of 1840–1841 Lincoln had been the sufferer and Speed had offered encouraging advice; now it was Speed who was at risk and Lincoln was trying to save his health and sanity."[24]

Fanny lived. More consequentially, with Lincoln's able assistance, embodied in a final prenuptial pledge that his "desire to befriend" Speed was "everlasting," and the sensible advice that Speed go through the ceremony "calmly, or even with sufficient composition not to excite alarm," his friend married.[25] In what might be rightly called Lincoln's swan song,[26] he wrote days after the marriage that his anticipation on Speed's behalf (news of the February 15 consummation did not arrive until the twenty-fourth) was such that "I opened the letter, with intense anxiety and trepidation—so much, that although it turned out better that I expected, I have hardly yet, at the distance of ten hours, become calm." Relieved that their "*forebodings*" were, in the end, "all the worst sort of nonsense," Lincoln offered one last bit of advice to calm Speed, who still seemed plagued by doubts. Speed had written that "something indescribably horrible and alarming still haunts [me]," and confessed his fear that the "Elysium" of which he had "dreamed so much, is never to be realized." Lincoln responded,

> Well, if it shall not, I dare swear, it will not be the fault of her who is now your wife. I now have no doubt that it is the peculiar misfortune of both you and me, to dream dreams of Elysium far exceeding all that any thing earthly can realize. Far short of your dreams as you may be, no woman could do more to realize them, than that same black eyed Fanny. . . . My old Father used to have a saying that "If

you made a bad bargain, *hug* it the tighter"; and it occurs to me, that
if the bargain you have just closed can possibly be called a bad one,
it is certainly the most pleasant one for applying the maxim to,
which my fancy can, by any effort, picture.

If their dreams of Elysium included an intense emotional bond with each
other, that too must be tempered with the bromide of homely maxims and
practical relations. Lincoln married Mary Todd, with whom he resumed a
courtship after Speed's marriage, in November 1842. His friendship with
Speed persisted throughout their lives, though it would never again, in
word or deed, match the emotional intensity palpable in that final blessing
of a devoted friend.

In terms of subtlety and indirection, Larry Kramer's rendering of the
Lincoln-Speed affair paled in comparison to Lincoln's letters and historians' interpretations of them. Indeed, Kramer, armed only with his queer
imagination and sharp tongue, ventured in bullish fashion with Wisconsin-
ites in tow where all others had feared to tread.[27] "Between 1839 and 1842
Abraham Lincoln and Joshua Speed loved each other." Far from being the
crucible of economic hardship, Speed's bed fostered a blossoming (and
hardly fraternal) love that began at first sight and was only sundered by
(tortured) political choices that required, among other sacrifices, wives.
"For years they shared a bed and their most private thoughts. They fell in
love with each other and slept next to each other for four years." Like
Lincoln scholars, Kramer substantiated his interpretation in part by reference to extant correspondence. "One only has to read the letters between these two to know the depth of their love." Unlike Lincoln scholars,
however, Kramer without qualification concluded that Lincoln and Speed
were gay.

More provocatively, Kramer's strikingly romantic narrative was pur-
portedly legitimated, and certainly amplified, by letters and diary entries
allegedly found buried beneath the floorboards of the old store and housed
currently in a private, unnamed collection in Davenport, Iowa. Lush with
witness to the love that dare not speak its name, those diary entries resolved any ambiguity about the nature of their friendship: "He ["Linc," as
Speed called affectionately called him] often kisses me when I tease him,
often to shut me up. . . . He would grab me by his long arms and hug and

hug." Anticipating the incredulity of posterity, Speed apparently writes, "Yes, our Abe is like a school girl."

Kramer's disclosure, of course, sought to titillate the historical imagination and provoke collective memory. I want to clarify, however, how it might be understood as a performance distinguishable from typical nonacademic discourses that grope for queer historical subjects. Kramer's lecture was not simply a manifestation of familiar gossip meant to intrigue by raising the specter of homosexuality; nor was it, in keeping with Kramer's long career of diatribe, a demolition of the historical closet designed to expose and condemn the hypocrisy of heteronormative power.[28] To the contrary, his protectiveness of the lecture, his uncharacteristically temperate persona, his evidentiary emphasis, and the care with which he constituted Lincoln's ethos reveal a political but not necessarily polemical motive.

Kramer offered what Roger Simon calls "insurgent commemoration": "attempts to construct and engage representations that rub taken-for-granted history against the grain so as to revitalize and rearticulate what one sees as desirable and necessary for an open, just and life-sustaining future."[29] Insurgency, in this sense, should not be construed as strategic *impiety*, to borrow Kenneth Burke's term. He did not, in other words, defile Lincoln's sacred memory for the sake of political confrontation. Rather, in filling a void perpetuated by the caretakers of official memory, Kramer exhibited a *will to piety*, which Burke characterizes as a "loyalty to the sources of our being. . . . [creating] the deep connection [with] . . . the 'remembrance of things past.'"[30] As Kramer argues, "To know that Abraham Lincoln and Joshua Speed were in love with each other for all of their adult lives and that no history book will record this essential truth that could so radically alter how gay people are accepted in this country that worships Lincoln is very painful."[31] "History is about possession," Kramer concluded. "History is about claiming what is ours."[32]

Proprietary claims are not novel in public memory. Indeed, their dynamic social construction and currency, and competition among them, provide the vital sustenance for memory's endurance. The agon of Lincoln's memory, as Barry Schwartz and Merrill Peterson's studies richly demonstrate, has long contributed fundamentally to his becoming an "inexhaustible resource," an exemplar so deeply forged, so iconic, so permanent, that he is unquestionably "part of the soul of American society."[33] It is noteworthy, however, that Kramer's countermemory, admittedly a radical reconfiguration of the American soul, provoked responses, especially by professional historians, attempting what I call *mnemonicide* to assuage the anxieties attending their homosexual panic.[34] Mindful of Schwartz's thoughtful reservations regarding the praxis of Bodnar's "official memory,"[35] I aim nonetheless to account for this rhetoric of control seeking to preserve Lincoln's and thus our own hegemonic heterosexuality.

This account begins with a simple question: Why would anyone care if a known gay extremist delivered a fantastic rendering of an American icon's homosexuality at a gathering of midwestern collegiate queers, a tale only repeated by the end of spring 1999 by the gay press, Madison's *Capital Times,* and the online magazine Salon.com? In response, I turn to the notion of homosexual panic, the homophobic terror of guilt by homosexual association that subtly governs our social bonds and warrants visceral and vicious responses to any potential encroachment by the queer contagion.[36] Given the magnitude of Lincoln's memory in forging our collective, national identity, with obvious implications for individual identity, conviction of his homosexuality would necessarily implicate us all, by means of this inescapable heritage, as practitioners and progenitors of same-sex love. The threat elicits not only fear of homosexual complicity but perhaps more consequentially that of normalizing and centralizing queerness as a national value. That said, my query reminds us that this panic, while potentially dispersed throughout a community, most keenly strikes locally those with particular proximity to the stakes. In this case, I highlight two of these panic-stricken communities to demonstrate mnemonicide at work.

You do not need to be a queer theorist to fathom the reaction of Springfield residents as they opened their Sunday *State Journal-Register* on May 16, 1999, to find, just beneath Lincoln's picture on the masthead, the headline "Writer Asserts Proof Lincoln Was Gay."[37] Staff writer Jefferson Robbins's judicious account[38] of Kramer's speech, its key arguments and the merits of its evidence as interpreted by historians, evoked a tirade by local residents sparked by an immediate and intense flash of homosexual panic. They answered this betrayal of their civic pride and collective memory with cancellations and a flurry of emails, phone calls, and editorials chastising the *State Journal-Register* for its sensationalism (what one woman described as "dredg[ing] up all the trash lying on the bottom of the ocean for the world to ponder"), its advancement of the gay "agenda," its endangerment of Springfield's prosperous tourism industry, and its "smearing of President Lincoln's reputation."[39] Even editor Barry Locher's immediate (if qualified) apology could not quell a feeling that most shared with a resident who wrote, "Honest Abe must be spinning in his Oak Ridge grave wondering what he did to Springfield to make them shame him in this manner."[40] What these local stewards of Lincoln did not articulate fully was the motive that animated so many of their explicitly pragmatic and patriotic appeals: to constitute Lincoln's memory is to be constituted by Lincoln's memory.[41] As one outraged subscriber astutely, if unfortunately, observed, "[F]amilies need good values, not gay values."[42]

The rather predictable volley of ad hominem and threat exhibits the limited rhetorical options available to those locals threatened by an "outlaw" memory, a flexing of vernacular muscle in the interest of bullying those who give it voice so as to insulate and protect the multiple (economic, social, familial) investments in a sanctioned and cherished memory.[43] Uninterested in the historical merits of Kramer's claims or their newsworthiness, Springfield residents did not seek to refute a competing memory out of existence; instead they formed a *posse comitatus* and performed the rhetorical equivalent of running the "outlaw" memory out of town on a rail.

Such tar-and-feather mnemonicide is not nearly as complex or interesting as that attempted by scholars who readily answered Kramer's folly. Any claim that professional historians suffered equally the moral, cognitive, and emotional constrictions of homosexual panic or, more precisely, that consequently they would deploy themselves, consciously or unconsciously, in the service of public memory's political battle over Lincoln, is tantamount to fighting words. Many historians would deny that, in the words of one London reporter, "scholars . . . consider it their business to safeguard the memory of the Father of the Nation."[44] Thomas Fleming, in distinguishing between the objectivity of history and the ideological labor of public memory, stated the case in unequivocal terms: "[M]y painfully acquired belief [is] that the historian's chief task is to separate history from memory. . . . memory is not history. It is too clotted with sentiment, with the kind of retrospective distortion that we constantly inflict on the past. History gives us, not the past seen through the eyes of the present, but the past in the eyes, the hearts and minds of the men and women who lived through a particular time, and experienced it."[45] Merrill Peterson maintains this distinction regarding the nation's memory of Lincoln, arguing that the "public remembrance of the past, as differentiated from the historical scholars', is concerned less with establishing its truth than with appropriating it for the present. . . . While heightening consciousness of the nation's heritage, it restages it and manipulates it for ongoing public purposes."[46]

Such, no doubt, is the professional response that should readily dismiss Kramer's queer memory of Lincoln, that all-too-familiar speculative imagining that has circulated at least since Carl Sandburg's capricious characterization of Lincoln and Speed as having "a streak of lavender, and spots soft as May violets" seventy-five years ago.[47] The seasoned and serious historian, with instant discernment, should rightly conclude with Lincoln scholar Douglas Wilson, "It sounds like this might be a case of taking a 19th century event and giving it a 20th century context."[48]

How, then, does one explain the passionate engagement of this controversy by historians? Without belaboring an obvious point, first it must be said that history is tropologically, ontologically, and ideologically *a rhetorical enterprise.*[49] The latter of these three dimensions that shape the historian-rhetor most concerns me here, generally because its presence in historiography remains closeted for many of its practitioners and specifically because of its profound implications for a queer past. At a minimum and without yet attributing nefarious motive, one can note with Dominick LaCapra that "[a]ny 'dialogue' with the past in professional historiography takes place in a larger social, political, economic, and cultural context that places severe restrictions upon it."[50] The degree to which a particular historical account is inflected by those constraints depends on the historian, but that those accounts are indeed inflected is difficult to gainsay. More pointedly, that the past—and its disciplinary recovery and representation—is usable and used ideologically often escapes notice except by those for whom a relevant past has been "consigned to oblivion."[51] Some historians' passionate differentiation between history and collective memory might be read as symptomatic of a fear that their ideological investments, however minimal, will be exposed in the comparison.[52]

In certain cases historians doth protest too much. Queer history and memory is certainly one of them. The story of GLBT historiography cannot be told but as one of struggle against discipline, a term that designates not only an academic field but the rhetorical efforts, often cloaked as "objective" praxis and judgment, that preserve hegemonic constructions of sanctioned domains of inquiry into the past.[53] Despite a contemporary climate of relative legitimacy, queer history continues to struggle, particularly in subfields like Lincoln studies. Philip Nobile has argued, "Ever since talk about Lincoln's possible bisexuality crept into the mainstream circa 1995 . . . Lincoln scholars have been unanimously skeptical and sometimes even hostile to the idea. Perhaps the best word to describe their reaction is homophobic, that is, fear of a lavender Lincoln."[54]

That homophobic fear when intensified becomes homosexual panic, as I believe occurred in the wake of Kramer's speech. Threatened by memory-making that claimed historical authenticity of Lincoln's homosexuality by virtue of documentary evidence, Lincoln scholars blurred Peterson's distinction between establishing history's truth and appropriating, restaging, and manipulating the nation's heritage for ongoing ideological purposes. I would argue that Joshua Speed's diary entries, upon which Kramer's public memory rests and which historians have not seen, mark that collision of history and memory that is born of the most dangerous forms of "insurgent commemoration." Speed's diary portends a radical disruption and transformation—a revolution, we might say—of national collective identity as constituted by Lincoln's memory. Given the stakes—what one author astutely labeled the "second Civil War"[55]— Lincoln scholars, many of whom as American citizens share the values embedded in the dominant memory of Lincoln, have reacted to their own homosexual panic by forming the last battalion capable of preserving Lincoln's heterosexual ethos.

Because, as David Thelen has observed,[56] historians professionally are most concerned with the accuracy of memory, their ethos when defending a particular version of the past derives from the same source, namely the legitimacy of a detached voice authorizing the verified remembrance of the historical subject. In the face of what could amount to exculpatory evidence, namely Speed's alleged diary, we find a consistent gesture toward the *plausibility* of Kramer's narrative, remote as historians may will it to be, that preserves this ethos of objectivity. Michael Burlingame, who wrote a psychobiography of Lincoln, for instance, comments, "If this is an authentic diary and it does contain homoerotic passages, I'm willing to believe it if the evidence is there."[57] Others, like Illinois state historian Thomas Schwartz, establishes similar ethos by clarifying the burden of proof: "You can't prove a negative. There's always a possibility that anything exists, until you can absolutely demonstrate it not being true. On the other hand, if the thing does exist, it's really incumbent upon Kramer to prove his assertion rather than for others to disprove it."[58] Beyond good method, however, these expressed deferrals of judgment serve to cloak the ideological work that will get done in the explicit judgments that follow nonetheless. This rhetoric of objectivity and deferral strategically grounds even as it is belied by enthusiastic arguments that aim precisely to prove the negative in Lincoln's case.

In varying degrees of development and sophistication, historians have challenged Kramer's memory without waiting for Kramer's disclosure of Speed's diary. Lincoln was "very, very unlikely" a gay man, they argue, for the following circumstantial reasons: because nineteenth-century frontiersmen typically slept in the same beds for the same reason Lincoln did—economic necessity; because Lincoln courted women, several prior to Mary Todd, and then fathered four children with her; and because the "very personal and very rough politics of the time" would have produced evidence of blackmail had there been a romance between Lincoln and Speed.[59] Each of these arguments provides useful contextual frames through which inferences regarding the Lincoln-Speed relationship and their texts (extant correspondence) might be derived. As Thomas Schwartz rightly observes, "History is always interpreted. Facts don't speak for themselves. Evidence has to be cemented together with imagination and interpretation."[60]

What marks these accounts ideologically, however, is their rather indiscriminate if not desperate application, their insistent tone. Although the contextual frames are not mutually exclusive in their relation to a queer reading of Lincoln and Speed, nor are they comprehensive, they are presented *as if* that were the case, meant to raise doubt sufficiently to eliminate homosexuality as a credible inference. The issue of romance is particularly illuminating. Michael Burlingame forcefully dismisses the possibility of Lincoln's homosexuality by asserting that "there is too much evidence that Lincoln was strongly attracted to women."[61] In his book *The Inner World of Abraham Lincoln,* however, he unambiguously charts the tortured history of Lincoln's relationships with women, aptly summarized in the opening sentence of the chapter-long discussion: "Abraham Lincoln did not like women." He quotes one love interest from the 1830s who observed that Lincoln seemed to be "a very queer fellow" and another whom Lincoln courted in Springfield during his residency in Speed's bed: "While he was never at ease with women, with men he was a favorite companion." Complexities he methodically elucidates for a narrower audience are absent in summary judgments that appear in mass-mediated sources to seek foreclosure of same-sex desire as a dynamic force in Lincoln's heterosexual congress.[62]

Perhaps more telling, Burlingame offers as evidence of Lincoln's heterosexuality his love affair with Ann Rutledge, which has long been contested by historians on evidentiary grounds. In his book Burlingame endorses those Lincoln scholars who rebut James G. Randall's skepticism regarding the veracity of the affair. Among those favored revisionists is Douglas Wilson, who argues that Randall "insists on an extremely high standard of proof" that befits legal judgment but not historical inquiry. Wilson, who considers the Rutledge story a "positive gain for all who seek to understand the man and the circumstances that brought him forth," dismisses Randall because "[o]bserving the evidentiary safeguards of a criminal trial would, after all, bring a substantial portion of historical inquiry to a halt, for much of what we want to know about the past simply cannot be established on these terms. Abraham Lincoln's early life is a perfect example." By stark contrast, both Burlingame and Wilson seemingly impose Randall's impossibly rigorous standards in interpreting the evidence—of comparable if not sounder documentary merit from the same time period—of Lincoln's relationship with Speed. Their heterosexist—if not homophobic—bias is unmistakable here and tells us much about the largely invisible ideological assumptions at work in their historical method.[63]

Others have employed definitional argument to limit interpretive ground for assessing such evidence. Thomas Schwartz, for example, is more forthright than Burlingame in dealing with the complexities of Lincoln's love affairs, only to dismiss them as a definitional warrant for a queer reading. "I don't think anyone would deny that you find [in Lincoln] an ambivalence and awkwardness toward women. Whether you could make the case that he experienced not only homosexual attraction but also had homosexual partners is something else." Lest that case be made, Michael Rogin deepens the definitional burden: "There may be evidence of male-male desire, but that's not gay. If 'gay' is going to mean anything it's got to mean orgasms with other men. There's got to be some sense of transgression and forbiddenness."[64] The ambiguity of establishing "something else" or the impossibility of discovering in some archive the fluid proof of "transgression and forbiddenness" insulates Lincoln and his custodians from interpretation that defies heteronormative memory.

Beyond the convulsions that have passed during this homosexual panic as coolly objective responses to Kramer's assertions, this discourse exhibits further assurances that control is both means and end in this struggle. Absent silencing Kramer by way of an authoritative historical interpretation of Lincoln's love for Speed, contingency plans lurk everywhere among circumstantial and evidentiary claims. First, ad hominem and well-poisoning abound, as one historian proclaimed on the *History News Network:* "[E]very gay historian, or gay activist who claims to be an historian, wants to 'out' all of our great historical figures."[65] Second, an admonishment against certain revisionist history, which Gabor Boritt articulates in *The Lincoln Enigma:* "Lincoln strongly bonded with men but what may suggest homosexuality in our time most likely did not so much occur to most people in his time. . . . In history, context is all-important and the first duty of the historian is to understand the past in terms understood by those who lived in the past."[66] Finally, queer distinctions are distinctions without meaningful difference. As Harold Evans argues, "If it was an isolated, earlier event that occurred decades before a person rose to prominence, the public should use their own good judgment and common sense and not take it very seriously."[67]

Fearing their incapacity to discipline memory, historians have sought the diminution of any queer interpretive context that would sustain the meaning for collective memory potentially derived from counterevidentiary authority. Ironically, Lincoln scholars have embodied their critique of Kramer. As Norman Hellmers, superintendent of the Lincoln Home National Historic Site, put it so well: "People find it useful to exploit Mr. Lincoln for their own purposes. They'll do whatever it takes to make the connection."[68] In this case, we witness not a disciplining or domestication of memory's imaginative excess but the assassination of memory, or mnemonicide, for the sake of perpetuating a hegemonic connection to our ostensibly straight past.

By way of conclusion, let me make a few relevant clarifications and point out some implications. I am not claiming that historians are *necessarily* elites whose standard practice, whose guiding impulse—as Bodnar might argue—functions as the ballast of hegemonic memory. Indeed, I have in principle much sympathy for Timothy Garton Ash's characterization of Holocaust historians: "Thank God for historians . . . [their] fairness, representation, completeness . . . the historians are our protectors. They protect us against forgetting—that is a truism. But they also protect us against memory."[69] Gay and lesbian historians have, in this spirit, labored to discover a past that both founds queer memory and dismantles the myths that have trivialized and scapegoated homosexuals into obscurity. I join Martin Duberman in pressing for the "right of a people to a knowledge of its own history (its *memory*), an indispensable prerequisite for establishing collective identity and for enjoying the solace of knowing that we too have 'come through,' are the bearers of a diverse, rich, unique heritage."[70] But I also draw from this study of Lincoln's memory the inherent danger in historians' ability to "protect us against memory." Induced (perhaps unknowingly) by circumstance into the political fray, bolstered by a professional ethos that positions them as arbiters and advocates of memory's struggle, they threaten to become the midwives of the forgotten.

For Larry Kramer, recuperating Lincoln was necessary not foremost as a form of gay protest but as a mandate that gays and lesbians, in order to survive, must learn to remember: "A lot of our brothers and sisters, the generations that came before us, our blood kin, died, and we must never for one second forget the fact that each and every one of us is related by blood to every single other gay man and lesbian who not only died from AIDS but who has ever lived."[71] His astuteness regarding the moral and rhetorical imperatives inherent in such a mandate of memory is revealed in his repeated use of the Gettysburg Address: "It is for us the living, rather, to be dedicated here to the unfinished work which they who fought here have thus far so nobly advanced. It is rather for us to be here dedicated to the great task remaining before us—that from these honored dead we take increased devotion to that cause for which they gave the last full measure of their devotion—that we here highly resolve that these dead shall not have died in vain."[72] Kramer's radical appropriation of Lincoln would extend beyond this rather typical if meaningful invocation of sacred words; indeed, like Lincoln himself, he would *innovate* in deploying the usable symbolic resources of the past as an organizing principle in the present and moral vision for a sustainable queer future.

Notes

For epigraphs, see Abraham Lincoln, "My Childhood—Home I See Again," in *Collected Works of Abraham Lincoln,* ed. Roy P. Basler (New Brunswick: Rutgers University Press, 1953), 1:367; Emile Durkheim, *The Elementary Forms of Religious Life* (1915; New York: Free Press, 1965), 55.

1. Paul Monette, *Last Watch of the Night* (New York: Harcourt Brace and Company, 1994), 147–49.

2. David W. Blight, "'For Something beyond the Battlefield': Frederick Douglass and the Struggle for the Memory of the Civil War," *Journal of American History* 75 (March 1989): 1159. See also Frederick Douglass, "Oration in Memory of Abraham Lincoln," in *The Life and Writings of Frederick Douglass,* ed. Philip S. Foner (New York: International Publishers, 1955), 4:309–19.

3. Monette, *Last Watch of the Night,* 149.

4. Martin Duberman, *Stonewall* (New York: Plume, 1994), xvii.

5. For an excellent analysis of the AIDS Quilt and public memory, see Marita Sturken, *Tangled Memories: The Vietnam War, the AIDS Epidemic, and the Politics of Remembering* (Berkeley: University of California Press, 1997); Peter S. Hawkins, "Naming Names: The Art of Memory and the NAMES Project AIDS Quilt," *Critical Inquiry* 19 (summer 1993): 752–79.

6. John Cloud, "Why Milk Is Still Fresh," *Advocate,* November 10, 1998, p. 33.

7. John Nichols, "History Out in the Open; AIDS Activist Says the Missing Chapters on Gays Must Be Written," *Capital Times* (Madison, WI), February 26, 1999, p. 11A; Larry Kramer, "Yesterday, Today, and Tomorrow," *Advocate,* March 30, 1999, p. 67.

8. See Charles B. Strozier, *Lincoln's Quest for Union: A Psychological Portrait,*

2nd ed. (Philadelphia: Paul Dry Books, 2000), 53–65; Jonathan Ned Katz, "No Two Men Were Ever More Intimate," *Love Stories: Sex between Men before Homosexuality* (Chicago: University of Chicago Press, 2001), 3–25; Douglas L. Wilson, *Honor's Voice: The Transformation of Abraham Lincoln* (New York: Knopf, 1998), 245–59; Charley Shively, "Big Buck and Big Lick: Lincoln and Whitman," *Drum Beats: Walt Whitman's Civil War Boy Lovers* (San Francisco: Gay Sunshine Press, 1989), 71–88; Robert L. Kinkaid, *Joshua Fry Speed: Lincoln's Most Intimate Friend* (Harrogate, TN: Department of Lincolniana, Lincoln Memorial University, 1943).

9. Douglas L. Wilson and Rodney O. Davis, eds., *Herndon's Informants: Letters, Interviews, and Statements about Abraham Lincoln* (Urbana: University of Illinois Press, 1998), 588–91.

10. In addressing the bed question, Charles Strozier is the most sensible of Lincoln scholars, most of whom refuse to consider its emotional dimensions: "Social custom and individual experience, however, are not always congruent. Just because many men slept together casually in inns and elsewhere during this period by no means proves that it was unimportant that Lincoln lay down in a crowded bed night after night for well over three years with his best male friend, whom he trusted above all with his deepest feelings. The question is, what does it mean?" Strozier, *Lincoln's Quest for Union,* 57.

11. Wilson, *Honor's Voice,* 245.

12. Ward H. Lamon, *The Life of Abraham Lincoln: From His Birth to His Inauguration as President* (1872; Lincoln: University of Nebraska Press, 1999), 231.

13. Herndon here exhibits irritation about the implications of the term "intimacy." Although this must be read in its cultural context, it might be understood as the first of many that resist depictions of same-sex affection or desire. For the purposes of my argument, it is all the more interesting for its injunction against the excesses of memory:

Who authorizes H. and N. to assert what they do assert? How do H. and N. know that Lincoln and Speed poured out their souls to one another? If to tell a friend some facts in *one line* or direction constitutes *intimate* friendship, then Lincoln always, before and after Speed left Illinois, had *intimate* friends, and if Lincoln's refusal to tell all the secrets of his soul to any man shows a want of intimate friendship, then Lincoln never had an intimate friend. Poetry is no fit place for severe history. I think the truth is just here, namely, that under peculiar conditions and under *lines of love* and in that direction they were *intimate* friends. No man pours his whole soul to any man. (William H. Herndon to Jesse W. Weik, January 22, 1887, in *The Hidden Lincoln: From the Letters and Papers of William H. Herndon,* ed. Emanuel Hertz [New York: Blue Ribbon, 1940], 159.)

14. Abraham Lincoln to Joshua Speed, February 13, 1842, in Basler, *Collected Works of Abraham Lincoln,* 1:269.

15. Wilson, *Honor's Voice,* 195–264; Strozier, *Lincoln's Quest for Union,* 41–65. Others suggest that Lincoln's struggles with women spanned his lifetime and stemmed not merely from anxiety about sex. See Katz, *Love Stories,* 14; Burlingame, *The Inner World of Abraham Lincoln,* 123–46.

16. Strozier, *Lincoln's Quest for Union,* 56.

17. Quoted in Wilson, *Honor's Voice,* 247.

18. See Douglas L. Wilson, "Abraham Lincoln and 'That Fatal First of January,'" *Lincoln before Washington: New Perspectives on the Illinois Years* (Urbana: University of Illinois Press, 1997), 99–132; Wilson, *Honor's Voice,* 233–38; Strozier, *Lincoln's Quest for Union,* 58–59; David Herbert Donald, *Lincoln* (New York: Simon and Schuster, 1995), 86–88; Katz, *Love Stories,* 18.

19. William H. Herndon to Isaac N. Arnold, November 20, 1866, in Hertz, *The Hidden Lincoln,* 37.

20. Abraham Lincoln to John T. Stuart, January 23, 1841, in Basler, *Collected Works of Abraham Lincoln,* 1:229.

21. Wilson, *Honor's Voice,* 251–59; Donald, *Lincoln,* 89–90; Strozier, *Lincoln's Quest for Union,* 60–65; Katz, *Love Stories,* 18–24.

22. All quotations from Abraham Lincoln to Joshua F. Speed, January 3?, 1842, in Basler, *Collected Works of Abraham Lincoln,* 1:265.

23. All quotations from Abraham Lincoln to Joshua F. Speed, February 3, 1842, in Basler, *Collected Works of Abraham Lincoln,* 1:267–68.

24. Donald, *Lincoln,* 89.

25. Abraham Lincoln to Joshua F. Speed, February 13, 1842, in Basler, *Collected Works of Abraham Lincoln,* 1:269–70.

26. All quotations from Abraham Lincoln to Joshua F. Speed, February 25, 1842, in Basler, *Collected Works of Abraham Lincoln,* 1:280.

27. Kramer has refused to provide a transcript of this speech or the chapter on Lincoln in his unpublished work-in-progress *The American People.* Excerpts and description of the speech are found in Samara Kalk, "Lincoln Was Gay, Activist

Contends," *Capital Times* (Madison, WI), February 23, 1999, p. 2A; Kate Kail, "Lecturer Suggests Lincoln Was Gay," *Cardinal News* (Madison), February 23, 1999; Nichols, "History Out in the Open," 11A; Carol Lloyd, "Was Lincoln Gay?" http://www.salon.com/books/it/1999/04/30/lincoln/index.html.

28. For Kramer's rhetorical career, see Larry Kramer, *Reports from the Holocaust: The Making of an AIDS Activist* (New York: St. Martin's, 1989); David Bergman, "Larry Kramer and the Rhetoric of AIDS," in *AIDS: The Literary Response*, ed. Emmanuel S. Nelson (New York: Twayne, 1992), 175–86; Lawrence D. Mass, ed., *We Must Love One Another or Die: The Life and Legacies of Larry Kramer* (New York: St. Martin's, 1997).

29. Roger I. Simon, "Forms of Insurgency in the Production of Popular Memories: The Columbus Quincentenary and the Pedagogy of Counter-Commemoration," *Cultural Studies* 7 (January 1993): 76.

30. Kenneth Burke, *Permanence and Change: An Anatomy of Purpose* (Los Altos, CA: Hermes Publications, 1954), 71, 74.

31. Larry Kramer, "Yesterday, Today, and Tomorrow," *Advocate*, March 30, 1999, p. 67.

32. Nichols, "History Out in Open," 11A.

33. Merrill D. Peterson, *Lincoln in American Memory* (New York: Oxford University Press, 1994); Barry Schwartz, *Abraham Lincoln and the Forge of National Memory* (Chicago: University of Chicago Press, 2000).

34. In using the term *mnemonicide,* I mean to imply the rhetorical nature of collective forgetting or repression of memory and thus retain and emphasize a sense of agency in thinking about the social construction, transmission, and erasure of memory as it occurs at a specific historical moment. I recognize that the rhetorical acts I explore are part of the broader social/cultural dynamics of collective "amnesia" that can occur over much longer periods of time. See Michael Schudson, *Watergate in American Memory: How We Remember, Forget and Reconstruct the Past* (New York: Basic Books, 1992); Barry Schwartz, "Deconstructing and Reconstructing the Past," *Qualitative Sociology* 18 (1995): 263–70.

35. Schwartz qualifies Bodnar and other theorists of the politics of memory who emphasize the retention of state hegemony in social constructions of an "official past": "Collective memory is in truth an effective weapon in contemporary power struggles, but the battlefield image of society, taken alone, distorts understanding of collective memory's sources and functions, leaving out, as it does, the cultural realm within which the politics of memory is situated."

Schwartz, *Abraham Lincoln and the Forge of National Memory,* 15–17. See John Bodnar, *Remaking America: Public Memory, Commemoration, and Patriotism in the Twentieth Century* (Princeton: Princeton University Press, 1992).

36. Homosexual panic functions by means of an ideologically driven fear that one might be homosexual, harbor homosexual longings, or, most important, be perceived as homosexual by others. It thus bolsters and perpetuates heteronormativity through its terrorizing discourse or by force of gay bashing. See Edward J. Kempf, *Psychopathology* (St. Louis: Mosby, 1920), 477–515; Eve Kosofsky Sedgwick, *Between Men: English Literature and Male Homosocial Desire* (New York: Columbia University Press, 1985), 83–96; Charles E. Morris III, "Pink Herring and the Fourth Persona: J. Edgar Hoover's Sex Crime Panic," *Quarterly Journal of Speech* 88 (May 2002): 228–44. See also Eve Kosofsky Sedgwick, *Epistemology of the Closet* (Berkeley: University of California Press, 1990), 182–212.

37. Jefferson Robbins, "Writer Asserts Proof Lincoln Was Gay/Gay Activist Claims Mystery Diary Shows Recollections of Affair," *State Journal-Register* (Springfield, IL), May 16, 1999, p. 1.

38. Robbins detailed the relationship and the controversy in three articles published in the same edition. Robbins, "Writer Asserts Proof"; Jefferson Robbins, "Joshua Speed Was Longtime Friend, Prototypical Frontier Settler," *State Journal-Register* (Springfield, IL), May 16, 1999, p. 1; Jefferson Robbins, "Joshua Speed Suffered a Case of Cold Feet before His 1842 Marriage to Fanny Henning," *State Journal-Register* (Springfield, IL), May 16, 1999, p. 6.

39. For editorial responses, see *State Journal-Register* (Springfield, IL), May 20, 1999, p. 6; Stephanie Simon, "Lincoln Country Aghast as Local Paper Prints Gay Allegation; Activist Claims He's Seen the Diary of the 16th President's Homosexual Lover. Historians Deride the Idea as Springfield Fumes," *Los Angeles Times,* June 22, 1999, p. A5.

40. Barry Locher, "Claims about Lincoln Deserved Investigation," *State Journal-Register* (Springfield, IL), May 20, 1999, p. 7.

41. On the relationship between identity and memory, see Maurice Halbwachs, *On Collective Memory,* ed. Lewis A. Coser (Chicago: University of Chicago Press, 1992); John R. Gillis, "Memory and Identity: The History of a Relationship," in *Commemorations: The Politics of National Identity,* ed. John R. Gillis (Princeton: Princeton University Press, 1994), 3–24.

42. Quoted in Locher, "Claims about Lincoln," 7.

43. Bodnar's discussion of vernacular memory is useful here, however in this

instance we witness a struggle between two vernacular memories, one of which (in Springfield) mirrors and supports rather than disrupts the "official" memory. Bodnar, *Remaking America*. My rendering of Kramer's countermemory of Lincoln as an "out-law" memory is in keeping with Sloop and Ono's broader conception of "out-law discourse." John M. Sloop and Kent A. Ono, "Out-law Discourse: The Critical Politics of Material Judgment," *Philosophy and Rhetoric* 30 (1997): 50–69.

44. Andrew Gumbel, "Abe Lincoln's Home Town Outraged at His 'Outing,' " *Independent* (London), June 27, 1999, p. 21.

45. Thomas Fleming, "History and Memory: They're Different," http://www.historynewsnetwork.org/articles/article.html?id=159.

46. Peterson, *Lincoln in American Memory*, 35.

47. Sandburg wrote, suggestively, "A streak of lavender ran through him [Speed]; he had spots soft as May violets. . . . Lincoln too had . . . a streak of lavender, and spots soft as May violets. . . . Their births, the loins and tissues of their fathers and mothers, accident, fate, providence, had given these two men streaks of lavender, spots soft as May violets." Carl Sandburg, *Abraham Lincoln: The Prairie Years* (New York: Blue Ribbon Books, 1926), 1:166–67. For an analysis of the homoerotic subtext here, see Katz, *Love Stories*, 354.

48. Quoted in Lloyd, "Was Lincoln Gay?"

49. See Michel Foucault, *The Archaeology of Knowledge* (New York: Pantheon, 1972); Hayden White, *Metahistory: The Historical Imagination in Nineteenth-Century Europe* (Baltimore: Johns Hopkins University Press, 1973); Hayden White, *The Tropics of Discourse: Essays in Cultural Criticism* (Baltimore: Johns Hopkins University Press, 1978); Dominick LaCapra, *Rethinking Intellectual History: Texts, Contexts, Language* (Ithaca: Cornell University Press, 1983); Hayden White, *The Content of Form: Narrative Discourse and Historical Representation* (Baltimore: Johns Hopkins University Press, 1987); Allan Megill and Donald N. McCloskey, "The Rhetoric of History," in *The Rhetoric of the Human Sciences*, ed. John S. Nelson, Allan Megill, and Donald N. McCloskey (Madison: University of Wisconsin Press, 1987), 221–38; Michel de Certeau, *The Writing of History* (New York: Columbia University Press, 1988); E. Culpepper Clark and Raymie E. McKerrow, "The Rhetorical Construction of History," in *Doing Rhetorical History: Concepts and Cases*, ed. Kathleen J. Turner (Tuscaloosa: University of Alabama Press, 1998), 33–46.

50. Dominick LaCapra, "Rhetoric and History," *History and Criticism* (Ithaca: Cornell University Press, 1985), 42–43.

51. I borrow the phrase from Gillis, *Commemorations,* 9. Although his focus concerns literary studies, Eagleton's insights on ideology and academic writing are relevant here. Terry Eagleton, "Ideology and Scholarship," in *Historical Studies and Literary Criticism,* ed. Jerome J. McGann (Madison: University of Wisconsin Press, 1985), 114–25.

52. On the rhetorical similarities between history and collective memory, see Marouf Hasian Jr. and Robert E. Frank, "Rhetoric, History, and Collective Memory: Decoding the Goldhagen Debates," *Western Journal of Communication* 63 (winter 1999): 95–114.

53. See Blanche Wiesen Cook, "The Historical Denial of Lesbianism," *Radical History Review* 20 (spring/summer 1979): 60–65; Lisa Duggan, "History's Gay Ghetto: The Contradictions of Growth in Lesbian and Gay History," in *Presenting the Past: Essays on History and the Public,* ed. Susan Porter Benson, Steven Brier, and Roy Rosenzweig (Philadelphia: Temple University Press, 1986), 281–92; George Chauncey Jr., Martin Bauml Duberman, and Martha Vicinus, introduction to *Hidden from History: Reclaiming the Gay and Lesbian Past,* ed. Martin Bauml Duberman, Martha Vicinus, and George Chauncey Jr. (New York: NAL Books, 1989); John D'Emilio, "Not a Simple Matter: Gay History and Gay Historians," *Making Trouble: Essays on Gay History, Politics, and the University* (New York: Routledge, 1992), 138–47; Lisa Duggan, "The Discipline Problem," *GLQ: A Journal of Gay and Lesbian Studies* 2 (August 1995): 179–91.

54. Philip Nobile, "Don't Ask, Don't Tell, Don't Publish: Homophobia and Lincoln Studies?" http://www.historynewsnetwork.org/articles/article.html?id=97.

55. Lloyd, "Was Lincoln Gay?"

56. David Thelen, "Memory and American History," *Journal of American History* 75 (March 1989): 1117–29.

57. Quoted in Robbins, "Writer Asserts Proof," 6. Burlingame implies that documentary proof is self-evident, obscuring the politics of interpretation that he exercises in other statements. The resiliency of ideology in the face of such "proof" can be witnessed in the controversy over Thomas Jefferson's memory. See Jan Ellen Lewis and Peter S. Onuf, eds., *Sally Hemings and Thomas Jefferson: History, Memory, and Civic Culture* (Charlottesville: University of Virginia Press, 1997).

58. Quoted in Robbins, "Writer Asserts Proof," 6.

59. Among the Lincoln scholars making these claims are Gabor Boritt,

Douglas Wilson, Michael Burlingame, and Gene Griessman. See their testimony in Lloyd, "Was Lincoln Gay?"; Stephanie Simon, "Lincoln Country Aghast as Local Paper Prints Gay Allegation," *Los Angeles Times,* June 22, 1999, p. A5; W. Scott Thompson, "Was Lincoln Gay?" http://www.historynewsnetwork.org/article. html?id=96; Gabor Boritt, *The Lincoln Enigma: The Changing Faces of an American Icon* (New York: Oxford University Press, 2001), xiv–xvi.

60. Hilary Shenfeld, "Lincoln's Love Life: A Lesson in Historical Interpretation," *Chicago Daily Herald,* July 8, 1999, p. 3.

61. Quoted in Lloyd, "Was Lincoln Gay?"

62. Michael Burlingame, *The Inner World of Abraham Lincoln* (Urbana: University of Illinois Press, 1994), 123–24.

63. Burlingame, *The Inner World of Abraham Lincoln,* 135–36. Douglas L. Wilson, "Abraham Lincoln, Ann Rutledge, and the Evidence of Herndon's Informants," in *Lincoln before Washington,* 74–98.

64. Schwartz, quoted in Simon, "Lincoln Country Aghast"; Rogin, quoted in Lloyd, "Was Lincoln Gay?"

65. Glenn Williams, "Gay Myths," http://www.historynewsnetwork.org/ articles/comments/displayCommen t.html?cmid=70.

66. Boritt, *The Lincoln Enigma,* xv–xvi.

67. Quoted in Shenfeld, "Lincoln's Love Life," 3.

68. Quoted in Gumbel, "Abe Lincoln's Home Town Outraged at His 'Outing,'" 21.

69. Timothy Garton Ash, "The Life of Death," *New York Review of Books,* December 19, 1985, 39.

70. Martin Bauml Duberman, "'Writhing Bedfellows' in Antebellum South Carolina: Historical Interpretation and the Politics of Evidence," in *Hidden from History: Reclaiming the Gay and Lesbian Past,* ed. Martin Bauml Duberman, Martha Vicinus, and George Chauncey Jr. (New York: New American Library, 1989), 168.

71. Kramer, "Yesterday, Today, and Tomorrow," 66.

72. Abraham Lincoln, "Gettysburg Address," in Garry Wills, *Lincoln at Gettysburg: The Words That Remade America* (New York: Touchstone, 1992), 263.

5

Shadings of Regret
America and Germany

Barry Schwartz and
Horst-Alfred Heinrich

Why should we assume the faults of our friend, or wife, or father or child, because they sit around our hearth, or are said to have the same blood? All men have my blood and I all men's. Not for that will I adopt their petulance or folly, even the context of being ashamed of it.

Ralph Waldo Emerson, *Self-Reliance*

The Spur of Regret

Never before have American leaders and officials apologized for so many things. Shortly after President Ronald Reagan expressed remorse over the internment of Japanese Americans during World War II, Americans observed the five-hundredth anniversary of Christopher Columbus's voyage to the New World by acknowledging his atrocities against its native people. As American Lutherans rejected the anti-Semitism of their founder, Martin Luther, and the Southern Baptist Convention formally apologized for sanctifying slavery, an interfaith delegation visited Japan to apologize for the bombing of Hiroshima and Nagasaki. In Sand Creek, Colorado, whites offered regrets to Native American descendents of the Cheyenne and Arapaho Indians massacred there a century before. More recently, President William Clinton apologized for America's many moral failings in Africa; Aetna, Inc., apologized for issuing insurance policies on slaves' lives. The list of regrets seems endless.[1]

During most of America's history, political and civil institutions resolved conflicts through formal treaties, restitution, or tacit understanding. Only during the last two decades of the twentieth century have formal, public apologies become necessary. What are we to make of this growing wave of repentance? Emile Durkheim led us to believe that "a man is surer of his faith when he sees to how distant a past it goes back and what great things it has inspired."[2] Remembering noble deeds, he said, elevates the community's dignity and moral values. How, then, are we to explain the spreading contamination of the past, the discovery in every nook and crevice of the memory landscape a new atrocity to be regretted, a new wrong to be set right?

The swelling wave of repentance corresponds to the outpouring of collective memory literature in the 1980s and 1990s, and both developments are part of the late twentieth-century "sensitivity revolution," with its unprecedented concern for minority dignity and rights.[3] As old forms of religious and class conflicts evolve into ethnic, racial, and gender conflicts, disadvantaged groups become increasingly aware of the uses of public discourse. References to past injustice and suffering are particularly useful because they legitimate new distributional policies (affirmative action, including racial and gender quotas and preferences), new civil demeanor and discourse (political correctness), new interpretations of minority contributions to history, new heroes, new villains, new insights into America's criminal history. Such is the background of the new ritual apology. The spur of regret intensifies as the "dominant culture" comes under attack.

In their broadest sense, America's repentance gestures are aspects of what James Hunter calls its culture wars—the conflict between "progressive" and "orthodox" (traditional) conceptions of moral authority. In the orthodox vision, moral authority arises from a "dynamic reality that is independent of, prior to, and more powerful than human experience."[4] Whether it be a religion, a nation, or a political movement, this reality surpasses the existence of the individual, dignifies him, and promotes within him a sense of purpose and wholeness. Embracing absolute definitions of right and wrong, the orthodox reject relativism, multiple truths, and "alternative lifestyles." In the progressive vision, all racial, religious, ethnic, and gender boundaries are arbitrary but, ironically, must be maintained in a diverse and equal society. Progressives are suspicious of tradition, dedicated to minority rights, receptive to negative information about historically oppressive majorities, and inclined to relate minority shortcomings to majority oppression.[5] Ritual apologies, because they recognize oppression and its consequences, provide symbolic support for the progressive agenda.

Articulating the tension between traditional and progressive strains of American culture, Hunter's thesis rings true for many issues. But this thesis is self-limiting: by focusing on institutional policies, it downplays individual beliefs and underestimates their consensus.[6] Hunter observes that controversial issues have "become institutionalized chiefly through special-purpose organizations, denominations, political parties, and branches of government,"[7] but to assume that institutions are the only significant participants in matters of moral authority is to skirt too many issues, including questions about the clash among culture, memory, and morality on the one hand and institutional and individual definitions of moral responsibility on the other.

We questioned university students in the United States and Germany to determine how different combinations of culture and historical experience lead to different perspectives on personal responsibility. Comparing state discourse to the beliefs of informed citizens, we do not assume that one level of responsibility is more authentic than another; we seek rather to understand how these different levels relate to one another. Our argument is simple: political exigencies, particularly international and internal political pressures, operate on American and German governments to express regret officially, while cultural values induce individual Germans to take seriously claims that Americans are hard-pressed to understand, namely, that people can be morally responsible for events in which they did not participate. Taking the German sample as our point of reference, we emphasize the American findings. The American state is ready and willing to express regret for past wrongs; the American citizen is decidedly unwilling to do so. On a broader level, this means that collective memory can have no significance apart from the relation among what historians say about the past, how political elites represent the past, and what ordinary people, constrained by their nation's experience and cultural values, think about the past. Regret and responsibility, properly understood, refer to the relation among these three elements. Such is the claim we wish to defend.

Individual and Collective Responsibility

Moral responsibility, according to Leszek Kolakowski, is a natural sentiment having nothing to do with one's conduct or the timing of one's birth. "Our primary relationship to the world," he believes, "is that of responsibility voluntarily assumed. [To live is] to take on the debts of the world as our own."[8] Is Kolakowski saying that the sharing of shame and responsibility is a universal disposition, applicable to everyone in all times? If so, his burden of proof is heavy indeed.[9]

Assertions about moral responsibility are difficult to defend when applied universally. Oskar von der Gablentz, referring to the National Socialist era, therefore limits his claim: "Every member of the body politic is responsible according to his function, from the absolute ruler to the common voter."[10] Even von der Gablentz's conception, however, is problematic. It is one thing for a state and its agents to assume responsibility for historical wrongdoing; it is another for an individual to assume responsibility for state misdeeds committed before his or her birth.

Gesine Schwan declares that moral guilt can never be transmitted across generations, but "the psychological and moral consequences of treating it with silence harm even the subsequent generation and the basic consensus of a democracy."[11] In this same connection, Jürgen Habermas used the image of history as a supermarket: we cannot pick out just what is convenient for us; on the contrary, democratic societies need to deal with the negative aspects of their past, especially when victims of earlier atrocities are still alive and still citizens.[12]

From the standpoint of both social identity theory[13] and self-categorization theory,[14] Schwan's argument makes sense. Since our self-image consists of both an individual and a group component, identification with social groups can support or undermine self-esteem, depending on what those groups have accomplished historically.[15] As individuals identify with the past of their family, community, or nation, they enhance their sense of responsibility as group members. But how, precisely, does an open confrontation with guilt protect new generations and sustain democracy? Can one imagine a point at which constant invocation of past wrongs backfires, inhibits rather than promotes recognition of moral responsibility? Might a measure of silence—not total silence but partial relief from the clamor of self-condemnation—be necessary rather than harmful to the consensus of democracy?

Schwan's formulation, like von der Gablentz's and Kolakowski's, connects the burgeoning of regret to accelerating ethnoracial movements, human rights discourse, decolonization, and the politics of recognition; but it ignores the question of how accountability of the state and community can be convincingly extended to individual citizens. Michel-Rolph Trouillot asserts that collective bodies have traditionally assumed responsibility for harms committed against one another's members, but these bodies are incapable of emotions that convert formal admissions of regret into expressions that injured parties can recognize. Ritual apologies involve a fatal abstraction: representatives of past perpetrators offering apologies to representatives of past victims conceal the affective trauma of the original offense. Apology rituals are abortive because they symbolize injuries no one can really feel and regrets no one can deeply affirm.[16] Kolakowski, von der Gablentz, and Schwan overestimate the strength of the linkage between institutional and individual regret; Trouillot underestimates it. If ritual apologies were as empty as he claims, recipients would not react to them and they would have ceased long ago.[17] Instead, the demand for contrition seems to grow stronger with each apology offered.

Under what conditions and at what levels is moral reconciliation possible? Jeffrey Olick and Brenda Coughlin have recently argued that in matters of the politics of regret, states take the lead and individuals follow. ("[T]he confessional individual mimics the regretful state.")[18] In fact, the situation turns out to be more complex. By locating philosophical assertions within different cultural contexts, we try to contribute, in some slight and tentative way, to the analysis of this question.

Time Frames of Responsibility

Americans typically reject moral responsibility for the misconduct of others, especially their ancestors. This resistance is not an isolated trait to be dismissed as a moral failing; it reflects a cultural pattern made up of individualism and liberalism—a pattern that focuses so closely on individual rights and individual responsibilities as to distinguish the United States culturally and historically from other democracies.[19]

Traditional societies, which bind present generations to the values and programs of the past, are familiar to us through Old Testament affirmations of fathers' sins being visited upon their posterity, and through medieval notions of collective guilt, including the eternal guilt of the Jew as Christ's killer. Enlightenment ideals, by contrast, denounce the dead hand of the past. Characteristic of every Western society, the Enlightenment's antitraditional animus is most prominent in the United States. Lacking feudalism's rigid status system and traditions, America's historical development promoted unique forms of present-centered individualism.[20]

While traveling in America Alexis de Tocqueville realized that the aristocrat "almost always knows his forefathers and respects them; he thinks he already sees his remote descendants and he loves them. He willingly imposes duties on himself towards the former and the latter and he will frequently sacrifice his personal gratifications to those who went before and to those who will come after him."[21] Aristocratic belief stems from the dependency of aristocratic communities, where all citizens occupy fixed positions dependent on patronage from above and cooperation from below. Having never known the profound inequalities of Europe, however, Americans have convinced themselves of their self-determination and have "acquired the habit of always considering themselves standing alone. . . . [N]ot only does democracy make every man forget his ancestors, but it hides his descendants and separates his contemporaries from him; it throws him back forever upon himself alone and threatens in the end to confine him entirely within the solitude of his own heart."[22]

That de Tocqueville had Thomas Jefferson in mind when he wrote about American individualism is doubtful, but he would have understood Jefferson perfectly. Jefferson believed it to be "self-evident that the earth belongs in usufruct to the living: that the dead have neither powers nor rights over it."[23] If past debts, financial and otherwise, are not to burden the present generation, Jefferson believed, federal and state constitutions must be rewritten every nineteen years. How else can men and women renounce the past and govern themselves? "By the law of nature, one generation is to another as one independent nation is to another."[24] Ralph Waldo Emerson's American Scholar address echoed Jefferson and de Tocqueville: "Each age, it is found, must write its own books; or rather, each generation for the next succeeding. The books of an older period will not fit this."[25]

Nathaniel Hawthorne also raged against the past. In *The House of the Seven Gables* he demands to know, "Shall we never, never get rid of this past? It lies upon the present like a giant's dead body! In fact, the case is just as if a young giant were compelled to waste all his strength in carrying about the corpse of an old giant, his grandfather. . . . Just think, a moment; and it will startle you to see what slaves we are to by-gone times."[26] Hawthorne was referring to his family's sins, which he wished to redeem, while at the same time wishing to eliminate the pastness of the family itself. At fifty-year intervals "a family should be merged into the great, obscure mass of humanity, and forget about all its ancestors." Likewise, public buildings, symbolizing public affairs, should be made of inferior materials that "crumble to ruin once in twenty years, or thereabouts, as a hint to the people to examine into and reform the institutions which they symbolize."[27]

A century later anthropologist Florence Kluckhohn distinguished American culture by its tendency to deemphasize the past and segment it from the present.[28] So, too, sociologist Robert Bellah observes: "We live in a society that encourages us to cut free from the past, to define our own selves, to choose the groups with which we wish to identify."[29] When psychologist Thomas Cottle invited his American subjects to order past, present, and future in terms of separate (atomistic), touching (continuous), or overlapping (integrated) circles, 60 percent construed the circles atomistically; 27 percent, continuously; and 13 percent, integrated.[30] When Mikyoung Kim and one of the authors asked Korean students to do the same, only nine percent separated past, present, and future; 11 percent conceived time as continuous; and 80 percent integrated the three time spheres—the extreme opposite of the American pattern.[31]

Segmenting time affects the way Americans disconnect themselves from the sins of the past, but how wide is the gap separating official expressions of regret from individual feelings of regret?

Gathering Clues

To assert that American culture weakens the relation between the living and the dead does not mean that Americans never think about their relation to the past; it means that that relation means less to them than it does to people elsewhere. Culture's influence on memory is best documented among nations in which judgments of the past differ despite similar religious cultures, economic and educational systems, levels of democracy, and penchants for self-criticism. In this regard, Americans' sense of remorse over and liability for past oppression of minorities can be usefully compared to Germans' sense of remorse over and liability for National Socialism and the Holocaust. Such close comparison helps us distinguish the culture of memory from the institutional politics of memory.

Between 1998 and 2001, we administered different versions of a questionnaire titled "Judging the Past" to 1,215 University of Georgia undergraduates. Our sample, which approximates the composition of the College of Arts and Sciences, is 88 percent white, eight percent black, and four percent Asian. The sample contains upperclassmen, but the majority, in almost equal proportion, are freshmen and sophomores. Female respondents slightly outnumber males, and the majority of all respondents (70 percent) were born in the South.

Given our topic, the following point warrants emphasis. The University of Georgia serves a conservative state, but its social science and humanities faculties have instituted liberal academic programs. As its faculty and administrators are acutely aware of the state's history of slavery and segregation, graduation requirements include several hours in courses with multicultural content, which includes material relevant to African Americans, Native Americans, Hispanic Americans, and Asian Americans. Ideologically, the student body leans slightly to the left: 53 percent of the students describe themselves as liberal or very liberal.

German data were drawn from four sources. The first set of data includes questionnaires administered to 360 undergraduate students in 1998. This sample includes mainly freshmen, 55 percent of whom were enrolled in sociology courses in the formerly West German city of Giessen; the remaining 45 percent of the students studied in Leipzig, an East German university. As is usual in Giessen social science courses, most students (79 percent in our case) were women oriented toward careers in public education. The student body leans decisively to the left, with 84 percent of the Giessen students defining themselves as moderately to very liberal; 16 percent, conservative. In gender, ideology, and occupational goals, Leipzig students are comparable to Giessen's. In a second (1999) sample, 44 Giessen students answered short questionnaires on specific aspects of German and American history. The third group of respondents comprises 110 students from the University of Stuttgart, an institution oriented toward technology, science, and the humanities alike. Most of the students were freshmen, evenly divided by gender, intending to major in political science and seeking careers in government, university teaching, or research. Stuttgart's students were no less liberal than the Giessen and Leipzig students, but their teachers were noticeably more conservative. Our fourth source of German data is a nationwide survey containing questions about national identity and attitudes toward the National Socialist era. These data were collected in 1995 and consist of 649 respondents.

Our student samples, drawn on the basis of availability, are sources of imperfect clues rather than clean, comparative evidence. Generalization is the most significant limitation: American and German university students do not and cannot represent the general population of America and Germany. We assume, however, that our data are defensible in one respect: the difference between American and German students' judgments of the past approximates the difference between judgments of all American and German adults.

Degrading Events

Asked to name the "three events in American history of which you do not merely disapprove but which, in your opinion, degrade the United States and arouse in you as a citizen (rather than private individual) a sense of dishonor, disgrace, shame, and/or remorse," 41 percent of American students named slavery; 34 percent, the Vietnam War; 32 percent, offenses against American Indians. The next five most commonly mentioned events, named by less than 20 percent of the respondents, were segregation, the Civil War, internment of Japanese Americans, the use of the atomic bomb, and Watergate.

The conspicuous feature of the events condemned by Americans is their historical diffusion. Three of the eight events displayed in table 1—slavery, treatment of Indians, and Civil War—occurred in the nineteenth century; three events, segregation, internment of Japanese Americans, and the use

Table 1
Percentage of Respondents Naming Sources of Dishonor, Disgrace, Shame, and/or Remorse in American History
(N = 1,109)

Event	Percentage
Slavery	41.2
Vietnam War	34.0
Treatment of Indians	32.1
Segregation	17.4
Civil War	12.7
Internment of Japanese Americans	11.9
Use of atomic bomb	9.1
Watergate	7.3

of the atomic bomb occurred in the mid-twentieth century; the other two, in the late twentieth century. To this broad range of events corresponds a broad range of victim communities, from African and Native Americans to Hispanic and Japanese Americans, to citizens of Vietnam and Japan.

In contrast, the three events that German students mention most frequently—World War II, the National Socialist regime, and the crimes of the regime—correspond to a narrow twelve-year period starting with Adolf Hitler's assumption of power in 1933 and ending in 1945 with his death and Germany's surrender (see table 2).

To determine how American and German students feel about the events they named, we asked three sets of questions. The first set, administered in the United States, includes: "I personally feel that my generation is morally responsible for treating the effects of past discrimination against all minority groups." In Germany the parallel question was: "My generation is responsible today for dealing with the fascist past."[32] Seventy-one percent of Germans compared to only 23 percent of Americans agreed that their generation is responsible for past offenses of the state. Comparable questions posed to a German national sample two years earlier yielded comparable responses.[33]

"Americans tend to think too much about the mistakes of the past. It is time to look more to the future." The German version of this question

Table 2
Percentage of Respondents Naming Sources of Dishonor, Disgrace, Shame,
and/or Remorse in German History
(N = 333)

Event	Percentage
World War II	48.1
National Socialist crimes	46.7
National Socialism in general	38.1
Present xenophobia in Germany	24.2
World War I	16.1
Present German policy	5.8

was: "After 1945, Germans have dealt with their past too much." With
these statements 74 percent of the Americans and 29 percent of the Germans, respectively, agreed. The final question posed to Americans was:
"Nothing can be done to offset the effects of past discrimination." This
question confounds belief that dwelling on the past is a waste of time with
readiness to compensate for past wrongs. Forty-one percent agreed. The
German version was more concrete but within the same realm of content:
"The persecution of Jews by Germans is a huge guilt that cannot be extinguished historically."[34] Eighty-two percent agreed.

Next, we asked students to characterize their nation's past as a whole.
Do the shameful and dishonorable events of the past outweigh events
evoking a sense of pride and honor? Fifty-three percent of the American
students disagreed with a statement defining the past as being more a
source of shame and dishonor than pride and honor. Corresponding per-
centages for Giessen-Leipzig and Stuttgart students are 26 and 34 percent
respectively.

Contexts of Regret

Many factors affect German and American judgments of the past. First,
the negative parts of Germany's past are concentrated in one time period,
ending in 1945. In the United States, events are diffused over centuries,
and the event deemed most serious, slavery, ended more than 135 years
ago—before many American families' ancestors arrived in the United

States and after many family lines existing in 1865 had died out. Americans learn most of what they know about their country's crimes at school, not home. Although German students also gain information about their country's crimes at school, many are exposed to oral family histories. In these histories some discover authentic family secrets; for others, the silence of the home is a defense against guilty knowledge.

Second, Germans have been confronted with continual discourse about their moral guilt and collective responsibility for both the Holocaust and fascist military aggression. As Germany is geographically contiguous to eight of the nations it attacked and occupied during World War II, reconciliation was politically and economically imperative. German leaders, accordingly, undertook moral recovery campaigns in the nation's press and mass media and through state rhetoric and policies. This intensive public discourse about National Socialism is supplemented in German school curricula and textbooks.[35] By contrast, America's crimes, committed largely against its own inhabitants, harmed no other nations; therefore, the American people have experienced no external pressure to recognize their misdeeds. American textbooks emphasizing the cruelties of the past did not appear until late in the twentieth century and expressed indigenous pressures that arose during a "rights revolution" emphasizing inclusion, diversity, and multiculturalism.

The quality of American and German offenses also differs. The National Socialist regime conducted war and persecutions that led to the death of at least 36 million people,[36] mostly civilians, and included the murder of six million Jews and hundreds of thousands of non-Russian communists, Gypsies, dissidents, and others. American slaveholders, in contrast, valued their bondsmen's lives, although denying them human quality. On the other hand, slavery's seriousness cannot be underestimated: the number of persons enslaved at a given period of time never exceeded four million, but far more than 100 million were enslaved during the era of slavery.

The difference among slavery, indiscriminate killing, and murder might go some way toward explaining why Americans are less inclined than Germans to accept responsibility for past wrongs, but it does not go far enough. Presently, slavery appears in the American media, school curricula, and textbooks as an absolute sin and the source of present racial troubles. This is not to mention media and textbook coverage of the oppression of Native Americans and the internment of Japanese Americans.

In terms of objective harm to human life, Americans and their German counterparts should feel comparable, if not identical, moral responsibility, but one recalls that a distinctive culture of memory reinforces the conditions leading Americans to consider themselves historically innocent. The cultural background of contemporary Americans, as Seymour M. Lipset tells us, revolves around the ideal of individualism.[37] Since the single individual strives to be self-reliant, to reach his goals independently of family or community, past failures of family and community members mean less to him than similar failures do to his German counterpart. This cultural trait powerfully affects the way American students attribute responsibility to young people in other nations.

Americans Judge Germans

Twelve different versions of our questionnaire were distributed among several University of Georgia samples to determine whether responses varied according to (1) *personal* or *generational* responsibility and (2) whether preceded or not by a question sensitizing respondents to their debt to the past (American soldiers killed during World War II). No differences were associated with these two split ballots. When comparisons were made among students defining themselves as liberal and conservative, only slight differences appeared.

If slavery and the oppression of minorities seem less serious to Americans than the mass murder of Jews, and if this difference affects ideas about moral responsibility, then American students would attribute less moral responsibility to themselves for slavery and minority oppression than they attribute to Germans for the Holocaust. Between University of Georgia students' assessment of their own and other nations' responsibility, however, there is little difference. Nine percent of the students agreed with the statement, "My generation is [or: I personally feel] morally responsible for the enslavement of tens of millions of black people over more than one hundred and fifty years." The level of agreement with the statement, "My generation is [or: I personally feel] morally responsible for the internment of Japanese-American men, women, and children in prison camps during World War II" was nine percent. Eleven percent agreed with the statement, "My generation is [or: I personally feel] morally responsible for the killing, forced expulsion, and other maltreatment of millions of Indians."

When we asked Georgia students about Japanese and German young people's moral responsibility for the atrocities in Asia and the Holocaust, we found a lower level of attribution: 5 and 3 percent, respectively, agreed with statements asserting that Japanese and German young people were responsible for their nations' past wrongdoing.[38] The tendency for American students to judge themselves more harshly than they judge others is a fact that we note but leave unexplained (see table 3).

Denying and Affirming Responsibility

The fact that different people give the same response to a question does not mean they think about it in the same way. After eliciting responses to closed questions about moral responsibility, we asked a new block of University of Georgia students to "Explain in a few words your answer to the above question. Why is the present generation of Americans (or you personally) morally responsible or not responsible for slavery?" We randomly asked comparable questions about the oppression of Native Americans and internment of Japanese Americans, and we received comparable answers (see table 4).

Responses fell into four categories, the simplest of which was "I wasn't born yet." Thirty percent of Americans gave this type of response. For American students, "not born yet" means "not present," "no control," "not alive," "had nothing to do with it," was "not part of it." The passage of time itself made a difference: "It was a different era," "Before our time," "It's in the past." Sometimes the respondent deprecated the questioner by posing and answering a question of his own: "How can a present generation be responsible for any event in the past? Only past generations can be looked upon as responsible." Other respondents were more emphatic, declaring it "absurd" or "obviously" wrong to assign responsibility to unborn generations. In some cases, birth and choice went together. "Everyone has the right to make choices independently, so my ancestors' choices don't make me responsible." "My generation was not born. It was not our choice."[39] No respondent in this category, however, mentioned the harmful consequences of that choice.

Our second group of respondents, 42 percent of the total, recognized the offenses that occurred in the past but claimed moral innocence because they could not see themselves committing them. "My race was responsible, but not me as an individual." The pattern is redundant: "That

Table 3
American Students' Attitudes toward Moral Responsibility for Past Wrongs

"My generation is [or: I personally feel] morally responsible for the enslavement of tens of millions of black people over more than one hundred and fifty years."

(N = 383)

Strongly agree	7	6	5	4[a]	3	2	1	Strongly disagree
–		2.1	3.6	3.6	5.2	7.0	19.2	59.3	–

"My generation is [or: I personally feel] morally responsible for the internment of Japanese-American men, women, and children in prison camps during World War II."

(N = 382)

Strongly agree	7	6	5	4	3	2	1	Strongly disagree
–	2.6	2.6	3.9	3.9	8.6	23.6	54.8	–

"My generation is [or: I personally feel] morally responsible for the killing, forced expulsion, and other maltreatment of millions of Indians."

(N = 383)

Strongly agree	7	6	5	4	3	2	1	Strongly disagree
–	3.1	2.1	6.0	5.0	9.1	20.9	53.8	–

"I believe the present generation of Japanese [or: Japanese young people] is morally responsible for Japan's war crimes against Chinese and Korean civilians during World War II."

(N = 106)

Strongly agree	7	6	5	4	3	2	1	Strongly disagree
–	1.0	1.0	2.8	9.4	9.4	21.7	54.7	–

"I believe the present generation of Germans [or: German young people] is morally responsible for the Holocaust—Nazi Germany's murder of six million Jews during World War II."

(N = 95)

Strongly agree	7	6	5	4	3	2	1	Strongly disagree
–	1.0	1.0	1.0	2.1	8.5	25.4	61.0	–

[a] Responses are arrayed along a 7-point scale ranging from strong agreement (7) through a midpoint indicating neither agreement nor disagreement (4) to strong disagreement (1).

Table 4

Reasons for Denial or Acceptance of Moral Responsibility for Past Wrongs

Reasons	Americans assessing own responsibility (N = 87)	Americans assessing German and Japanese responsibility* (N = 162)	Germans assessing American responsibility (Stuttgart, N = 108)
1. Respondent (or subject) not born at the time of offense. Not morally responsible.	29.9	54.9	28.7
2. Respondent recognizes (or subject should recognize) the gravity of the offense and condemns its perpetrators but is not morally responsible for it.	42.5	24.1	13.0
3. Respondent feels (or subject should feel) obligation to address present wrongs and to prevent reoccurrence of past wrongs but is not morally responsible for past wrongs in which he or she had no part.	18.4	17.3	37.0
4. Respondent feels (or subject should feel) obligation to redress present wrongs, prevent reoccurrence of past wrongs because he or she is morally responsible for them.	9.2	3.7	21.3

*Pooled frequencies based on comparable distribution of responses.

was my ancestors' doing." "My ideals and values completely differ from the attitudes of most of my ancestors." "I feel guilty about what my ancestors did, but I do not feel responsible for their actions." "I consider my heritage responsible for slavery, but not myself." Students did not confine their references to ancestors in general; they dissociated themselves from specific relatives. "Being a white from the South, I know that parts of my family were once involved in slavery, but . . . I do not share the views of my ancestors." These are the reactions of principled minds, but they are inner-directed minds indifferent to the conditions of their day, including minority disadvantages related to past abuses.

A third group of respondents denying moral responsibility, 18.4 percent of the total, not only recognized past wrongs but also felt a moral obligation to redress them. "I hold my ancestors responsible. . . . I want to try to make right what they did wrong." "The only thing I can be responsible for is the present." Multiculturally oriented respondents, while declaring themselves innocent of past wrongs, strove "towards racial equality and diversifying all parts of the American way of life."

The fourth group of respondents, nine percent of the total, accepted responsibility. "Although I do not believe that very many of my ancestors were involved in slavery, I believe that it was wrong and that our country as a whole should take responsibility for slavery." "I am a Caucasian woman and I am ashamed of the fact that my ancestors caused minority groups so much pain and suffering." Such logic was rare; most students conceding moral responsibility referred to present consequences of past oppression. "They have to accept responsibility for what their ancestors did. Good or bad. Not only do they benefit from what their ancestors did but it is their responsibility to correct the things of the past." Another respondent held himself morally liable because his generation "facilitates this oppression and continues the cycle of inequality"; another, "because we have seen the benefits of our ancestors owning slaves." Yet another declared, "Discrimination is embedded deep into our roots; therefore, each generation is a contributing factor to this segregation."[40] Guilt over undeserved benefits and the assumption that existing inequalities between whites and blacks are due to slavery find frequent expression: "As a white person, I still enjoy preference and special privilege over minorities that were created and still perpetuated by institutions such as slavery. Therefore, I am still responsible for taking part in that aspect."

Germans Judge Americans

Americans apply to German contemporaries the same reasoning they apply to themselves: no one can be responsible for events in which they take no part. What logic do German students apply?

We addressed this question in two steps. We asked a sample of 44 Ger-

Table 5a
German Students' Attitudes toward Moral Responsibility for Past Wrongs
(Total sample, N = 44)

"In the United States young people are morally responsible for the enslavement of tens of millions of black people over one hundred and fifty years" and
"German youth are responsible today for dealing with National Socialism."

American youth responsible								
Strongly agree	7	6	5	4	3	2	1	Strongly disagree
—	2.3	2.3	4.5	20.5	2.3	9.1	59.0	—
German youth responsible								
Strongly agree	7	6	5	4	3	2	1	Strongly disagree
—	43.2	20.5	11.4	4.5	13.6	2.3	4.5	—

mans to respond to two statements: "In the United States young people
are morally responsible for the enslavement of tens of millions of black
people over one hundred and fifty years" and "German youth are responsible today for dealing with National Socialism." Seventy-five percent of
the German students accepted the proposition that German young people
are responsible for the crimes of National Socialism (see table 5a). However, German responses to the question about American responsibility depended on question order. When the question about American responsibility for slavery appeared *before* the question about German Holocaust
responsibility, four percent of German students agreed that Americans
are responsible for historical wrongs. When the question about American
responsibility appeared *after* the question about German responsibility, the
percentage of German students agreeing that Americans are responsible
rose to 13.5 percent, while the percentage falling into the ambivalent/
neutral category (four in a 1 to 7 scale) increased from nine to 32 percent.
The percentage disagreeing fell from 86 to 55 percent (see table 5b).

Changing question order affects response distribution because it transforms the questions' moral context. Asking about German responsibility
invokes a framework within which all subsequent questions must be considered. However, no question-ordering effects appeared when the split-

Table 5b
German Students' Attitudes toward Moral Responsibility for Past Wrongs
(Split sample, N = 22)

"In the United States young people are morally responsible for the enslavement of tens of millions of black people over one hundred and fifty years" and "German youth are responsible today for dealing with National Socialism."							
German responsibility, if slavery question is asked first							
Strongly agree	7	6	5	4	3	2	1	Strongly disagree
—	0.0	0.0	4.5	9.1	0.0	4.5	81.9	—
German responsibility, if National Socialism question is asked first							
Strongly agree	7	6	5	4	3	2	1	Strongly disagree
—	4.5	4.5	4.5	31.9	4.5	13.6	36.5	—

ballot procedure was used on a new sample of 276 University of Georgia respondents. Whether slavery or Holocaust questions appear first or second, the same percentage denied that their German contemporaries are responsible for ancestors' wrongdoing.

The numbers on which this analysis is based are small, but the direction and magnitude of the result warrant confidence. German students disdain National Socialism, but their qualified beliefs about American responsibility betray ambivalence. German youth commonly ask themselves why people of other nations are so eager to remind them of their forebears' crimes, even while knowing they were not alive during their commission. Logically, German students have no more right to hold their American peers responsible for slavery than to hold themselves responsible for the Holocaust; yet when reminded of the Holocaust their reasoning changes: they believe young people elsewhere must be responsible for their own ancestors' misdeeds. "Since others point to us and declare us guilty," they would say, "these people must be guilty, too."

The tone of the University of Stuttgart and University of Georgia responses could not be more different. When we asked American students to explain why they rejected moral responsibility for past oppression, we received straightforward, innocent, simple, unemotional, sincere answers:

typically, "I wasn't born yet," or "I didn't do it," or "I'm only responsible for today's problems." German students' responses were more diverse, complex, and perturbed.[41] Many German students believed that American young people are, like themselves, innocent because of the time of their birth; others couched this belief within a system of ideas unknown in America. To accept responsibility for past wrongs in Germany or America, they said, is to embrace the "controversial" and "reactionary" concept of *Erbschuld*—inherited guilt—an idea connoting "the commercialization of grief."[42]

For some students the coupling in the questionnaire of American crimes and National Socialist crimes produced resentment. "Americans are responsible because one should be conscious about one's own history/past; one should be conscious of one's own fallibility. The United States, in contrast, insolently intervenes in international policy; assumes the role of world police." Americans need to be taken down a peg or two and reminded of their own failures: Because they "are so proud on the one part of their history they have to bear responsibility for the other." Slavery, segregation, endless racial injustice, the murdering of Indians and theft of their land, the imprisonment of their survivors on reservations—these are dark matters. "As Americans show an exaggerated national pride, it is reasonable to remind them of the circumstances in their history which can be neither ethically nor morally supported." Present practices are also questionable. "Young U.S. citizens do not stand up for human rights in the U.S.; consider the death penalty in Texas." German students are more willing than their American peers to face the past and fulfill their obligation to deal with it; yet German responses are tinged with an aura of resentment.[43] "Every generation deserves a chance of rehabilitation. Americans, yes. We Germans should get this chance, too, which is, however, often refused to us." If Americans and Germans must be held responsible for past wrongdoing, "[t]he American generation has only the advantage insofar as others do not fling the mistakes of the Americans' ancestors in their face."

Martin Walser's concept of *Moralkeule*—morality as a weapon—captures the many nuances of victimization through attribution of guilt.[44] Walser asserts that the Holocaust was an unmitigated moral wrong, but he believes that Germany's neighbors have for too long used morality as a weapon to crush the dignity of its people. When Germans themselves recognize past atrocities and so carry Germany's burden privately in their conscience, there will be no need for their country's neighbors, or for the state itself, to remind them of their debts. Whether self-imprisonment by internalizing the guilt of an earlier generation is a "breakthrough" (*Befreiungsschlag*), as Walser believes, is contestable; whether repentance can be privatized let alone instilled and maintained without educational and ritual reminders is doubtful. The majority of German students, in any case, reject Walser's argument.

One cannot read German students' responses without being reminded of anthropologist Ruth Benedict's distinction between shame cultures and guilt cultures. "Shame is a reaction to other people's criticism. . . . Where shame is the major sanction, a man does not experience relief when he makes his fault public even to a confessor."[45] In contrast, guilt results from an internalized censor, a conscience or superego, criticizing one's ego independently of others' knowledge of wrongdoing. Benedict stresses that people everywhere experience shame and guilt under different circumstances, but the emphasis falls differently in different countries. Japan's is a shame culture while Germany, with its strong Protestant and Catholic roots, is, relative to Japan, a culture of guilt. On the other hand, Germany shares with Japan a feudal past in which relations governed by shame norms remain relevant. Sensitivity to the judgment of other nations is a sure sign that the shame dimension of German culture remains viable. That Germans, like Japanese, often feel resentment toward their judges and the obligations placed upon them is equally evident and no less an aspect of shame.

In summary, American and German responses fall into two categories: a majority denying responsibility and a minority accepting responsibility for the wrongs of the past. Open-ended responses, however, show that the size and makeup of the two categories differ. Twenty-one percent of the German students believe their American peers are morally responsible for historical wrongs against African and Native Americans, but only nine percent of the American students can think of reasons why they should be. Thirty-seven percent of the German students believe their American peers should feel an obligation to address present wrongs, even if not morally responsible for their causes; 18 percent of the Americans actually do. Germans, then, are more likely than Americans to recognize an obligation to deal with historical injustice (see table 4). Americans' sense of obligation to the past is considerably more casual than Germans think it should be.

Conclusion

Assessing the way students think about responsibility is more than a mapping of the working of the mind; it is a way of knowing how human beings use their minds—symbol-making, conceptualizing, meaning-seeking—to fix personal experience at a definite time within the experience of the nation. Different combinations of culture and experience, we have found, lead to different perspectives on causation, blame, accountability, and, above all, community. Since the national community, as Robert Bellah conceives it, is a community of memory, it continually retells "its constitutive narrative, and in so doing it offers examples of the men and women who have embodied and exemplified the meaning of the community. These stories of collective history and exemplary individuals are an important part of the tradition that is so central to a community of memory. . . . And if the community is completely honest, it will remember stories not only of sufferings received but of sufferings inflicted—dangerous memories, for they call the community to alter ancient evils."[46] In question is not whether Americans and Germans remember ancient evils but how they relate themselves to them, and this relationship is complex, reflecting many aspects of American and German culture, including the reckoning and framing of time itself.

American culture and German culture can be located on a continuum limited at one pole by traditional, "postfigurative" consciousness and at the other by modern, configurative consciousness. In "postfigurative" cultures, past and present are integrated into a single realm of experience.[47] Programs for the present are modeled on the past; thoughts of the present and memories of the past commingle with no boundaries distinguishing their contents. "Integrators" experience today's projects, no matter what their goals, no matter when conceived and formulated, as continuations of yesterday's events. At the other extreme are configurative cultures in which things of the past and things of the present exist in two untouching worlds. Guided by peers as much as predecessors, "segmenters" reserve a separate time zone for each. As segmenters cannot live in the present and past simultaneously, they cannot bask in the glow of past achievements; cannot assume guilt for past misdeeds; and cannot connect themselves to history in any causal or morally meaningful way. Segmenters know the past but do not—cannot—conceive themselves a part of it.[48]

Articulating responsibility is a form of boundary work, a way of expressing beliefs about the proper relation between the living and the dead. All cultures segment and integrate time, but American culture is largely a segmenting culture in which the living feel few obligations to the dead and assume few obligations of the dead. German culture, in contrast, is rooted in the residue of European status systems, with their strong traditions of status, honor, exclusion, and mutual obligation.[49] Assuming responsibility for peers enhances status solidarity as it enables all groups, whether ordered vertically, from the aristocratic ruling class to the peasantry, or horizontally by ethnicity or religion, to lessen the precariousness of life and manage conflict. German culture is an integrating culture in which the call to assume past debts, however strongly resisted, is more difficult to ignore than it is in America.

Culture is a context, not a cause, of national differences in historical consciousness. Before the 1960s German young people were far less sensitive to National Socialism and Americans less sensitive to slavery than are their successors. Within the same political structure, contrasting cultures of memory lead to different judgments of the past. Furthermore, institutions and individuals segment and integrate past and present differently. Regret, as noted, is orchestrated by institutions, including universities, media, and religious and political associations, but many individuals reject their premises. Many individuals cannot hold their generation let alone themselves responsible for past wrongdoings, but to say that organizations are for this reason morally superior to their members is misleading. To assert that accepting responsibility for the past is more virtuous than denying responsibility is equally misleading. Kolakowski, von der Gablentz, and Schwan, among many other moral philosophers, rely on this assumption, but their views apply more to Germany than to America. Admission of responsibility for present wrongs alone is rooted in ideas of what it means morally to be an American, what defines the good society, on what basis citizens are to live together, what claims one set of citizens may place on another, what rights it may demand of another. These moral ideas are not equally compelling to every American, but they are no less moral than beliefs about collective liability, to which many American institutions, especially American universities, are committed.

Beginning with the 1960s, new history teaching standards have thrown unprecedented light on the underside of America's past. The New American History, structured by a logic of inclusion and cultural diversity, not only condemns historical events that promoted exclusion and consensus but also defines these events as characteristic features of American history.[50] This "new history," a product of late twentieth-century progressivism, provides the intellectual basis for affirming regret, but it has not negated the logic of "traditional history," whose narrative links public wrongdoings to individual failings, redeemable by holding the nation's offenders, not the nation itself, responsible. The ideal of individual responsibility, then, is necessary to the way Americans conceive and relate themselves to events. Americans conceive all events, even random events like automobile accidents,[51] as products of individual responsibility and fit them into the way they run their institutions and socialize their children. The individual, not the society, is for most Americans the relevant agency of moral obligation.

Is a perspective that so radically denies the past viable? On the one hand, Americans' belief that every generation is responsible for itself lessens appreciation of the legacy of the past and erodes motivation to sacrifice for posterity. On the other hand, Americans' belief in the sanctity of the individual, forever free from the wrongdoings of his or her ancestors, mitigates racial, ethnic, and religious resentments and accelerates the quest for an inclusive society. Societies of unlimited inclusion require limited liability for past wrongs.[52]

Notes

The authors are grateful to the German Science Foundation (Peter Schmidt, Principal Investigator, Grant No. Schm 658/4-3) and the German Marshall Fund of the United States (Grant No. A-0375-17) for their generous support of this project. Denise Burgert of Freiburg University and Michelle Petrie of the University of Georgia contributed to the data analysis.

1. In Europe similar rhetoric is exemplified by French Prime Minister Jacques Chirac's apologizing for French complicity in the Holocaust and expressly repudiating former Prime Minister Mitterand's assertions of French innocence. Among scores of similar gestures are German President Roman Herzog's regretting formally the Luftwaffe's devastation of Guernica, public demands for acknowledgment of the German Army's World War II atrocities against the Greeks, and Polish President Kwasnietzky's public admission of wartime anti-Semitic pogroms by the Polish inhabitants of Jedwabne. Elsewhere, New Zealand officials apologized for British expropriation of Maori land and awarded the Maoris $112 million and 39,000 acres in compensation. In Australia, white reformers rejected official apologies to aborigines for not going far enough.

2. Emile Durkheim, *The Elementary Forms of the Religious Life* (1915; New York: Free Press, 1965), 420.

3. For detail, see Barry Schwartz, ed., "Introduction: The Expanding Past," *Qualitative Sociology* 19 (fall 1996): 275–82; Barry Schwartz, "Postmodernity and Historical Reputation: Abraham Lincoln in Late Twentieth-Century American Memory," *Social Forces* 77 (September 1998): 63–103.

4. James D. Hunter, *Culture Wars: The Struggle to Define America* (New York: Basic, 1991), 120.

5. Ibid., 122–27.

6. For a critical overview of the culture wars thesis, see Rhys H. Williams, ed., *Cultural Wars in American Politics: Critical Reviews of a Popular Myth* (New York: Aldine de Gruyter, 1997), esp. 63–100. For a general (balanced) overview, see James L. Nolan Jr., ed., *The Culture Wars: Current Contests and Future Prospects* (Charlottesville: University Press of Virginia, 1996).

7. Hunter, *Culture Wars,* 290.

8. Leszek Kolakowski cited in Gesine Schwan, *Politics and Guilt: The Destructive Power of Silence,* trans. Thomas Dunlap (Lincoln: University of Nebraska Press, 1997), 11.

9. Friedrich Nietzsche already in the nineteenth century characterized Christian norms of regret as a triumph of "slave morality" that subordinates noble achievement to the resentment of history's losers. In contrast, Richard McKeon locates moral responsibility historically by defining it as an attribute of demo-

cratic, not Christian, culture. As the word "responsibility" appeared in English and French in 1787 in connection with new, reciprocal relations between the individual and the state, there arose the corresponding idea of a self-conscious "cultural" or "collective" responsibility. "The concept of responsibility relates actions to agents by a causal tie and applies a judgement of value to both. . . . The agent may be an individual or a group acting in the context of a society or a political state, or an individual, group, or community acting in the looser association of free individuals or independent communities or states whose actions affect each other." "The Development and the Significance of the Concept of Responsibility," in *Freedom and History and Other Essays,* ed. Zahava K. McKeon (Chicago: University of Chicago Press, 1990), 82.

10. Oskar H. von der Gablentz, "Responsibility," in *International Encyclopedia of the Social Sciences,* ed. Edward L. Sills (1968; New York: Macmillan, 1979), 497.

11. Schwan, *Politics and Guilt,* 7–8.

12. Jürgen Habermas, "Grenzen des Neohistorismus." Interview with J. M. Ferry, in *Jürgen Habermas: Die Nachholende Revolution: Kleine Politische Schriften* (Frankfurt am Main: Suhrkamp, 1990), 7:149–56.

13. Henri Tajfel and John C. Turner, "The Social Identity Theory of Intergroup Conflict," in *Psychology of Intergroup Relations,* ed. Stephen Worchel and William G. Austin (Chicago: Nelson-Hall, 1986), 7–24.

14. John C. Turner, Michael A. Hogg, Penelope J. Oakes, Stephen D. Reicher, and Margaret S. Wetherell, *Rediscovering the Social Group: A Self-Categorization Theory* (Oxford: Basil Blackwell, 1987).

15. Bertjan Doosje, Nyla R. Branscombe, Russell Spears, and Antony S. R. Manstead, "Guilty by Association: When One's Group Has a Negative History," *Journal of Personality and Social Psychology* 75 (1998): 872–86; Eviatar Zerubavel, "Social Memories: Steps to a Sociology of the Past," *Qualitative Sociology* 19 (fall 1996): 283–99.

16. Michel-Rolph Trouillot, "Abortive Rituals: Historical Apologies in the Global Era," *Interventions* 2, no. 2 (spring 2003): 171–86.

17. For a useful if not altogether satisfactory discussion of the conditions under which apologies succeed or fail, see Nicholas Tavuchis, *Mea Culpa: A Sociology of Apology and Reconciliation* (Stanford: Stanford University Press, 1991).

18. Jeffrey K. Olick and Brenda Coughlin, "The Politics of Regret: Analytical Frames," in *The Politics of the Past,* ed. John B. Torpey (Lanham, MD: Rowman and Littlefield, 2003). The rise of regret, in their view, is a characteristic of our age,

"an age of shattered time and shifting allegiances, indeed of skepticism toward allegiances at all" (37–62).

19. Seymour Martin Lipset, *American Exceptionalism: A Double-Edged Sword* (New York: W. W. Norton, 1996).

20. Louis Hartz, *The Liberal Tradition in America: An Interpretation of American Political Thought since the Revolution* (New York: Harcourt, Brace, 1955).

21. Alexis de Tocqueville, *Democracy in America* (New York: Knopf, 1945), 2:104–5.

22. Ibid., 2:105–6.

23. Thomas Jefferson, "Letter to James Madison," in *The Portable Thomas Jefferson,* ed. Merrill D. Peterson (New York: Penguin, 1975), 445.

24. Ibid., 448.

25. Ralph Waldo Emerson, "The American Scholar," in *Selections from Ralph Waldo Emerson,* ed. Stephen Whicher (1837; Boston: Houghton-Mifflin, 1959), 67.

26. Nathaniel Hawthorne, *The House of the Seven Gables* (1859; New York: New American Library, 1962), 162.

27. Ibid., 163.

28. Florence Kluckhohn, "Dominant and Variant Value Orientations," *Social Welfare Reform* (New York: Columbia University Press, 1951), 97–113.

29. Robert N. Bellah, Richard Madsen, Ann Swidler, and Steven M. Tipton, *Habits of the Heart: Individualism and Commitment in American Life* (New York: Harper and Row, 1985), 154.

30. Thomas J. Cottle, *Perceiving Time* (New York: Wiley, 1976), 85–94.

31. Barry Schwartz and Mikyoung Kim, "Honor, Dignity, and Collective Memory: Judging the Past in Korea and the United States," in *Culture in Mind: Toward a Sociology of Culture and Cognition,* ed. Karen A. Cerulo (New York: Routledge, 2001), 218.

32. With a similar statement, "My generation is responsible today for dealing with the National Socialist past," 71 percent agreed.

33. In a German national sample, drawn and analyzed by Peter Schmidt and his associates, 64 percent of the respondents agreed with the statement, "I personally feel the persecution of the Jews by National Socialists is a very heavy burden." Seventy-five percent agreed with the statement, "The persecution of the Jews by the National Socialists is a great crime, which historically cannot be eradicated." In contrast, more respondents (49 percent) disagreed with the statement, "After 1945, the Germans have been too preoccupied with their own

history" than the number of respondents agreeing with it (33 percent). Only 19 percent agreed with the statement, "Guilt over National Socialism has been implanted in us by Allied powers."

34. When "fascists" is substituted for "National Socialists," the same result, 76 percent agreement, obtains.

35. For detail on the geopolitics of memory, as they distinguish Germany from Japan, see Akiko Hashimoto, "Japanese and German Projects of Moral Recovery: Toward a New Understanding of War Memories in Defeated Nations," *Occasional Papers in Japanese Studies* (Cambridge, MA: Edwin O. Reischauer Institute of Japanese Studies, Harvard University, March 1999).

36. Wolfgang Michalka, *Deutsche Geschichte 1933–1945: Dokumente zur Innen- und Aussenpolitik* (Frankfurt am Main: Fischer, 1993), 380.

37. Lipset, *American Exceptionalism.*

38. A slightly different version of the Indian and Holocaust question produced similar results: 15 percent of the American students agreed that "American citizens today bear moral responsibility for the killing, forced expulsion, and other maltreatment of millions of Indians." Five percent agreed with the statement, "I believe that German citizens born today bear moral responsibility for the Holocaust—Nazi Germany's murder of six million Jews during World War II."

39. Denying responsibility for the past does not necessarily mean that one feels no connection to it. As one denier put it: "I take pride in my history and ancestors when a minority forces me to think about it. For example, blacks run around saying we owe them for past abuse we didn't even commit. I don't agree and that upsets me that they really think that." The offense of this respondent's ancestors is less relevant to him than the fact of their kinship.

40. Slavery is not only transmuted into the present-day problem of segregation; "[s]lavery still exists for many people based on gender."

41. We did not ask German students expressly to explain their own sense of responsibility; however, when explaining whether or not they considered Americans responsible for their country's historical offenses the students' responses were peppered with comments about their felt relation to Germany's past.

42. *Erbschuld* (charge or encumbrance on an estate) is a legacy (the prefix, *erb,* refers to inheritance) differing from Thomas Jefferson's "natural law" of the earth belonging to the living unencumbered by the debts of the past. *Erbschuld* is a vehicle of guilt distinguishable from other legacies, including *Erbfall* (heritage),

Erbbesitz (hereditary possession), *Erbrecht* (right of succession), etc. Only when *Schuld* (guilt) is the suffix does legacy become negative—"inadequate," "needless," and "coercive." *Zwanghaft* and *haftbar* likewise refer to moral responsibility as a libel immorally imposed. The German vocabulary of denial is rich and deep: to be held responsible for the distant past is to be responsible for "killing a people that is already dead." Against this libel some German respondents, thinking of their own country's past, referred to the "Mercy of a Late Birth" (quoting Helmut Kohl's remark to an Israeli audience).

43. Americans and Germans can also be linked by their common background. "The American majority has emerged from European tradition or the European value system with its latent sense of superiority." In both cases the obligation to express oneself publicly, a duty routinely ignored during the National Socialist era, becomes critical. "People cannot be accountable for past sins, but people can be held responsible where they shut their eyes and do not take an initiative." This respondent offers as his example the Americans' silence on capital punishment, which reminds him, as it does other German students, of the necessity to deal with the National Socialist past.

44. Martin Walser, "Erfahrungen beim Verfassen einer Sonntagsrede," *Dankesrede. Friedenspreis des Deutschen Buchhandels* (Frankfurt am Main: Börsenverein des Deutchen Buchhandels, 1998), 37–51.

45. Ruth Benedict, *The Chrysanthemum and the Sword: Patterns of Japanese Culture* (Cleveland: World Publishing, 1946), 223. No analytic distinction has been more misrepresented than Benedict's distinction between shame cultures and guilt cultures. Tavuchis, *Mea Culpa o,* 37, and Ian Buruma, *The Wages of Guilt: Memories of War in Germany and Japan* (New York: Farrar, Straus, Giroux, 1994), 116–17, for example, are influential authors, but they are so concerned about "national profiling" that they consider the existence of a single guilt-ridden Japanese or a single shamed German as evidence of Benedict's cultural prejudice and inadequate concepts.

46. Bellah et al., *Habits of the Heart,* 153.

47. Margaret Mead, *Culture and Commitment: A Study of the Generation Gap* (New York: Doubleday, 1970).

48. For a discussion of integration and segmentation in the realm of home and work (private time and work time as opposed to present time and past time), see Christena E. Nippert-Eng, *Home and Work: Negotiating Boundaries through Everyday Life* (Chicago: University of Chicago Press, 1995).

49. Max Weber, "Class, Status, Party," in *From Max Weber: Essays in Sociology,* ed. Hans Gerth and C. Wright Mills (New York: Oxford University Press, 1958), 186–91.

50. Gilbert T. Sewell, *History Textbooks at the New Century: A Report of the American Textbook Council* (New York: American Textbook Council, 2000).

51. Joseph Gusfield, *The Culture of Public Problems* (Chicago: University of Chicago Press, 1981).

52. "Surfeit of memory" is the term Charles S. Maier uses to portray the recent celebration of minority glories and sufferings. Such self-indulgence, Maier believes, diverts attention away from transformative politics. "It testifies to the loss of a future orientation, of progress toward civic enfranchisement and growing equality. It reflects a new focus on narrow ethnicity as a replacement for encompassing communities based on constitutions, legislation and widening attributes of citizenship." Maier, "A Surfeit of Memory," *History and Memory* 5 (1993): 150. Maier is right about the dimensions of the problem but wrong about causal direction. The surfeit of memory is the effect, not the inhibitor, of narrow ethnicity.

2

The Publicness of Memory

6

The Appearance of Public Memory

Charles E. Scott

In this essay I address public memory as it both shapes and is shaped by our attempts to address it. I shall advance three claims. (1) Public memory (or "memorial life") is best approached not in terms of a subject-object structure but rather as nonsubjective enactment in and as such things as institutions, practices, and discourses. (2) Insofar as what is public appears and insofar as any appearing carries with it dimensions of loss and nonpresence, our approach to public memory, our speaking from it and to it, should be attentive to the dimension of fragility and fragmentariness that characterizes appearing occurrences. (3) By virtue of two particular forms of address, the middle voice and the subjunctive mood, our language offers resources to speak appropriately of the nonsubjective and appearing aspects of public memory. I attempt throughout the essay to engage these resources as I encounter the ways in which public memory happens.

In a way, in this essay I consider a dimension of public memory that I believe we enact in this collection. I am not, however, entirely sure whether to say "we enact" or "a dimension of public memory that enacts us." Either phrasing has its problems. If I say, "we enact a dimension of public memory," the transitive grammar makes us appear as agents who carry out and establish by action a dimension of public memory. We who enact seem to stand in some vague way outside of the object of our action, that is, outside of public memory. Can "we" appear in our language, thought, and scholarship and in that sense happen publicly, outside of public memory? I will answer that question with a qualified "no" in the course of these remarks.

If I say, however, that a dimension of public memory enacts us, the grammar joins the meaning of subjectivity with that dimension. A dimension of public memory would appear to carry us out and establish us publicly. That is, this dimension becomes public in this language in a transitive form of subjectivity, and "we" appear as an objective "us" in connection with an enactment of public memory. Are "we"—indeed am I as I write and speak these words—an object of public memory's enactment? That phrasing seems to say too much.

My language in the last two paragraphs has been controlled by the active voice. We or I or public memory does something—acts—and one of these nouns receives the action. And all the while the language in those statements is making "us" and the meaning of "public memory" public in a voice of activity that manifests a subject that is not the object of its action.

I expect that we agree that there is something wrong with this way of making "us" and "public memory" public in this way. I expect, too, that you have noticed that "appear" plays an important but understated role in these remarks so far, that I have equated "making public" and "appear" and that I have suggested—or the language has suggested (we're not yet clear about that)—that as language happens appearing happens; and in the case at hand appearing is shaped by an active, as distinct from a passive, voice.

A middle voice that is neither active nor passive is probably not foremost in your thoughts at this point. Since these remarks must be short, I will state directly what I have in mind about grammatical voices, this kind of systematic inflection, in order to set forth a territory of observation in which we might make an initial exploration regarding the occurrence of public memory. First, articulate language is best understood as an appearing event that gives things to be public, that is, perceptible and able to be understood in specific and definable ways. Second, appearing events are not primarily active or passive, and they are obscured in their dimension of eventuation if they are described primarily in active and passive voices. Third, middle voice constructions are usually better for addressing appearing events when we want to consider the way appearing occurs; and since "appearing" and "making public" say almost the same thing, middle voice constructions are most appropriate when we speak of events of public memory with primary attention, not to the contents of a public memory but to the ways public memory appears and takes place.

I make these statements in a context of asking about the manners in which making public occurs in our addressing the topic of public memory. I hope to arrive at a point where we can hear the sense of saying that public memory happens in and as appearing, that public memory occurs as an appearing event. If I succeed in this intention, when we wish to understand "public," our attention will be drawn not so much to the content of public memories as to their appearing enactment.

When I say "middle voice" I evoke the grammatical inflection of enactment in which an action reverts to the subject as, for example, in the transitive, middle-voiced statement, the cook cooks for himself, or in the intransitive, the window shuts, the country sleeps, or birthing happens. We might also say—awkwardly in our active-passive-controlled manner of speech—appearing appears.

In the present context I could say that appearing publicly takes place or happens as articulate language occurs. Appearing publicly is not a subject that does something actively to something else, and language, in being public, does not do something to an object called public. And if I say "public," the word says, among other things, exposed with people and available for their perception. To say "public memory" is to say at once memory of people, people in memory, and memory that is not a private domain or a hidden possession. In the occurrences of public memory, people happen memorially. They appear in an unpossessable, historically dynamic transfer of past events, and these past events that are not themselves present compose people as people, compose a public world in which and as which people live. So when we say that a public memory happens as this practice or that institution or as these words, we speak in, among other memories, a grammatical memory of a kind of happening that is neither subjective nor objective.

This kind of linguistic memory gives us to know that when birth or death or language happens, there need be no subject who does something to something else. Rather, peoples' lives are eventuating—are taking place—in specific ways; they appear dying, birthing, or languaging.

Before saying more about memorial life, I turn to "culture" in order to elaborate a meaning of "public" in the context of memories that are embedded in the occurrence of linguistic establishments.

To speak of culture and memory is to speak of care. Care is a disturbing word. In its history of meaning it suggests loss and grief—it derives from the Old High German word *kara,* which means "lament." Blended into its meaning are experiences of uncertainty, apprehension, and responsibility. "Care" contains a suggestion of anxiety and watchful attention. To have a care is to look out for danger and adversity. To be careful is to be solicitous of things that can suffer damage and loss. To feel care is to feel concern and uncertainty.

Culture and *cultivate* have the sense of tillage, breaking, preparing, and tending ground for planting and growth, for careful nurturance and production. In its broader usage, *culture* means, of course, development and transmission of practices, beliefs, and knowledges. The word also carries in its history the sense of *wheel.* It derives in part from the ancient Greek word *kyklos* (circle, wheel). There is in *culture* an overtone of recurrence, return, and revolving movement. It suggests a defining force of movement on a pivot or axis and in which people are returned to something recalled. Culture, in this suggestion, thus directs us to memory and its power. For when we bring together culture and care, we arrive at a basic meaning that is found in the word *memory,* which connotes returning to something vital for people but something that is lost in its earlier and initiatory presence.

This word *memory* has in its history the ancient Greek word *mermeros,* "care for" something losable, from which the Latin *memoria* derives. In its many overtones, the word *memory* suggests mourning, remainder, solicitude, and mentation. The basic meanings of memory in this context are those of presencing with a loss of original presence, continuation with absence of guaranteed continuity, and return to beginnings with absence of a primary origin. When something happens in memory, it is presented in the absence of its original presence.

I have made these philological observations in order to hold in mind from the outset that when we address the topic of public memory we are addressing appearing, cultural memories, and in such address, culture and human care are reverting to themselves. I mean that public memory appears as we engage the topic of public memory, and it appears as the care of culture takes place. I also want to remind myself and us together that there is no available, original reality called cultural or public memory toward which we can make our way as though toward a timeless essence. We are culturally and memorially enmeshed immediately. When we speak of cultural memory, there is a return, even a revolution of cultural memories. We are enmeshed in memories that are transmitted nonvoluntarily by words in their histories of suggestion. The word *culture,* for example, signifies (and, I will say, remembers) not only labor that is required for human survival—tilling occurs in the absence of paradisiacal plenty—but also recalls in its usage the definitive importance for people's survival of a steady repetition of knowledges and behaviors that help them and define them. Culture is like the repetitive movements of a fairly balanced, if somewhat wobbly, wheel, movements that revert to themselves, that is, movements that appear as recall and reversion to certain experiences and meanings that happen only in these appearing movements. And with that memory of the need of constructive repetition, there is another one, the memorial knowledge that practices and values by which we survive must be produced and nurtured; the wheel of repetitive cultural movement finds its shape, dynamics, and beginnings within its own, limited figurations, not outside. The word *culture,* then, eventuates as a prevoluntary and prereflective memory of pervasive danger, loss, care, and struggle as well as memory of the value of produced and nurtured continuity and stability. To say that people are cultural means in the word's significance that people survive in occurrences of dynamic and public contexts of recall, that we are formed in memorial processes of return and recurrence, and that we are living memories of manners of survival in the immanence of disaster. As cultural, people happen in what I might call the middle voice of public memories, as memories, in appearing, revert to themselves, giving people to live as memorial eventuations.

By holding in mind that I am speaking in cultural memories as I address the topic of public memory, I also intend to bring into close proximity a slippage and transformation that appear to accompany memorial events. When, for example, the word *culture* recalls tillage, nurturance, and possible disaster, a person might experience vague, nonvoluntary images of someone's preparing a field or an educational institution or a room in an art gallery. Perhaps not even such vague images but inchoate feelings occur of rightness and high-mindedness that are accompanied by a sense of distaste for crude and low behavior. "Culture" often brings with it a sense of light and a sense of something vaguely darker and opposite—a feeling for what is "uncultured." My guess is that such vague feelings and images flicker in some brain processes even in people who are working in as disciplined and objective a manner as possible with the facts that define a cultural situation. Regardless of the feelings and images, it is surely the case that none of us stands outside of the nonvoluntary force of the word *culture* in its significatory life as we consider cultural and public events. That is a force that is carried in the word's use and in its position in a system of rules, inflections, references, and connotations. It is a force of meaning that invests our intelligence and affections and that lives as a part of our brain and composes part of our physical life. In the enactment of the word *culture,* many nonvoluntary meanings and memories appear and are available for all manner of perceptions. In a phrase, the word *culture* happens culturally.

In addition to the memories of meanings in "culture," there is also a memorial dimension in occurrences of appearing that does not seem to be dependent on what is appearing. You might recall that I used the phrase "appearing appears" when I described the middle voice. The two descriptive claims that I wish to make are these: the ways in which appearing happens are public—of people—and are thus available for understanding; and the occurrence of appearing happens memorially.

Memorial in what sense?

There is in the occurrence of appearing a vexing aspect that is filled with discomforting implications: in appearing, I have said, something is always at a remove from full presence and possession. I find this aspect vexing because appearances can be so full. There are things that appear solid and stable—floors, earth, well-built structures, thoroughly trusted friends, certain inevitabilities like the sun, moon, and tide—not to mention such regularities as occurrences of death, lightning, and desire. My point is not that we know that these occurrences could change or that the very place of death could cease. I want to note, rather, that in their fullness, appearing things also recede, that an appearance never fully encompasses and exhausts a thing's happening, no matter how stable the thing appears.

Appearing gives both presence and loss of presence at once. In an appearance of stability, for example, stability also comes to pass. I will say more in a moment about the memorial aspect of the recession of appearing in the happening of appearing. For now I note that in appearing, things come forth at a distance—the *appearing* thing is not *the* thing. They happen with an elusive and unpossessable quality, even in their full-seeming stability. The lives of things as they appear seem always to elude full encompassment by their appearing. Appearing happens in a recession of complete presence in what appears.

Appearing things happen mutably and transitorily. As far as I can tell, appearing gives what is in appearing to come to pass and come to pass because it is really, genuinely, unpossessably, palpably appearing. Whatever appears seems to be subject always to alteration. Appearing thus seems to happen with a peculiar memory; its occurrence recalls the mutability of everything that is manifest, as though appearing were a circle of temporality that wheels whatever appears by an axis of perishability, returning even the most persistent appearances to the reminders of non-appearing and the need for care.

I would like to bring together with the meaning of the word *subjunctive* the recession of appearing in appearing, mutational transitoriness, and memory. I make this move because I want to show that the very happening of public things is memorial—that when we speak of memory we might speak not only of mental events and dynamic institutional formations but also of memory in the eventuation of appearing itself. And I wish to show that the subjunctive mood is especially fitted for expressing the memorial happening intrinsic to appearing. For as appearing happens publicly, happens with people and their ways of life, a surprising nonfactual aspect also takes place. By giving accounts of appearing we can also give accounts of a memorial dimension in our lives that is not circumscribed by any one group of human practices. This is a dimension of nondetermination in the occurrence of appearing that I am figuring with the words *mutability* and *transitoriness*. It is a dimension of elision that escapes declarative language and direct, objective engagement.

Although in this discussion I am limiting the field of appearing to words and the memorial histories of significance that they bear, you can see that I am also shaping an approach to public memory that is a grandchild, if not a great-grandchild, of a way of thinking that gives a methodological priority to the dynamics and qualities of appearing. Presently, I want to indicate that the subjunctive mood can serve to recall an aspect of appearing that is important when we consider the meaning of "public" and as we think of the memorial aspect of appearing.

I choose subjunctivity as a collecting and integrating word because in naming a grammatical possibility, it recalls a nondeclaratory dimension of events that is not subject to more literal occurrences—occurrences that are just as we say they are. Or, to put the matter more formally, the subjunctive is a mood of noncompletion contrary to fact. It names a dimension of occurrences outside the range of declarative statements. Subjunctive phrasing indicates or betokens indeterminate contingency, possibility, and mood. So when I said a moment ago that in appearing, the mutability of everything that is manifest happens as though appearing were a circle of temporality that wheels whatever appears by an axis of perishability, you probably recalled nonvoluntarily that the verb *were* indicated not a fact but a nonliteral, metaphorical possibility. The subjunctive mood subjoins indeterminacy with a determinate state of affairs and expresses something by reference to an elision, a gappiness, which is said to be in the way something happens. This grammatical trope integrates by signifying an elision of factual literalness and direction in factual events. The subjunctive mood recalls a nonfactual dimension of facts. Or, I could say, the subjunctive mood is a trope that bespeaks a withdrawal of factuality in the occurrence of facts.

I have named aspects of subjunctivity in appearing: "recession," "mutability," and "transitoriness." And I have pointed out that the subjunctive mood recalls us to an indeterminacy in factual situations. Appearing things—public events—*as appearing,* embody a recall, a continuous return to the very qualities of life that make us care, to the instability of stabilities, to things' always coming to pass. Appearing carries memory of the necessity of culture, and culture reminds us constantly and publicly that ours is a fragile, appearing world with indeterminacy and mere possibility as well as factual determinacy. Whatever appears, all public things—axioms, values, meanings, scientific methods, bodies, facts, beliefs, and established practices—in their appearing come to completion in passage and change and can never be held in a perfection of presence, an exactness of designation, or a language of engagement. This subjunctive quality of appearing suggests that what is public might be otherwise, is not only factual and might be found, as it were, in *might* rather than *is*.

I will close with some observations on the recession of appearances in appearing and a consideration of the significance of this recession for our accounts of public memory.

In my remarks I have joined recession with the meaning of palpable and suggested that the reality of what happens, the concreteness of experiences and appearing lives, is found in an eventuation that can be expressed by the middle voice and the subjunctive mood. I have said that there is a happy coincidence of this mood with a voice that is controlled by neither subjectivity nor objectivity. How are we academic disciplinarians to live with that? If the things that we want to understand are, by virtue of appearing and becoming public, forever coming to pass and disappearing, if the very occurrence of the culture that we express and the life to which we contribute bear witness to the care-filled incompletion of all things, if appearing comprises a nonfactual determination of all public events, how might we speak knowledgeably of public memories?

I expect that we must take into account the ways in which appearing happens and make that account a definitive part of our scholarly work. If we make, for example, public memory into a quasi-essence by reifying it into something like an historical subjectivity, or if we expect to comprehend appearances as though they were completely present, then the knowledge that we produce will embody a degree of forgetfulness of the mutable and recessive, appearing lives that we address. We will have overlooked a nonfactual dimension of what is public. Such knowledge would forget the *appearing* culture that we bespeak. Our scholarly care will take forms that are not attentive enough to the memory of our culture as it appears. And the structures of objectivity that we in our disciplines intend will miss the voice of eventuation that does justice to the incompletion of whatever is public that we wish to understand.

I think that Foucault, for example, knew that. In his broken prose and rambling empiricism he continuously found broken continuities. He found continuities *in* their broken and rambling appearances. He found fragments of unifying disciplines, shards of practices, happily inconclusive matrixes of contradicting values, and instances of cruelty in processes that were also charitable and anguished with good intent. There are many others on the scene who have found in the incompletion of language and appearing things avenues to considerations of lives in their striking appearing and withdrawal from anything that would engulf them with meaning, value, and status: Deleuze, Blanchot, James, Derrida, Heidegger, Dewey, Nancy, to name a few. One issue upon which they insist places the language of our knowledge at the fore of what appears: articulate language gives publicity, is intrinsic to what is known and meant, and is filled with memories that are seldom cohesive and always forceful. It appears that in our speaking, we remember much more than we can know as we make things public in our many ways. This surplus happens, and no one does it. And with the surplus come the passing incompletions of whatever becomes public.

The question that I wish to underscore is: how might we care for those vast and conflicting memories in appearing of loss as we speak of public memory? How might we best give voice to the incompletions of those memories and of the things that appear with them as we attempt to make public memory manageable in our disciplines of address?

One way to address such questions would be to give accounts of the withdrawal of public memories as they appear, to show that *public* no more means full presence than *memory* does and, perhaps, to show that making public appears to lose what is public in its publicity, that our issue is a people's issue of how to address the inevitability of loss and incompleteness as well as address what is lost, and not to forget the loss in such a way that we become engulfed by our truths and objectivity. I am suggesting that the life of public memory depends on lives that are never fully public, on a recession in publicness, and on losses that can never be restored. Alert to these aspects of public memory we might—here's the subjunctive again—find that to speak well of public memory we need to learn how to speak in regard for nothing public at all. As appearing reverts to itself in its occurring it is as though nonappearing were remembered, as though a public place were not literally a place, and as though we were public no where else than in appearing.

7

The Voice of the Visual in Memory

Barbie Zelizer

For as long as collective memory has been an area of scholarly concern, the precise role of images as its vehicle has been asserted rather than explicated. This essay addresses the role of images in collective memory. Motivated by circumstances in which images, rather than words, emerge as the preferred way to establish and maintain shared knowledge from earlier times, it offers the heuristic of "voice" to help explain how images work across represented events from different times and places. The essay uses "voice" to elucidate how the visual becomes an effective mode of relay about the past and a key vehicle of memory.

On the Boundaries of Memory

Memory works through the various vehicles that give collectives a sense of their past. Addressed already in the work of Frances Yates, who showed how material artifacts in classical Rome facilitated the capacity to remember,[1] the material object has long been seen as a stand-in or synecdochic representation of larger events, issues, and settings. That notion has been elaborated by contemporary scholars; Paul Connerton, Barry Schwartz, and Jacques Le Goff underscore the instrumentality of remembering complex events through vehicles of collective memory.[2] In particular, Pierre Nora's notion of "lieux de mémoire," or "sites of memory," has helped demonstrate the linkage between the ability to remember and the places—conceptual and physical—where shared memory is lodged.[3]

This scholarship postulates that different vehicles of memory offer different ways of making sense of the past. From portraits to bodily habits, collective memories take shape at the intersections created by the different vehicles involved, with remembering through public monuments assumed to be a qualitatively different experience than remembering through films.[4] How these vehicles equip publics to remember thereby foregrounds different stress points in the memory work under question. Images are one such vehicle, the various forms—portraits, pictures, photographs, films—which constitute a cogent means of tackling the past and making it work for the present. But how we remember through images remains powerfully different from how we might remember the same event were images not involved.

How Images Work

Theories of visual representation have long been occupied with delineating how images work differently than words. Much recent scholarship has been drawn to the place at which words and images meet, arguing that side by side the cogent dimensions of each representational template emerge.[5] Such an intersection has generated similar interest in scholarship on memory, where the entanglement of words and images plays upon the respective representational strengths of each memory vehicle.

Indeed, the value of considering how images work by comparing and contrasting them with words dates back at least to the work of Gotthold Lessing. In his early essay on the Laocoon, he argued that painting differs from poetry simply because it "can use but a single moment of an action, and must therefore choose the most pregnant one, the one most suggestive of what has gone before and what is to follow."[6] In other words the visual, unlike the verbal, might best tell a story by strategically catching things in the middle. It depicts for its onlookers a moment in an event's unfolding to which they attend while knowing where that unfolding leads. This means that visual work often involves catching the sequencing of events or issues midstream, strategically freezing it at its potentially strongest moment of meaningful representation.

This point is crucial for explaining the role of images in memory. It suggests that images help us remember the past by freezing its representation at a powerful moment already known to us. Indeed, Lessing's ideas are particularly interesting because we do not encounter images in contemporary experience devoid of other memory vehicles. Rather, images about the past appear alongside other visuals, words, sounds, and artifacts in an array of settings—legal discourse, religion, politics, and journalism, to name a few. Individuals and publics thus often know more about the past than what is actually depicted in a given image, perhaps having read of the depicted, seen a different visual representation of it, or even visualized depictions associated with similar mnemonic schemata. An unusual relationship is created between spectator and image that positions spectators in the peculiar circumstance of knowing more than they see while positioning images between what the spectator knows and does not know. When it comes to viewing images of the past, of which at least some information may be familiar, spectators are thereby led to suspend knowledge so as to encounter the depiction upon spectatorship.

Against this background, theories of visual representation have long held that images work through a combination of two forces. On the one hand, images, particularly photographs, work through a denotative force that is connected with verisimilitude, or the ability of the image to reference things "as they are." Also called the image's indexicality or referentiality, by which an image appears to capture life on its own terms, the power to represent is established through the assumption of a correspondence with real life events. On the other hand, we expect from images a certain connotative force too. Connected with symbolism, generaliz- ability, and universality, the image in this regard is assumed capable of invoking and repairing to broad symbolic systems that draw on certain meanings for the visual representations that are displayed.[7]

The tension between the denotative and connotative forces of the image has occupied scholars of visual culture for decades. Yet certain theorists of visual culture have remained bewildered by an additional force of the image, which Roland Barthes calls its "third meaning."[8] In Barthes's view, the image's third meaning compels viewers after they encounter and deplete both its literal/informational side and its symbolic dimensions. Barthes argues that the third meaning is difficult to locate because it is not situated structurally or in a certain place of the image. It is similarly difficult to describe because it involves what he calls the image's obtuseness, its accent or anaphoric side. It is thus no surprise that contemporary theories of visual representation generally have left the image's third meaning unexplicated.

It may be that visuals need more than just indicative and symbolic force to work in memory. We know that visual memory uses both indicative and symbolic parameters to assert itself in predictable and patterned linkages to the past.[9] But it is possible that such parameters come together systematically, picking up recurrent visual tropes over time and activating them across different events and places in a way that lends meaning to the recycling typical of memory. In other words, it may be that in memory images need more than their indicative and symbolic dimensions and depend on the successful activation of that third meaning to which Barthes refers.

Photographs and Memory

As vehicles of memory, images work in patterned ways, concretizing and externalizing events in an accessible and visible fashion that allows us to recognize the tangible proof they offer of the events being represented. Images actively depend on their material form when operating as vehicles of memory, with our ability to remember events of the past facilitated by an image's availability and interchangeability. In a sense, then, visual memory's texture becomes a facilitator for memory's endurance.

With photography this is even more the case, for the force of the photographic image is derived from its powerful capacity to represent the real. Often photography aids the recall of things and events past so effectively that photographs become the primary markers of memory itself. We need only think of the wide-ranging familiarity of the image of a small boy being herded out of the Warsaw Ghetto by Nazi soldiers to recognize how far a photograph can go in standing in for the event it depicts.

But difficulties arise when photographs shape a collective past. At best photographs are arbitrary, composite, conventionalized, and simplified glimpses of the past. They are "conventionalized, because the image has to be meaningful for an entire group; simplified, because in order to be generally meaningful and capable of transmission, the complexity of the image must be reduced as far as possible."[10] They are also schematic, lacking the detail of the images of personal memory. We do not remember the name of the South Vietnamese village where children ran screaming from their napalmed homes into the field of vision of a photographer's camera, nor the date or circumstances under which the photograph was taken. But its resonance as an image of war atrocity—and consequent invocation by *check*

Without Snowdown

U.S. antiwar groups during the sixties and seventies—stabilizes its meaning precisely along its more schematic dimensions. Collectively held images act as signposts within these limitations, providing a frame in which people can collectively appropriate images. That frame directs us to preferred meaning by the fastest if not the most all-encompassing route.

In events as wide-ranging as the Hindenberg explosion and the *Challenger* disaster, the collective's ability to remember through images depends on some recognized means of storage. For unless cultures have the "means to freeze the memory of the past, the natural tendency of social memory is to suppress what is not meaningful or intuitively satisfying . . . and substitute what seems more appropriate or more in keeping with their particular conception of the world."[11] Modern culture's capacity to freeze, replay, and store visual memories for large numbers of people—facilitated by museums, art galleries, television archives, and other visual data banks—has enhanced our ability to make the past work for present aims. Discussions of photographic memory thereby become at some level discussions of cultural practice—of the strategies by which photographs are made and collected, retained and stored, recycled and forgotten.

These points of emphasis have moved us substantially in our appreciation of how photographs work in memory. But they have also introduced certain blind spots into our understanding of photographs as vehicles of memory. Scholarship on photographic memory has emphasized the fact and actuality of photographic depiction to such an extent that it has left unaddressed its opposite—contingency. Defined as the quality of being uncertain, conditional, or possible, contingency softens the fact-driven force of the photograph by introducing chance and relativity into its appropriation by spectators.[12] Such "what if" dimensions of the image, however, are largely absent from theories of visual representation. Despite the lexicon that we have begun to develop for some dimensions of visual authority, there is still no term that complicates/modifies/qualifies what we see. Without it, all that contingency entails—possibility, qualification, imagination—is pushed aside to accommodate the blunt force of the photograph's depiction of the here and now.

Yet it is possible, even probable, that images function in memory precisely through contingency, when meaning settles not at the image's original point of display but over time in new contexts that are always altered,

re current 344 theme

sometimes playful, and often contradictory. By playing to the contingent aspect of a depicted event or issue, the image's capacity to speak for the past changes in its relation to the events it depicts. And when dealing with events of a tragic nature, contingency may be the best interpretive stance for which we can hope.

The Subjunctive Voice of Images

"Voice" offers a useful way of making sense of the image's role in memory. Seen here as the dimensions of an image that propel it to link with other events at other times and places, voice helps explain how the image takes on an already provided meaning upon its initial appearance. In this regard, voice can be seen as an assist that helps us understand both the image's third meaning and the role of contingency in visual memory.

It is important to note that what is here called "voice" in effect corresponds with a slew of linguistic terms—including voice, mood, tense, and aspect—that complicate and qualify the word of action in a statement. While in popular usage voice simply means articulation or expression, voice is defined grammatically as that which shows the relationship between the subject and the word of action in a statement.[13] Taken together, voice is extended here to refer to the relationship developed between the spectator and the image—involving state of mind, attitude, temporal and sequential positioning—and to those aspects of the image that help the spectator develop that relationship. This is key, for it offsets the limitations of the image itself. As Slavoj Zizek contends, "[V]oice does not simply persist at a different level with regard to what we see, it rather points to a gap in the field of the visible, toward the dimension of what eludes our gaze . . . ultimately, we hear things because we cannot see everything."[14]

Voice helps situate visual memory on the boundaries of the familiar, ensuring not only that new images build on a visual tradition in both form and content but on a series of related expectations for how we are willing to connect with the past and where our resistance for doing so can be found. At the same time, voice helps introduce the more amorphous aspects of visual depiction that are associated with what might be loosely called an image's mood, tense, and aspect.

If we are agreed that the domain of the visual is in need of explication for both an image's third meaning and its connection to contingency, it makes sense to search for a voice that accomplishes that address effectively. One such voice—the "subjunctive"—does so particularly well, as it is concerned with the capacity to couch what is represented in an interpretive scheme of "what could be." Grammatically, the subjunctive qualifies the word of action by situating it within the hypothetical, changing the statement "I shot that man" to "I might have shot that man." Usually signified in verbal language by auxiliaries such as "might," "could," or "should," by the substitution of "would have" for "had" and by the use of "if" clauses, depiction in images adds impulses of supposal, hypothesis, and possibility to photographic verisimilitude. The condition under focus is transformed from a reality or future certainty into a probability made possible by someone's desire, emotions, or imagination. Technically defined as the mood of a verb used to express condition or hypothesis, the subjunctive creates a space of possibility, hope, and liminality through which spectators might relate to images. Images that might not be inherently uncertain, hypothetical, or emotional become so due to the attitude of spectators. It allows them to move through what might be called the "as if" of visual representation and memory. The "as if" thrives on contradiction, on often illogical, unpredictable, and idiosyncratic connections, whereby the original use value of a piece of visual culture is easily negated and undermined. The "as if" has many helpers in photography, such as insufficient credits, overgeneralized captions, an imprecise relation between text and image—all the tools that blur an image's referentiality. In the subjunctive voice, questions about cultural authority are altered and muted, if not suspended. Spectators begin to ask not "What are we looking at?" but "What does this remind us of?" and "What possibilities does this raise?"

As a mode of tackling experience, the subjunctive has been addressed by numerous scholars concerned with meaning and representation. Anthropologist Victor Turner was instrumental in introducing the subjunctive to discussions of everyday life with his notions about ritual process and liminality.[15] Charles E. Scott, Roger Silverstone, and Michael Schudson each elaborated on the notion in the contexts of philosophy, cultural studies, and journalism, respectively.[16] Yet none considered the role that

I saw

have seen

the subjunctive might play in images and the domain of visual representation.

The subjunctive enhances the work of visual memory because it activates visual markers for subjunctive ends and thereby becomes well suited for representing complex events. Prominent when the visual retreats into the past, the subjunctive here depends on the texture and availability of images that are simplified, schematic, and often composite and that appear in an interchangeable array of paintings, icons, photographs, and video clips. In memory, the subjunctive voice connects across these dimensions in patterned ways. We come to remember whole events through condensed images that reduce complex and multidimensional phenomena into memorable scenes. Often they are memorable because they activate impulses about how the "world might be" rather than how "it is."

For example, when a depiction pauses on the "as if" dimensions of an image—coaxing spectators to consider how a depiction "might mean," "might be," "might look," or "might end"—it involves many sides of the imaginary. A photograph of a kiss, tendered in a public square at the end of World War II, draws imaginary visions of who the people might have been, what kind of relationship they might have had, or where their act might have led. Similarly, a photograph of a flag raising at the conclusion of a drawn-out battle conjures up thoughts about the flag raisers' experiences in battle and the world order that their action was hoping to set in place. Each of these examples illustrates what Lessing said long ago about the visual: Images break the sequencing of action in the middle. By freezing that sequencing midway at a particularly memorable representational moment, spectators are able to embellish numerous imaginary schemes on the "about to" moment that is depicted in the sequencing of action. In this sense they supply a contingent dimension to visual depiction. That contingent dimension, in turn, helps activate the image's third meaning that facilitates connections between images across times and places.

Visualizing the About-to-Die Moment

The possibilities raised here regarding the role of the image in memory—that it thrives on both the image's third meaning and its contingent dimensions—are key to understanding images over time. Yet both possibilities depend on representational decisions that strategically play to the kinds of images that typically emerge as effective vehicles of memory. Such images tend to be of the type described above: they freeze a particularly memorable moment of representation midway through the sequencing of action by representing it through the subjunctive voice. Typically, then, they build on the blunt force of photographic depiction—its concretization of the here and now—and soften that force with qualifiers that are suggestive of possibility, contingency, and hypothesis.

While such images come to the foreground in numerous kinds of visual representation, perhaps nowhere are their attributes as salient as in those visual images that depict individuals on the brink of death. From Phillippe Aries we have learned that the representation of death has long been codified in conjunction with broader notions about how life is supposed to be lived and ended.[17] The work of Jay Ruby has extended our understanding of how people use photographs of loved ones to mitigate the finality of their deaths.[18] Such assumptions play to the subjunctive voice and midway sequencing typical of images in memory. In other words, images of the about-to-die moment offer a content that is well suited to the form provided by images acting as memory vehicles.

First, the subjunctive voice offers an apt way of depicting the difficult topic of death. It allows us to recognize its finality while facilitating the inclusion of possibility, contingency, and even the illogical conclusion of its postponement. Visual images using the subjunctive voice to address death are thus possibly easier to view.

Second, freezing the sequencing of action midway means that these images purport to delay death's progression. It positions the action at the "about to" moment, the moment at which an individual or group is going to die, but not after they are already dead. By freezing the representation of death before people actually die, we mark the moment *before* death, rather than after, as the most powerful and memorable moment of representation in the sequencing of events surrounding human demise. And indeed, both the arts and scholarship on the death experience have long held one's final moment as crucially important, as it is assumed to offer a playback of one's life in which one's entire life flashes by in an instant. Individuals are often seen reflecting on personal accomplishments and failures at the moment they are about to die.[19] It is not only a point of transference but a boundary marker of crucial importance that marks significant aspects of all that has come before and all that is to follow.

This is a long way of saying that the moment before death has long been seen as one of the most perplexing, complicated, and interesting moments in contemporary civilization. Seen in many instances as the preferred version of death's representation, the final moment before death can be traced as an enduring trope in one of the classic representations of civilization—the Crucifixion. Although not all portrayals of the Crucifixion show an already dead Christ, a recurrent visual trope has been to depict Christ at the moment of his impending death.[20] In such images, Christ is portrayed as still alive and suffering rather than already dead, and the moment before his death is positioned as the preferred way of depicting death itself, death's opposite being used as its stand-in.

It is not surprising, then, that the aesthetic choice to frame the one already dead at the moment that the person is about to die has a long history in visual representation. Woodcuts from the fifteenth and sixteenth centuries—the *artes moriendi* that portrayed for the public the proper manner of dying—depict the traditional image of the deathbed and the deathbed scene as the preferred iconographic representation of death.[21] Similarly, numerous paintings from the late eighteenth and early nineteenth centuries reflect the decision to feature the moment before death as the stand-in for death itself.

For instance, a painting by Benjamin West titled *The Death of General Wolfe* (1770) portrays Wolfe's death in the midst of the siege of Quebec during the French and Indian War. West depicted the death of what he saw as the modern hero by portraying a dying Wolfe surrounded by adoring subordinates. Publics here were offered the same tension that had resonated earlier from the Crucifixion images, whereby the state of death was visualized by a still-live body. *The Death of Socrates* (1787) by Jacques Louis David portrays Socrates' last moments in a similar fashion. Despite the image's title, publics saw Socrates sitting upright and busily engaged with everyone around him, all of whom probably wondered when the hemlock he had just swallowed would take effect. The image was in keeping with Plato's account of Socrates' death, which maintained that the philosopher died as he lived rather than the other way around. Nearly thirty years later

Francesco Goya portrayed the horrors of the Napoleonic invasion by depicting a man stiffened with fear against the firing squad about to end his life. Titled *Third of May, 1808* (1814), the painting showed the man's last moment before being bayoneted by insurgent troops.

In considering the middle captured by each of these paintings, we are reminded again that it is their frozen motion that makes each image so striking, offering us, as Lessing suggested, what may in fact set visual representation and particularly the still moment apart from other modes of representation. Simply put, the image tells the story of what happened at a point just before the end of its unfolding. The power of the images is magnified by the deaths to which they lead, with death built on to accommodate broader subjunctive messages.

In each case of viewing the about-to-die image, we are drawn into an illogical spectator position that is simultaneously naive and all-knowing. That all-knowingness coaxes us to review what we know is about to happen and to think about what might have been had things happened differently. We entertain the irrational hope that death may not occur. As Lessing suggested, we are drawn here to what is by knowing what follows, suspending what we know is about to happen. This impossible contradictory stance is facilitated by the mood of contingency made possible by the subjunctive voice. As spectators, then, we are drawn to the "as if" of these representations, left to wonder how things might have looked different had death not occurred. And it is the subjunctive voice—the stance of contingency—that persists in memory. The "as if" is what gets recycled—on posters, collectors' volumes, photographic yearbooks. Subjunctivity, then, becomes a voice or trope through which to remember.

All of this suggests that the aesthetic choice to pitch an image of death as an about-to-die moment has been key. This is important, because it may have emerged as a choice producing a particularly powerful and emotional image of death. Moreover, this moment of about-to-die plays itself out across a wide range of depictions in culture, journalism among them. Even before the advent of photography in journalism, drawings of about-to-die moments appeared regularly. Among the most well-known examples was an illustration of President William McKinley's assassination in 1901, which a *Leslie's* magazine artist drew at the moment McKinley extended his right hand for a handshake with his about-to-be assassin.[22] Once photography became the preferred way of visualizing events in journalism, however, the opportunity for displaying about-to-die moments became more widespread.

Journalism and the About-to-Die Image

The inclusion of the about-to-die image in journalistic representations provides a particularly interesting illustration of the resonance of this particular type of depiction. When journalists include the about-to-die moment as part of their coverage, they in effect subvert journalism's own aims—which is to present depictions of that which is most newsworthy. What is most newsworthy for journalism is death itself. Yet its depiction may not coincide with that which is most visually powerful, suggesting that a journalist or news organization's decision to attend to the visually powerful in effect neglects that which is newsworthy. When that visually powerful image remains the primary iconic representation of the depicted event over time, questions arise concerning the documentary status of the news image in memory. Moreover, when that depiction uses the subjunctive voice—the "as if"—rather than the indicative—the "as is," on which journalism strongly relies—questions arise regarding the voice by which journalists typically establish their own authority.

This is no small matter, for photographic depictions of the about-to-die moment have literally cluttered the repository of photojournalism's high moments. Collections of the iconic images of photojournalism have long included versions of the about-to-die moment, where photojournalistic images have focused on the final moment before death, actual or presumed. Such images fill our collective memory: a young boy being herded from the Warsaw Ghetto under a Nazi machine gun; Lee Harvey Oswald about to be gunned down by Jack Ruby; a black man ascending the platform to his own lynching; a Palestinian child crouching in fear before he is shot to death by Israeli soldiers. In each case, the about-to-die moment recurs time and again as a memorable synecdochic stand-in for a range of complex, often contested events in contemporary history.

The about-to-die moment involves two aberrations to journalism. One concerns the violation of journalistic values of newsworthiness at the time of the photograph's initial display, either on the part of the photographer or the news organization, by which the about-to-die photo becomes the preferred way of visualizing the death at hand. In most cases this decision involves substituting depictions of the about-to-die photograph for other more newsworthy images of death itself. In part, such a decision depends on what Jessica Fishman has defined as an inhibition regarding the images of corpses in the news, whereby photographs of dead bodies are rendered the more offensive choice for journalists to make.[23] The second involves violating journalistic values of newsworthiness over time, whereby the less newsworthy photo, originally selected for initial display, becomes the iconic image by which the complex events surrounding death are remembered. Such photos of the about-to-die moment reappear in news retrospectives, anniversary issues, and other memory work conducted by news organizations over time.[24] Given that many of the events being depicted or remembered involve the tragic death of either large populations or prominent individuals, the selection and maintenance of photos that have been strategically chosen because they depict death in process rather than as a finished state is telling.

For instance, three of the four iconic images of the conflict in Vietnam captured individuals poised at the moment of death but not yet dead.[25] Each photo not only received widespread depiction at the time of the event's original unfolding but was recycled extensively over time, reappearing in retrospectives on the Vietnam War, newspaper and broadcast retrospectives of the sixties and seventies, and memorial volumes on Southeast Asia. Perhaps the most famous was the Eddie Adams photograph from 1968 of a South Vietnamese chief of national police—General Loan—shooting a Vietcong prisoner in the head. The picture, one of a sequence of still shots that Adams took at the time, rapidly became a potent symbol of antiwar sentiments and played a crucial role in turning U.S. public opinion against the war. Significantly, Adams shot numerous images of the Vietcong prisoner, already dead, which did not make it widely into print, while the about-to-die moment made it onto the front pages of nearly every newspaper across the United States. It appeared twice in one edition of the *New York Times,* both on the front page and on page 12, bracketed by photos that Adams had taken before and after the execution.[26] The photographer's provision of evidence of the dead prisoner was thus pushed aside to accommodate the about-to-die image. In somewhat of a reverse practice, when the shot was shown on NBC Nightly News the network blacked out its screen for three seconds, thereby increasing the photo's impact.[27] Not surprisingly, the photograph eventually won a Pulitzer and has since become one of the iconic representations of the Vietnam War.

Perhaps nowhere has the about-to-die moment been as aptly represented as in the visuals of the September 11 attacks on the World Trade Center and the Pentagon. Because the World Trade Center attack occurred in the midst of the nation's media capital, the *New York Times* felt that camera crews and news photographers "all had ample time to capture the most horrific moments."[28] Yet images of human death did not generally appear, other than one photo of a severed hand that appeared in the New York *Daily News.*[29] Depictions of body parts, blood, and gore were generally nowhere to be found. Possibly due to the trauma caused by the scope of the tragedy, depicting the loss of human life at a point *before* life was lost seemed to be simply easier than depicting death itself. It also reflected a longstanding reluctance, identified by Fishman, to depict images of human gore in the press and a tendency to target instead other focal points, such as inanimate objects or live bodies.[30] Hence, news executives admitted that video footage and photography of body parts were excised from public view. MSNBC's president said that his staff pushed aside numerous pictures showing blood and body parts to find the more antiseptic images. "We chose not to show a lot," he said. "How more horrifying and graphic can you get than a 110-story building, blowing up and disintegrating before your eyes?"[31] In other words, the about-to-die moment took precedence as a trope of visual representation from the beginning.

Nonetheless, the depictions that appeared in the days following the attacks were met with incredulity. As *Business Week* advised its readers, "Close your eyes and try to make the images go away—the jagged holes ripped in the twin towers by two hijacked airliners, desperate office workers jumping to their deaths, the buildings' eventual cascading collapse, scenes of panic in the streets, jumpy TV footage of injured Pentagon officers. You can't banish the horror."[32] Photographs connected to the attacks, though not depicting bodies, appeared with a systematic regularity that bordered at times on excess. Even by year's end the same images continued to be displayed because, in the *New York Times*'s view, "they freeze-frame a calamity so great that the mind struggles, even months later, to comprehend the data being sent by the eyes."[33]

The about-to-die depictions of September 11 had two photographic focal points: ill-focused shots of people about to die and images of the burning World Trade Center buildings, filled with individuals who were not visualized but poised in an imaginary or presumed space on the brink of death. These two sides of death's depiction—a first-order image depicting actual people on the way to their death and a second-order image depicting their presumed death in the buildings on the way to their collapse—were shown in complementary but different ways. It makes sense to consider them in turn.

First-Order About-to-Die Photos

The images of people on the way to their death in the World Trade Center provided a particularly horrific example of the force of photographic depiction that constituted a first-order representation of the about-to-die moment. Pictures of still-live bodies leaning from upper-story windows or tumbling from skyscrapers constituted a set of perhaps the most tragic depictions displayed in the aftermath of the attacks. Reminiscent of an earlier image in which people in a clothing factory gestured hysterically at bystanders from inside a fiery warehouse and jumped rather than burn to death,[34] these photos were nonetheless shocking for the magnitude of the loss of human life that they represented. Moreover, the pictures of people waving frantically as fire engulfed the buildings or jumping to certain death were particularly painful because they underscored the sheer hopelessness of both the people trapped inside and the people witnessing their demise.

Images of people about to die appeared first on television. During the first few hours after the attacks, certain broadcast and cable news organizations—CNN, Fox News, and CBS—initially showed moving images of people jumping from the center towers' upper floors to their presumed deaths on the pavement below. These pictures, which portrayed bodies like unreal stick figures tumbling jerkily into the gray sky from the side of the buildings, represented but did not depict actual death. No bodies were shown striking the pavement below, and little visual detail of those about to die was offered. The photographs were peculiar for the long view of action that they offered and for their failure to depict faces, identifiable human features, or detailing of clothing. At the same time the distance between the photographers and camera people, on the one hand, and the individuals on the towers' upper floors, on the other, ensured that the people remained anonymous and would not be recognized by relatives.[35] Spectators, instead, were expected to expand on the brutal fact of anonymous falling bodies with the presumption of their impending death on the pavement below. In a sense, then, these images that aptly captured the horror of the attack as it unfolded depended already at their original depiction on the spectator to fill in the narrative of a gruesome death beyond that actually depicted. Significantly, however, the image in its moving version was pulled from the television screen almost immediately after its initial broadcast. Both ABC and MSNBC decided not to show it at all, with executives at both news organizations wondering whether it was "necessary to show people plunging to their death."[36] NBC showed an image of one person jumping and then pulled it because, in one executive's view, it was "disturbing."[37] Although the image continued to be shown on some foreign broadcast networks, such as the BBC, on the home front it was deemed inappropriate and taken off air.

Yet the images of people jumping and hanging out of the towers experienced a peculiar short-life in the press that underscored the power of the subjunctive in helping people deal with the World Trade Center attacks. Two particular images made a comeback the day after the attack, when they were relegated as still photographs to the inner pages of certain daily newspapers. An Associated Press photograph of a solitary person tumbling headfirst out of one of the buildings, taken in two versions by Richard Drew, was reprinted more widely than other images of people about to die. The jumper, his legs poised as if in a graceful dance position, was depicted plummeting straight down the side of the building. The image appeared in the *Philadelphia Inquirer* on an inside page under the matter-of-fact title "A Person Falls from the World Trade Center's North Tower," alongside a much larger picture of a jetliner lining up to fly into one of the towers.[38] It also appeared in the *Chicago Tribune* and the *Washington Post,* where it was appended to an article pondering why people had chosen to jump.[39] A differently angled version of the same shot was displayed in the *New York Times* and the *Washington Post.*[40] *Time* labeled it "The Long Fall."[41]

A second image, taken by Reuter's Jeff Christiensen, was also reprinted widely in the first day or two after the attacks. The photograph showed

Figure 7.1. An unidentified man jumps to his death from one of the towers (Richard Drew, Associated Press/Wide World Photos).

people hanging out of the World Trade Center, waving frantically. Although Christiensen did not realize at first that his much larger shot of the building included in one corner scores of people caught between death by fire and death by jumping, the wire service blew up the smaller image, constituting one-fiftieth of the original frame, into its own image once alerted to its contents. The picture appeared twice in the *Washington Post,* the *Chicago Tribune, Newsweek,* and the *Boston Globe.*[42] Typically it received a caption that generalized the depicted scene: *Newsweek* called it "After the Blast."[43]

The images' immediate display in the press at first raised the question of how the photographic still image could suddenly make the horrific display presentable. Why did the image of people jumping, considered too powerful and inappropriate when positioned as part of a video sequence, become appropriate for public display a mere twenty-four hours later when transformed into a single, static shot? Those questions, however, were quelled by the fact that the static shots of people about to die reappeared in only a limited fashion.

Despite a short run in the press during the first day or two after the attacks, the photos did not proliferate widely. They were printed in only a limited number of newspapers, primarily New York papers and newspapers of record.[44] When they did appear, they were printed on inside rather than front pages and more often than not in black and white rather than color.[45] Finally, when they did run, they provoked reader complaints.[46]

By the weekend the images of people about to die virtually disappeared, appearing in very few of the newsmagazines, retrospectives, or other overviews of that first week's events.[47] By the time that many of the later retrospective volumes went into print three months later, they reappeared hardly at all. One memorial volume comprised nearly one hundred photos but not one portrayed the tumbling bodies.[48] Even an Associated Press retrospective, issued in September 2001, did not include the photograph of a solitary jumper taken by its own photographer.[49]

The contradictory display of the static shot—by which it appeared but without full force—is telling. On the one hand, its appearance could have been expected to be short-lived, given the reluctance in the press about showing human gore.[50] On the other hand, the reappearance of the about-to-die moment as a still shot offered a more subjunctive and contingent

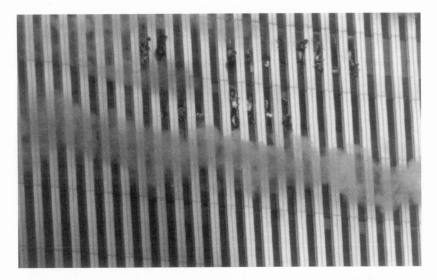

Figure 7.2. People poised between death by fire and death by jumping (Jeff Christensen, ©Reuters 2001, used by permission).

display of the image than was suggested in the image's moving version. While most spectators within a day or two were able to fill in the tragic details of the larger narrative—the fact that beyond the camera's frame lay the harsh pavement on which the bodies landed—there was little in the images themselves that forced spectators to face that aspect of the event. Rather, the static depictions allowed them to remain in a subjunctive space even longer than they had with the moving image. In that subjunctive space, the people portrayed were not yet dead and the depiction suggested the remote possibility that perhaps, as in one spectator's words, it was "all just a bad dream."[51] As one ABC news correspondent said, "[T]he most horrible thing was the sight of people hurling themselves from the building. I was telling myself maybe they weren't real people. They looked like little dolls."[52]

The tug of these two contradictory impulses facilitated the images' disappearance and brief return. However, the no-nonsense positioning of the bodies, some of them tumbling headfirst as they fell from the buildings, made it difficult to contain a subjunctive interpretation for long. What possibilities—other than certain death—could be entertained here? So bothered was the *New York Times* by the image that it ran an article detailing journalistic decisions to run the picture of jumping bodies.[53] While the *New York Times* justified its decision to publish because the photo appeared on an inside page and in black and white and *Newsday* justified it because it was a small image and the person unidentifiable, this was not enough for some readers.[54] As one person wrote to the *Denver Post*, "[T]his is nauseating. . . . Do you have no feelings, no sense of respect for the families of the loved ones lost?"[55]

Thus, the portrayals of jumping bodies disappeared a second time. In need of a visualization that could powerfully convey the tragic events as they unfolded, a second-order about-to-die moment emerged from the scores of photos being taken. It depicted the more imaginary or presumed aspect of impending death as embodied in the collapse of the World Trade Center itself. In other words, images of the buildings in which people were about to perish took the place of depictions of people about to die.

Second-Order About-to-Die Photos

Depictions of the buildings upheld a tendency in the press, identified by Fishman, to offset the visualization of dead bodies with a focus on inanimate objects.[56] But the buildings here took on a central role in visualizing the tragedy for a grieving public from the very beginning. Played over and over again on television, in newsmagazines, and in other venues of visual display, the towers provided a remarkable shot of impact that segmented the larger story neatly into before and after portions. At times the images seemed to function like "a kind of wallpaper."[57] And yet the repeated display of the shots helped offset people's persistent disbelief in what was happening. In MSNBC anchor Brian Williams's words, "[I]t just never ceases to amaze people to watch that piece of videotape."[58]

But as an about-to-die photo, the image of the fractured World Trade Center, its towers burning shortly before their monumental demise, had an additional function. It forced spectators to imagine or presume the precise circumstances of the individuals who faced their deaths rather than see the individuals as they were about to die. In much the same way that the moving images of jumping bodies offered less of an ability to pause subjunctively than did the still shots, so too the depiction of bodies offered less of a subjunctive space than did the inanimate buildings. Choosing to depict buildings instead of bodies prolonged the moment of contingency

Figure 7.3. The impending collapse of the World Trade Towers (Sean Adair, ©Reuters 2001, used by permission).

in which spectators could improbably hope that the buildings would not fall and the people not die. As one spectator said, "I kept looking and looking and wishing that the story would take a different turn."[59] Or, as a *New York Times* columnist commented on a moment in which the tape of the just-struck buildings played backward momentarily, "[W]e saw history reverse itself; the building appeared whole, as if in a wishful dream."[60]

These photos portrayed the looming facades of the twin towers in various stages of their demise. Certain photos showed them at the moment of impact of one or the other airliner; others showed them on fire after the planes struck; still others showed them as they began to crumble. The front pages of some newspapers elected to show a series of temporal moments of the buildings crumbling in sequenced succession.[61] Each depiction was an additional variance of the about-to-die moment, with spectators recognizing that the thousands of live people inside were experiencing horrific and life-threatening circumstances at the moment of the images' depiction.

The same images were shown repeatedly over the next few days. The day after the attacks, the burning towers appeared on nearly every front page of U.S. and foreign newspapers.[62] In viewing the images by that point, spectators clearly were forced to suspend what they knew—that the towers did in fact come down, killing all those still trapped inside. Yet the image persisted. The *Philadelphia Inquirer,* for instance, used the burning towers as its logo for days after the attacks, as a way of marking its daily inventory of the attack-related articles inside the newspaper.[63]

The burning towers were also seen in nearly every possible visual venue beyond the front pages of newspapers. They appeared on the covers of all of the major newsmagazines and as logos for most televised broadcast and cable coverage of the aftermath of the attacks.[64] The towers adorned the covers of retrospective memorial volumes over the months that followed.[65] The cover of *Newsweek*'s year-end double issue featured an overview of the year with the single word "September" affixed above a picture of the burning towers.[66] On December 31, the image topped a special *New York Times* section titled "The Year in Pictures."[67] The towers appeared not only on many volume covers but also on inside pages in the same volumes: a Reuters commemorative volume designated 10 percent of its more than 130 photos to the burning towers.[68] The images were also affixed to numerous popular cultural artifacts including calendars, buttons, t-shirts, and posters.[69]

But we need to ask why these images stuck in memory. Why did the burning towers persist as the reigning about-to-die moment of the September 11 attacks? It is probable that the images reigned as the preferred way of making sense of the attacks because they had the right "voice" for displaying the horror associated with the World Trade Center attacks. Not only did the images offer the appropriate degree of contingency for a message too harsh to be seen with the brute force of reality's depiction. As one spectator, trying to take his own photograph of the towers before they collapsed, wrote in the *New York Times:* "It had been a nice shot. And certainly it had been easier to shape the horror into an aesthetic distance and deny the human reality. There was safety in that distance."[70] But the image also cut—and depicted—the story at precisely its most powerful moment, pushing spectators to recognize what came later while allowing them to prolong the experience of what had been before. The images hence created a space of (im)possibility, whereby spectators were able to linger in a moment when the full scope of the tragedy was not yet upon them.

Conclusion: When Memory Freezes on Contingency

The substitution of buildings for people as the preferred representation of the about-to-die moment in the World Trade Center attacks makes sense when considering the role of the subjunctive in the popular imagination. Viewing the raw horror of bodies tumbling to their death was clearly problematic because their harsh depiction overwhelmed the subjunctive possibility of muting the finality of death for viewers. The buildings, by contrast, prolonged that subjunctive response, softening the reality of the response with the improbable—but comforting—sense that time might have thwarted death's intention.

It is important to realize that the contradictory display associated with these images was resolved by drawing from a robust tradition of earlier about-to-die photos where death was actual or presumed. Not a decision made on the backs of this event alone, the trajectory by which horrific tragedy came to be visualized through its "as if" rather than its "as is" dimensions has a long history connecting this event with other similar ones—wars, assassinations, natural tragedies, terrorist acts. The image's voice made available the parallels, making clear which filters were acceptable for drawing death's representation in the public sphere. Voice offered spectators the space of contingency for as long as they needed to be there, postponing the logical conclusion of the about-to-die image—death itself.

Significantly, however, as we have seen through the long and resonant tradition of such images, the about-to-die representation does not dis-

appear as we move into memory and into what should be a gradual acceptance of the horror of its underlying events. Despite its strategic representativeness for certain kinds of public events, when it is invoked the
about-to-die moment lingers as a marker of complex events in history. It
persists in manifold forms, turning, in journalism, into prize-winning
photos, celebrated images, and even iconic representations that become,
in one newspaper's words, "defining statements of the events from which
they have arisen."[71] This means that a subjunctive response to the horrors
they embody persists too, lingering as messages of contingency at a point
where contingency may no longer be the optimum response to the events
of mass destruction depicted in these images.

All of this should give us pause. For the powerful presence of the subjunctive within our capacity to remember the past suggests that we often
willingly engage in a kind of irrational game-playing with what we see,
projecting altered ends on the screens through which we see. The "as if"
permeates the core of our very encounters with the real world, molding
our capacity to remember long after it may have outlived its usefulness.
Often "we see" because "we should see." But our leap into the third meaning of the image, into an embrace of conditionality and hypothesis, is
worth pondering for what it suggests about the boundaries of memory.
For it may be that memory rests not only upon the boundaries of the
familiar but upon the boundaries of the impossible. And when dealing with
the memory of tragic events, we need to ask ourselves if that is the best
response we can muster.

Notes

This essay began as part of a keynote address for a conference on visual rhetoric in Bloomington, Indiana, and part of a talk for a conference on framing
memory at Syracuse University (both in September 2001). Thanks go to Barbara
Biesecker, John Lucaites, and Kendall Phillips for organizing my participation; to
Roger Abrahams, Larry Gross, and Amy Jordan for critiquing drafts of my ideas;
and to Bethany Klein for research assistance. A more extended discussion of these
ideas appears in Barbie Zelizer, *About to Die: Journalism, Memory, and the Voice of the
Visual* (Chicago: University of Chicago Press, in press).

1. Frances Yates, *The Art of Memory* (New York: Routledge and Kegan Paul,
1966).

2. Paul Connerton, *How Societies Remember* (Cambridge: Cambridge University Press, 1989); Barry Schwartz, "The Social Context of Commemoration: A Study in Collective Memory," *Social Forces* 61, no. 2 (1982): 347–402; Jacques Le Goff, *History and Memory* (New York: Columbia University Press, 1992).

3. Pierre Nora, *Realms of Memory* (New York: Columbia University Press, 1997–2000).

4. I have discussed this elsewhere. See Barbie Zelizer, *Remembering to Forget: Holocaust Memory through the Camera's Eye* (Chicago: University of Chicago Press, 1998); Barbie Zelizer, "Reading the Past against the Grain: The Shape of Memory Studies," *Critical Studies in Mass Communication* 12, no. 2 (1995): 214–39; and Barbie Zelizer, ed., *Visual Culture and the Holocaust* (New Brunswick: Rutgers University Press, 2001).

5. See, for instance, W. J. T. Mitchell, *Picture Theory* (Chicago: University of Chicago Press, 1994).

6. Gotthold Ephraim Lessing, *Laocoon* (New York: Noonday Press, 1961), 92.

7. See Stuart Hall, "The Determinations of News Photographs," in *The Manufacture of News,* ed. Stanley Cohen and Jock Young (Thousand Oaks: Sage, 1974), 226–43. Also see Allan Sekula, "On the Invention of Photographic Meaning," *Photography against the Grain* (Nova Scotia: Press of the Nova Scotia College of Art and Design, 1984); John Tagg, *The Burden of Representation: Essays on Photography and History* (New York: MacMillan, 1988).

8. Roland Barthes, "The Third Meaning," in *Image/Music/Text* (New York: Hill and Wang, 1977), 52–68.

9. See, for instance, Zelizer, *Remembering to Forget;* Marita Sturken, *Tangled Memories* (Berkeley: University of California Press, 1997); Karal Ann Marling and John Wetenhall, *Iwo Jima: Monuments, Memorials, and the American Hero* (Cambridge, MA: Harvard University Press, 1991).

10. James Fentress and Chris Wickham, *Social Memory* (Oxford: Basil Blackwell, 1992), 47–48.

11. Ibid., 58–59.

12. Richard Rorty, *Contingency, Irony, and Solidarity* (Cambridge: Cambridge University Press, 1989). Also see Judith Butler, Ernesto Laclau, and Slavoj Zizek, *Contingency, Hegemony, Universality* (New York: Verso Press, 2000).

13. This definition is paraphrased from *Webster's New Universal Unabridged Dictionary.* Also see Emile Benveniste, *Problems in General Linguistics* (Coral Gables, FL: University of Miami Press, 1981).

14. Slavoj Zizek, "I Hear You with My Eyes," in *Gaze and Voice as Love Objects,* ed. Renata Salaci and Slavoj Zizek (Durham: Duke University Press, 1996), 93.

15. Victor Turner, *The Ritual Process* (New York: Routledge and Kegan Paul, 1969). Also see Arnold Van Gennep, *The Rites of Passage* (New York: Routledge and Kegan Paul, 1960).

16. Charles E. Scott, *The Time of Memory* (Albany: State University of New York Press, 1989). Says Scott: "The subjunctive mood belongs to states of affairs in which incompletion and contingency, something not stately or directly statable, are joined with statement and fact" (279). Roger Silverstone, *Why Study the Media?* (Thousand Oaks: Sage, 1999); Michael Schudson, "When? Deadlines, Datelines, and History," in *Reading the News,* ed. Robert Manoff and Michael Schudson (New York: Pantheon, 1986), 79–108.

17. Phillippe Aries, *Western Attitudes toward Death* (Baltimore: Johns Hopkins University Press, 1974). Also see Aries, *The Hour of Our Death* (Oxford: Oxford University Press, 1981).

18. Jay Ruby, *Secure the Shadow: Death and Photography in America* (Cambridge, MA: MIT Press, 1995).

19. Aries, *Hour of Our Death,* 106. Literature, cinema, and theater abound with representations structured around the about-to-die moment. One recent example is the acclaimed play *Wit.*

20. See Leo Steinberg, *The Sexuality of Christ in Renaissance Art and in Modern Oblivion* (Chicago: University of Chicago Press, 1996); Mitchell B. Merback, *The Thief, the Cross and the Wheel: The Spectacle of Punishment in Medieval and Renaissance Europe* (Chicago: University of Chicago Press, 1999).

21. Aries, *Western Attitudes,* 34.

22. The illustration, by T. Dart Walker, appeared on the front cover of *Frank Leslie's Weekly,* September 21, 1901. Although first reports maintained that McKinley, who did not die for over a week, would recover from the assassination attempt, this about-to-die image was displayed simultaneously with his actual death.

23. See Jessica M. Fishman, "Documenting Death: Photojournalism and Spectacles of the Morbid in the Tabloid and Elite Newspaper," Ph.D. diss., University of Pennsylvania, 2001.

24. I have discussed these two modes of interpretation as a distinction between the local and the durational. See Barbie Zelizer, "Journalists as Interpretive Communities," *Critical Studies in Mass Communication* 10, no. 3 (1993): 219–37.

25. Other than the Eddie Adams shot discussed below, these included the photos of a Buddhist monk's self-immolation and of a group of women and children about to be shot in My Lai. When the former picture reached editorial desks, questions were raised about whether to print it. One Syracuse editor went on record saying, "If you can publish a picture of the crucifixion, you can publish this picture." See Vicki Goldberg, *The Power of Photography* (New York: Abbeville, 1991), 212.

26. Eddie Adams, "Shooting of General Loan" (Associated Press, 1968).

27. Goldberg, *Power of Photography,* 226.

28. Jim Rutenberg and Felicity Barringer, "The Ethics: News Media Try to Sort Out Policy on Graphic Images," *New York Times,* September 13, 2001, p. A24.

29. New York *Daily News,* September 13, 2001, evening edition.

30. Fishman, "Documenting Death."

31. Erik Sorensen, cited in Rutenberg and Barringer, "The Ethics."

32. "Terror in America," *Business Week,* September 24, 2001, p. 35.

33. Andy Grundberg, "Photography," *New York Times Book Review,* December 2, 2001, p. 35. Indeed, the number of photos that circulated was enormous, suggesting that public response to the tragedy was shaped by using photography to bear witness in a manner set up in 1945 following the liberation of the Nazi concentration camps. For more on this, see Barbie Zelizer, "Photography, Journalism, and Trauma," in *Journalism after September 11,* ed. Barbie Zelizer and Stuart Allan (New York: Routledge, 2002); Barbie Zelizer, "Finding Aids to the Past: Bearing Personal Witness to Traumatic Public Events," *Media, Culture and Society* (May 2002): 697–714.

34. The earlier incident, the Triangle Shirtwaist factory fire, occurred in 1911. Approximately fifty people jumped from the building to their death.

35. When interviewed, a Fox News Channel cameraman became teary when he described filming people jumping from the towers. "I stopped," he said, "but I saw 25 more jumping, holding hands, in groups" (Rob Ginnane quoted in "Behind the Camera," *TV Guide,* September 29–October 5, 2001, p. 15).

36. David Westin, president of ABC News, cited in Rutenberg and Barringer, "The Ethics."

37. Bill Wheatley, vice-president of NBC News, cited in Rutenberg and Barringer, "The Ethics."

38. The photo appeared in the *Philadelphia Inquirer,* September 12, 2001, p. A14.

39. The photo appeared in the *Chicago Tribune* on September 12, 2001, p. A12. It was appended to Gene Weingarten and David Von Drehle, "A Death Better Than Fate's," *Washington Post,* September 13, 2001, p. C1.

40. The photo appeared in the *New York Times,* September 12, 2001, p. A12. Pictures of the burning towers appeared on pages A1 and A8. The photo appeared in the *Washington Post* on September 12, 2001, p. A8. A slightly different photo of people jumping, taken by Getty Images, appeared in the *Los Angeles Times,* September 12, 2001, p. A13.

41. *Time,* special September 11 edition, n.p.

42. Reuters was alerted to the people in the shot by a European subscriber who noticed small incongruous blobs on the original larger print. See Valerie Basheda, "An Unforgettable Picture," *American Journalism Review* (October 2001): 27. The photo appeared in the *Boston Globe,* September 12, 2001, p. A8; the *Chicago Tribune,* September 12, 2001, p. A12; the *Washington Post,* September 12, 2001, p. A16 and September 13, 2001, p. C3.

43. *Newsweek,* September 24, 2001, Special Report, n.p.

44. See Alice Tugend, "The Simple Act of Getting to Work Was an Ordeal," *American Journalism Review* (October 2001): 25. The newspapers that ran the photograph included the *New York Times,* the *Detroit News, Newsday,* the *Denver Post,* and the *Philadelphia Inquirer.* The *Washington Post* included a front-page discussion of the bodies jumping (Barton Gellman, "I Saw Bodies Falling Out—Oh God, Jumping, Falling," *Washington Post,* September 12, 2001, p. A1), but the accompanying picture depicted two grieving women holding each other. The Reuters photo of people hanging out of the towers appeared on A16.

45. In one widespread collection of the front pages of newspapers the day after the attacks, not one of 122 national papers showed an image of people about to die on their front pages. See Poynter Institute, *September 11, 2001: A Collection of Newspaper Front Pages Selected by the Poynter Institute* (Kansas City: Andrews McMeel, 2001). The only newspapers in the collection that printed such images on the front page were foreign: Mexico City's *El Universal* showed the Reuters photo of people hanging out of buildings (September 12, 2001, p. A1), and Rio de Janeiro's *O Dia* showed the AP photo of a man falling headfirst to his death under the caption "Desperado" (September 12, 2001, p. A1).

46. See Tugend, "Simple Act of Getting to Work." Also see Rutenberg and Barringer, "The Ethics."

47. The image did appear in *Newsweek,* September 24, 2001, n.p., as a double-

page spread, and a different photo, taken by a photographer for Getty Images, appeared in *Time*'s special issue on September 11. But the image of people jumping did not appear in the regular issues of *Time, Business Week, People,* or *In These Times.*

48. Magnum Photographers, *New York: September 11, 2001; In the Line of Duty* (New York: Regan Books, 2001); and Reuters, *September 11: A Testimony* (Upper Saddle River, NJ: Pearson Education, 2002). In the Reuters volume the Jeff Christiensen shot of people hanging out of the windows was included (p. 13).

49. World Wide Photography and Associated Press, *Day of Terror* (New York: America Products, 2001).

50. Fishman, "Documenting Death."

51. Anonymous comment made at a public viewing of television coverage, University of Pennsylvania, Philadelphia, September 11, 2001.

52. Don Dahler, quoted in "Ground Zero," *TV Guide,* September 29–October 5, 2001, p. 39.

53. See Rutenberg and Barringer, "The Ethics."

54. Ibid.; Tugend, "Simple Act of Getting to Work," 25. By contrast, the *Philadelphia Inquirer* ran a column titled "The Most Horrific Images," in which it did not mention the bodies at all.

55. Cited in Rutenberg and Barringer, "The Ethics."

56. Fishman, "Documenting Death."

57. Deborah Potter, "It Isn't Over," *American Journalism Review* (November 2001): 76.

58. Quoted in "Terror Hits Home," *TV Guide,* September 29–October 5, 2001, p. 10.

59. Personal communication with author.

60. Caryn James, "Live Images Make Viewers Witnesses to Horror," *New York Times,* September 12, 2001, p. A25.

61. Such a representational template, in which sequenced shots showed the buildings being struck by the airplanes and then lit on fire on their way to collapse, was fairly common. The sequence appeared on the front pages of the *Los Angeles Times,* the *Lexington Herald-Leader,* the *Sacramento Bee,* the *Arizona Republic,* the *Tennessean,* the *Denver Post,* and the *Dallas Morning News,* among others.

62. In one widespread collection of front pages the day after the attacks, the burning towers appeared in nearly 85 percent of the newspapers displayed. See Poynter Institute, *September 11, 2001.*

63. The logo stopped appearing in the newspaper on September 16, at which point a similar image of the burning towers appeared on an internal page (p. 24).

64. The burning towers tended to appear on both the covers and multiple internal pages of the popular press. For instance, they appeared on the cover of *In These Times,* October 15, 2001, and again on pages 9 and 10; on the cover of *TV Guide,* under the title "Terror Hits Home," September 29–October 5, 2001, and again on three internal pages (8–9, 10, 18); the cover of *Business Week,* under the title "Act of War," September 24, 2001, and again internally on page 34; on the cover of *People,* under the title "September 11, 2001: The Day That Shook America," September 24, 2001, and again on pages 6–7.

65. They included the covers of Magnum Photographers, *New York: September 11, 2001* (New York: Powerhouse, 2001); World Wide Photography and Associated Press, *Day of Terror;* Editors of *New York* Magazine, *September 11, 2001: A Record of Tragedy, Heroism, and Hope* (New York: Henry N. Abrams, 2001); Ethan Casey, ed., *9:11 8.48 A.M.: Documenting America's Greatest Tragedy* (Booksurge.com, 2001).

66. *Newsweek,* December 31, 2001–January 7, 2002.

67. "The Year in Pictures," *New York Times,* December 31, 2001, sec. G.

68. Reuters, *September 11: A Testimony.* Also see World Wide Photography and Associated Press, *Day of Terror* and Magnum Photos, *New York: September 11, 2001.* In the latter, of the nearly 100 photos, 20 portrayed the burning or smoking towers. In a mnemonic pattern that was common to the memorial volumes, another 12 portrayed the towers before September 11.

69. Some examples included a World Trade Center 2002 Memorial Wall Calendar (Brown Trout Publishers); a Heroes 2002 Wall Calendar (Brown Trout Publishers); and *America 911: We Will Never Forget* (VHS).

70. Colson Whitehead, "The Image," *New York Times Magazine,* September 23, 2001, p. 21.

71. Richard Edward Larsen, "Did Palestinian Boy Die in Vain?" *Ventura County Star,* October 5, 2000, p. B9.

8

"A Timeless Now"
Memory and Repetition
Bradford Vivian

> When the shadow of the sash appeared on the curtains it was between
> seven and eight o'clock and then I was in time again, hearing the watch.
> It was Grandfather's and when Father gave it to me he said I give you
> the mausoleum of all hope and desire; it's rather excruciating-ly apt that
> you will use it to gain the reducto absurdum of all human experience
> which can fit your individual needs no better than it fitted his or his
> father's. I give it to you not that you may remember time, but that you
> might forget it now and then for a moment and not spend all your
> breath trying to conquer it.
>
> William Faulkner, *The Sound and the Fury*

Thus begins Quentin Compson's narrative in William Faulkner's *The Sound
and the Fury,* a literary masterpiece whose true subject, more than any
particular character, may be the poignant influence of memory on the
experiences of its various narrators. Faulkner's story comprises four sections, each with a different narrator, relating the events of four different days. The echoes of the past suffuse the narrative of a given day's
events, as if the nature and meaning of the present only coalesced out of
memory's reverberations. In the epigraph above, Quentin cannot hear
the ticking of his grandfather's watch without remembering his father's
words upon receiving the heirloom. He recalls the elder Compson's lu-
gubrious commentary on the significance of time to one's mortality whenever he touches or thinks of this small but momentous memento, "the

mausoleum of all hope and desire." With this gift, Quentin's father lends prophetic meaning to his son's entire life; his words resound endlessly within Quentin's consciousness, distressing his every passing moment with their gravity. Consequently, Quentin remains acutely aware of the watch's unstoppable progression, which transforms his days into "the reducto absurdum of all human experience": the understanding that time is finite and therefore futile, that even the most carefully measured life will culminate in a timeless end. Despite constant efforts, Quentin never honors his father's admonition, which was not to "remember time" by carrying the watch but to "forget it now and then for a moment and not spend all your breath trying to conquer it." For Quentin, attempting to forget time, to live outside of it, serves only to remind him of time's inevitable consequence, even as he tries to repress his awareness of it. Such repression merely stimulates memory anew while renewing its potency. Quentin wanders in and out of his own past and present according to the repeated interplay of time forgotten and the rush of memory this forgetting provokes.

The senses of time and memory in *The Sound and the Fury* are not explicitly public. In many ways, they are intensely personal and even resistant to public articulation. The virtuosity of Faulkner's novel derives from its invocation of a traumatic and haunting memoryscape that encompasses the consciousness of the primary narrative perspectives. Yet a "fictional technique," Jean-Paul Sartre wrote in an essay on *The Sound and the Fury*, "always relates back to the novelist's metaphysics." While Faulkner's work offers no explicit meditation on *public* memory, it nevertheless dramatizes what Sartre called "a metaphysics of time"—a system of values and ideals concerning the interrelated meaning of past, present, and future—which allows for reconsideration of the assumptions upon which the study of public memory is often based.[1]

Repetition offers the most provocative organizing principle of such metaphysics. Olga W. Vickery observes that although the four sections of *The Sound and the Fury* "appear quite unrelated," they do "repeat certain incidents and are concerned with the same problem," namely, the plight of the oldest Compson sibling, Caddy. "Thus," Vickery elaborates, "with respect to the plot the four sections are inextricably connected, but with respect to the central situation they are distinct and self-sufficient. As related to the central focus, each of the first three sections presents a version of the same facts which is at once the truth and a complete distortion of the truth."[2] Vickery's account suggests that the complex truth of memories depends on the distortions of repeated acts of recollection as much as any original or authentic perception. In this context, according to Cleanth Brooks, "the sense of enlightenment" that the novel produces "comes simply from the fact that we are traversing the same territory in circling movements."[3] The novel's repetition of frequently cryptic and disjointed recollections, its "circling movements," paradoxically induces a sense of lucidity and linearity, a kind of "enlightenment."

What is being repeated here? Is the original truth, meaning, or event somehow preserved through repetition or merely the value and pathos with which it is invested? Is the defining function of memory to preserve a truth when that truth may be engendered only by its "distortion," by mnemonic mutations inherent in every attempt to narrate the past? To what extent is the apparent lucidity, linearity, and perdurance of memory related to the fundamentally incoherent, fragmentary, and ephemeral nature of recollection? To what extent, moreover, does memory depend on forgetting, on a repeated inducement of amnesia like the kind that Quentin's father prescribes to his son? And in what manner does further meditation on the centrality of repetition to memory warrant closer inspection of the privileged ideals of public memory studies, including the objectivity of the past, its conformity with historical representation, and the ability to express memory in a normative or canonical form?

In what follows, I address these questions by attending to the different senses of repetition evident in a mode of collective memory apparently foreign to conventional Western forms of public commemoration. In order to do so, I turn in the next section from Faulkner's temporal metaphysics to a set of cultural practices that exemplify such metaphysics in the formation of collective memory. Specifically, I draw from a variety of studies focusing on Eastern European Gypsies in order to scrutinize the defining features of their collective memory. Gypsy collective memories exhibit a sense of time, memory, and community dramatically different from Western forms of public commemoration. The Gypsies' contrasting commemorative ideals are exemplified by their distinctive embrace of memory *work,* of the ritualized making and remaking of memory—in a word, of *repetition*—rather than its comparatively static and institutional-ized outcome: the codification of public memory central to Western com-memorative traditions. As such, I propose to augment the very concept of public memory by surveying the emergence and transformation of collec-tive memories that do not aspire to the iconic authority so often denoted by civic monuments or memorials but are nevertheless crucial to the maintenance of a given community and its heritage. The following, then, situates the concept of public memory in a broader and more sugges-tive frame of reference by surveying the dynamic relationships among memory, repetition, and collective life among Eastern European Gypsies. I intend to demonstrate that consideration of these dynamic relationships, far from amounting to a detour around the question of public memory, is essential to provoking further dialogue about its nature.

In order to conduct this demonstration, I argue that collective or public memories function *nomadically*. Like Quentin Compson, we wander about in the landscape of memory. We may remember the same events over and over again, but we remember them according to fluctuating conditions, in different times and places, in response to changing needs and desires. Acts of recollection invariably transform the nature of memory because memory's changing incitements and purposes ensure that we remember in different ways, even if we remember the same event. Rather than pre-serving an identical meaning or truth, the modes of repetition by which memory emerges and endures in the service of diverse social interests imbue it with inevitable mutations. Collective or public memory is inher-ently nomadic because it encompasses a mnemonic landscape comprised not of stability but ongoing redistribution or, better still, *re*-membering.

The following consideration of repetition in the enactment of public memory contributes far more to memory studies than mere semantic dis-tinctions. Observing such concepts in practice, I am convinced, allows one to apprehend the ethical and political dynamics inherent in memory work, though not with the intention of establishing a normative ethical and po-litical prescription. The claim that public memory is often (if not always) socially contested, and therefore politically inflected, is hardly novel. In a fundamental sense, public memory is *political* memory. Yet ethical and po-litical prescriptions modeled on privileged forms of memory tend to sug-gest correct and incorrect ways to remember (not to mention correct and incorrect ways to forget) and therefore make themselves available for the founding of mnemonic dogma. Such dogma is sometimes aggressively enforced when various social groups contest the normative codes of a public memory. The analysis to come, however, reveals that public memory is most productively evaluated on the basis of categories other than simple right and wrong, accurate or inaccurate. Instead of reducing memory to either one of these categories, I offer an account of the formative and transformational influence of repetition on public memory that mnemonic dogma would suppress. By surveying the nomadic interplay of authenticity and forgery or continuity and discontinuity from which memory emerges, this essay seeks to apprehend the formative ethical and political conditions by which public memory is engendered instead of endorsing a privileged commemorative ethics or politics. In sum, the essay interrogates memory's debt to repetition by exploring both the processes of remembering that take place in forgetting and the sort of amnesia upon which even the most hegemonic or transparent memories are based.

The Permanent Present

Public memory scholars have long recognized the fundamental relationships among place, historical memory, and the maintenance of community. In a Western frame, communities cohere around the formation of a civic domain, and their history unfolds according to its maintenance. These relationships among place, history, and community assume a different character in the context of Gypsy collective memory. Some scholars believe the Gypsies became itinerant not by choice but because they were repeatedly driven away from whatever land they had come to occupy.[4] Today, in the volatile topography of post-Communist Eastern Europe, this trend continues.[5] The Gypsies' perpetually displaced status leaves them without proven ethnic and geographic origins, despite compelling circumstantial evidence tying them to northern India.[6] How does one preserve and profess the distinctive character of one's people without recourse to a transparent civic origin, a common commemorative grounding?

Ceremonial professions of a common cultural identity contribute to its renewal. This process of cultural renewal is maintained through the repetition of collective rituals that preserve a given unity of memory, place, and community. Such unity depends for its preservation on the authority of an unmediated historical origin. The authority of this origin governs the coherence of collective memory in its historical unfolding. Cultural reproduction so conceived personifies the Platonic logic of an ideal model approximated by a lineage of diminished copies, for what is repeated is always the same: the ideal and original form that transcends the mottle of every repetition and retains its essence in doing so. Repetition as such, in Gilles Deleuze's words, occurs "in relation to something unique or singular which has no equal or equivalent. This is the apparent paradox of festivals: they repeat an 'unrepeatable'. They do not add a second and a third time to the first, but carry the first time to the 'nth' power."[7] The festival commemorates an origin through ceremonial repetition, thereby preserving its sense and value, while the origin, which cannot be repeated but merely symbolized in memory, transcends the very ritual, the repetition, that renews its power and dominion.

Despite whatever conflicting testimony they might provide, the Gypsies lack the unity of memory, place, and community that would legitimate such a repetition—and thus preservation—of their culture. Here I do not wish to suggest that specific places are unimportant to Gypsies as the loci of memory. Instead, I wish to underscore the absence of an ideal and original place with respect to Gypsy memories: the lack of a transparent spatial and temporal origin to which the Gypsies can trace the rise of their people and preserve their culture through its ritual commemoration. In Angus Fraser's estimation, "If a people is a group of men, women and children with a common language, a common culture and a common racial type, who can be readily distinguished from their neighbors, it is a long time since the Gypsies were that."[8]

The Gypsies' lack of an objective origin likely explains the instability of myth as an organizing principle of their culture. "Gypsies have no myths about the beginning of the world," Isabel Fonseca explains, "or about their own origins; they have no sense of a great historical past. Very often their memories do not extend beyond three or four generations."[9] Michael Stewart highlights the radical juxtaposition between Judeo-Christian notions of time and remembrance—poetically figured in Walter Benjamin's vision of "an angel of history, with his face turned toward the past, helplessly observing the debris of historical events as it accumulates skyward"—and the dramatically different Gypsy experience of passing time: "For the Gypsies, there is no history, nor is there a past to be redeemed. They live with their gaze fixed on a permanent present that is always becoming, a timeless now in which their continued existence as Rom is all that counts."[10] The Gypsies possess their distinctive histories and memories because they forget and therefore continually reinvent them, not because they remember the past in a canonical or uniform sense. Gypsies do not repeat the past in order to remember; they forget the past in order to repeat its mythic invention. A given repetition, an ostensible reproduction of Gypsy culture, repeats only the novelty of "a timeless now." For the Gypsies, that is, the inconstancy of the present does not emerge from the stability of an easily retrievable past; according to their sense of history and memory, the past only comes into being as it suits the changing needs and desires of the present.

Gypsies regard the archives of official memory, with their stores of authoritative documents, as barren edifices. The Gypsy taboo against writing, against documentation, is illustrated by the story of Papusza, who, according to Fonseca, was "one of the greatest Gypsy singers and poets ever and, for a while, one of the most celebrated."[11] But when Papusza wrote down some of her poems and allowed them to be published by the Polish poet Jerzy Ficowski in 1950, her people soon turned on her.[12] Fonseca explains that there are no Gypsy words for "to write" or "to read"; "Gypsies borrow from other languages to describe these activities."[13] Gypsy culture is largely maintained by the unfettered license of their oral practices, which remain open to constant embellishment and revision. Writing is nonsensical to the Gypsies and carries a stigma of arresting or pinning down. They have no use for graphic memory, for a transparent public record. Thus, "Papusza was put on trial" and with "little deliberation, she was proclaimed *mahrime* (or *magherdi* among Polish Roma), unclean: the punishment was irreversible exclusion from the group."[14] Committing Gypsy narratives to writing objectifies the memories they dramatize by establishing a fixed interpretation of the past. Many Gypsies would regard the civic archive as a house of dead letters. Hence, Papusza's crime was to reduce the distinctive repetition of Gypsy culture, a repetition of difference and mutation, into a repetition of the same, of an official document.

The Gypsies are remarkable storytellers, despite a lack of empirical evidence or coherent memory concerning their origins. Although they purport to account for such origins, Gypsy folktales often raise more questions about the past than they answer. Konrad Bercovici recorded a rendition of perhaps the best known such tale by Macedonian Gypsies in the 1920s.[15] Legend has it that Roman soldiers went looking for black-smiths to forge the nails that would be used in the crucifixion of Jesus Christ. After two Jewish blacksmiths and a Syrian refused to make the nails for this purpose, a Gypsy apparently agreed to do so. The soldiers com-missioned four nails, but before the last nail cooled they rushed out of the Gypsy's tent (recall that Jesus was crucified with only three nails). No matter how much water the Gypsy poured on the fiery nail, it continued to glow; no matter where or with whom he left it, the nail followed him. Thus, the legend concludes, "[T]hat nail always appears in the tents of the descendents of the man who forged the nails for the crucifixion of Yeshua ben Miriam. And when the nail appears, the Gypsies run. It is why they move from one place to another."[16]

Three features of this legend in particular deserve commentary because they illustrate the distinctive characteristics of Gypsy folktales in general. First, its apparent account of the Gypsies' nomadic ways actually accounts for very little; the Gypsy in the story is named as a Gypsy, so it begs the question as to how his people came to be even as it purports to ex-plain their creation. Second, the symbolism of the nail is certainly evoca-tive; because it is not a Christian folktale, however, one wonders what exactly it means. Why is this essentially biblical account of any importance to the Gypsies? Third, the elliptical nature of this legend reflects its sus-ceptibility to adaptation. When Fonseca rehearsed the tale for modern-day Macedonian and Bulgarian Gypsies, she learned that some characters had changed over time to include Communist dictators from those regions. Like all myths, the story lends itself to variations in which the general plot stays the same while particular elements are revised; but *unlike* most other myths, the story is characterized by a paucity of information concern-ing the history and genealogy it is supposed to preserve. Indeed, the Gypsy in the story, its presumed main character, is introduced almost as an afterthought. As such, the tale invokes not the authenticity of the Gyp-sies' origins, but a simulacrum thereof.

This simulacrum, which distinguishes so many Gypsy narratives, belies the fact that Gypsies lack a common sense of identity and thus of culture and memory. To be sure, I am not claiming that Gypsy communities evince no sense at all of a defining identity, culture, or memory; recalling his time among Hungarian Gypsies, Stewart writes, "For them, identity was neither primordial nor essential, though it was no less deeply felt for that."[17] My purpose, rather, is to highlight the fragmented and dispersed mnemonic *conditions*—the lack of a transcendent origin, the distrust of archival memory, the highly mutable and often elliptical nature of cultural folktales—that prevent Gypsy identity, culture, or memory from achieving the stable or uniform sense and value that such phenomena acquire in Western communities.

Romani, the language of the Gypsies, imperfectly reflects the long and complex chronology of such fragmentation and dispersion. Because the Gypsies keep no records of events, Romani provides crucial clues about the Gypsies' wanderings throughout the landscape of history. Scholars have identified a number of ancient Indian roots in Romani, along with several Persian elements, a smattering of Turkish words, a peppering of Armenian, and many Greek components dating back to the Byzantine Empire.[18] The sheer variety of Gypsy dialects sprouting from these diverse linguistic seeds offers an index of the Gypsies' difficulty in forging and professing the transparent ethos of identity, culture, and memory so esteemed in the Western tradition. According to Jean-Pierre Liegeois, "There is no single word for 'Gypsy' in all Romany dialects. In some dialects, the word 'Rom' is a noun meaning 'Gypsy', its plural being 'Roma.' But not all Gypsies call themselves Roma, and to complicate matters there is a sub-group of Gypsies who do call themselves Rom (in the singular and plural alike), but use the designation to set themselves off from other Gypsy groups."[19] Simply put, the meaning of being Gypsy resists signification: as a group, Gypsies lack a proper name and therefore a proper history—a unified memory. In light of such lacunae, some scholars even contend that it makes no sense to refer to the Gypsies as a common cultural group. Gypsy culture and memory thus lack that which is so essential to the Western tradition: a transcendent logos. At best, the Gypsies can only aspire to the semblance of such logos and the authenticity it confers on their shared identity and collective memories.

Consequently, the collective memories of Gypsies are often derived not from an essential and unbroken heritage, but from the slander of outsiders. Much of the familiar lore about Gypsies purports that they are liars and swindlers by trade. Gypsy stereotypes "of wanton women, of carrion-eaters, and even those among them who had a 'relish for human flesh' "[20] can be found in European folklore from medieval times through the early modern periods. The lingering memory of such tales accounts, in large part, for the Gypsies' continued persecution today. Gypsies, however, seldom offer a competing narrative, a countermemory, in response to such folklore. On the contrary, the oral culture of Gypsies and the slander of outsiders throughout the centuries have come to appear like different sides of the same tapestry: identifying where one ends and the other begins would be impossible. Perhaps this common tapestry helps explain the legend of the Gypsy blacksmith, a time-honored, though dubious, folktale in which the forefather of one's people participates in the death of another culture's central religious figure.

Mimicry and adaptation have always been principles of Gypsy survival. According to Fonseca, "When they first appeared in Europe in the fourteenth century, the Gypsies presented themselves as pilgrims and told fortunes: two winning professions in a superstitious age. Their leaders called themselves Counts and Princes and Captains. These were not expressions of Gypsy values so much as further evidence of their (often underemployed) talent for adopting local moods and hierarchies in order to sustain their ever-precarious prestige."[21] Rather than demanding recognition for a unique and unbroken heritage, Gypsies often sustain their communities by testifying to the authenticity of a counterfeit heritage. The public pronouncement by Yugoslavian Gypsies, in the late 1980s, of an ancient Egyptian ancestry exemplifies the political utility of such mnemonic forgery. Wim Willems explains that when the Serbs came to power after the fall of the Soviet Union, the so-called Yugo-Egyptians reached back to "reclaim an old, alternative identity."[22] This declaration of an alleged Egyptian heritage provided the Gypsies with an alternative fate to either assimilation or expulsion; as "Yugo-Egyptians," they were able to contend that their ancient Egyptian heritage must be protected. That they supposedly reclaimed this ancestry by appropriating Westerners' habitual, though erroneous, attribution of an Egyptian past to the Gypsies (a misconception phonetically crystallized in the very term "Gypsy") was likely no accident. The opportunism of Gypsy collective memories dramatizes James Young's distinction between collective and *collected* memories: the nature of Gypsy memories, that is, draws attention to the material *accumulation* of memory in the face of changing social and political exigencies rather than its ostensibly institutionalized and transhistorical manifestation.[23]

Insofar as they claim to be unburdened by the past, the Gypsies' very lack of a coherent and unified historical consciousness enables them to adapt to the burdens of the present. Such adaptation, however, carries a heavy price, namely, the indifference of many Gypsy communities to political organization, despite repeated persecution. To be sure, certain Gypsy organizations have initiated nationalist and human rights movements in recent decades. These organizations have even established archives and museums housing Gypsy art, history, and folklore, especially in Eastern Europe. But without the consolidating power of a shared past, without the sense of meaning and destiny signified by common memories, a transnational and politically viable Gypsy consciousness has yet to emerge.

Indeed, Gypsy communities often lack a collective investment in the evidentiary power of the past—a manifest politics of remembrance, in other words. Traditionally, the Gypsies only exist as they do because they forget. Apparently, not even the horrors of the Holocaust could induce a lasting commemorative consciousness in Gypsy culture. The Gypsies were the first population slated for extermination by the Nazis specifically on the basis of their race, and they suffered the loss of a higher percentage of their people than any other such population.[24] Fonseca reports that Polish Gypsy survivors of what they call the *porraimos,* or "the devouring," today expend minimal effort attempting to pass on collective memories of the Nazis' genocidal programs. "The Second World War and its traumas are certainly within memory," she writes, "but there is no tradition of commemoration, or even discussion."[25] So dominating is the influence of what Stewart calls "the timeless now" on the Gypsies' commemorative economy that many find no benefit in reliving their harrowing past.

Again, this is not to deny that certain Gypsy organizations have taken measures to preserve evidence, and thus memory, of the Nazi atrocities against Gypsies in select archives and museums. Despite the scattered preservation of memory as such, the whole of Gypsy culture has, for one reason or another, evinced little ability or aspiration to establish a uniform memory of their wartime past. A simple contrast makes the point: unlike the monumental relationship that Jewish Holocaust survivors have established with that past, the massive symbolic weight of which has quite literally been concretized again and again in their many public memorials, the Gypsies are collectively tethered to the same unspeakable events by little more than a diaphanous gauze of remembrances.[26] Rather than modeling their communal ethic and social agenda on a continuity between past and present, Gypsies traditionally have placed a premium on breaking with the past as a means of escaping its trials.[27] This Gypsy proclivity for forgetting, however, should not be interpreted as a form of resignation. Such forgetting nonetheless represents a certain politics of re-membering, albeit a politics invested in something far more fragmented and transitory than a democratic consensus sanctioned by a uniform moral interpretation of the past. "Among Roma," Fonseca writes, "forgetting does not imply complacency: its tenor is one of—sometimes buoyant—defiance."[28]

Perhaps this defiance in forgetting appears less complacent when compared with the obstacles other Gypsies have faced while working for recognition of the *porraimos* in international Holocaust commemorations. True to their legendary flair for adaptation, the Gypsy "art of forgetting," as Fonseca puts it, suggests a political response to a democratic politics of memory, which, in laboring to remember the past so as not to repeat it, reproduces familiar forms of exclusion by endowing particular kinds of memory with political priority. Consider: not one Gypsy was called to testify in the Nuremburg Trials; since World War II ended only one Nazi has been convicted for crimes of genocide against Gypsies; those Gypsies who petitioned the United States Holocaust Memorial Council for involvement and representation in its museum met with prolonged resistance and dubious results; and violence against Gypsies has only increased in the newly democratic regions of post-Communist Eastern Europe. Surely all these facts and more serve as warrants for at least some Gypsies' defiant forgetting, if this is what a democratic politics, presumably committed to the equitable representation of diverse commemorative interests, will make of memory.[29] In short, perhaps the fact that the Gypsies' victimization prior to, during, and after the Holocaust is so little remembered by those democratic alliances pledged to the preservation of its fatal lessons is proof enough that Western institutions habitually mistake a necessarily partial and privileged account of the past for its transparent and universal truth. Whereas Gypsy collective memories are sustained by the repetition of *difference,* by an investment in the politics of forgetting and the incorporation of new mnemonic elements, traditional Western forms of public memory remain invested in a repetition of *the same,* in a transcendent mnemonic logos whose pretensions to transparency and universality obscure its fundamental debt to partisan commemorative values and politics.

Despite their reputation for wanderlust, the nomadic travels of Eastern European Gypsies were dramatically and sometimes violently curtailed during the twentieth century. In countries like Czechoslovakia, for instance, the Gypsies were forced to settle and assimilate under the Communist regime. Following these events, romantic tales of a bucolic Gypsy life in which, as Konrad Bercovici muses, "[t]he Gypsy has locked himself out of the gates of modern civilization and roams freely on the highways and byways of the world" could not be more misleading.[30] Stewart advises, "Forget romantic notions of the careless freedoms of caravans and campfires; the Gypsies' lives were hard and sometimes brutal."[31] The sudden eruptions of ethnic hatred in post-Communist Eastern Europe form a tragic contrast with such "romantic notions."[32]

Yet in the landscape of memory the Gypsies remain essentially nomadic. Rather than a repetition of the same, of static and transparent recollections, Gypsy memories are engendered by the continual repetition of difference, "a timeless now" in which the Gypsy past is solicited and revised according to the changing needs and desires of the present. The eternal recurrence of this timeless now is even symbolized on the Gypsy flag in the figure of a wheel—the emblem of a people whose only unifying past is invoked by their travels away from it, and in every repetition of their culture, of its apparent sameness, difference returns, eternally.

Forgetting to Remember

Regardless of the seemingly alien nature of their commemorative practices, one would be mistaken in regarding the Gypsies' collective memories as inconsequential to more conventional discussions of public memory. To the contrary, Gypsy collective memories prompt one to question whether even the most transparent or monolithic memories are engendered by the very obfuscation of memory. In order to pursue this notion with greater clarity, I turn now to an additional disciplinary perspective on the relationship between memory and repetition that will enable further reconsideration of the premises and values central to conventional conceptions of public memory.

Although it concerns individual memories, psychologist John Kotre's research on autobiographical memory provides yet another instructive demonstration of the metaphysics of time and memory that I have been surveying throughout this essay, specifically according to the trope of repetition.[33] One might even say that Kotre's work on autobiographical memory amounts to a dispersion of individual memory as such and an affirmation of its inherently collective and nomadic character. By drawing from some of the terminology featured in his research, I plan to more explicitly define the principles of repetition inherent to the formation of memory and its ensuing nomadic capacities.

Kotre posits that we often remember not on the basis of stable and transparent recollections, but by virtue of a kind of amnesia. A "commonplace" phenomenon known as cryptomnesia refers to recollections in which "you remember *what* someone told you but you forget *that* you were told."[34] Our most intimate memories often function as the mediations of others' recollections and are shaped by processes of forgetting: "[A]n individual starts to remember what he heard in a hallway conversation or a group meeting, but he forgets where he heard it, and even that he heard it. An old idea becomes his original creation."[35] Renowned psychologist Jean Piaget once wrote that he grew up with a vivid memory of narrowly escaping a kidnapping when he was two years old. During his childhood and adolescence, he could recall his nurse heroically fending off the would-be kidnapper. Piaget even recalled that his nurse's face was scratched during the attack. The nurse, however, wrote to Piaget's parents when he was fifteen and admitted that the story was fabricated.[36] Citing this anecdote, Kotre observes: "The clarity with which Piaget had seen the event in his memory, and the personal conviction that he had about its truth, was no proof that it ever happened."[37] Amazingly, even the visceral clarity of memories relating to personal trauma, which would appear to preserve the experience of an unmediated event, belies the fact that such memories may well exist in a state of translation, of migration, from one locus of memory to another. "Because of cryptomneisa," Kotre concludes, "it's possible to believe that a picture actually planted in your memory by a photograph, a film, or someone else's words originated in a direct experience of your own. Nor can you tell if a memory has been cryptically implanted by the way it looks or feels. Unreal memories look and feel like real ones."[38] Perhaps this account even warrants consideration of whether or not categories such as "real" and "unreal" prevent a deeper understanding of memory's nomadic character, of its formation and function as it is adapted from one context to another.

According to Kotre, cryptomnesia is only one form of the mnemonic "reconstruction" present in every act of recollection: "[M]emories don't sit inertly in our minds the way they do on an audiotape or the shelves of a library," he says. "They are constantly refashioned."[39] The irony here is profound: the memories from which we derive our most fundamental sense of self may simulate the memories of others, attain a significance completely altered from their "original" import, and even refer to a different time and place than they once did. Indeed, the vividness and coherence of such reconstructed memories are predicated upon scattered instances of amnesia. Memory, rather than repeating an ideal and original impression ad infinitum, rather than repeating *the same* or an "unrepeatable" event, is engendered and preserved by mutation—a repetition that generates memory precisely through a series of mnemonic differences and transformations. In Faulkner's *The Sound and the Fury,* Quentin Compson's efforts to forget the defining episodes of his past merely stimulate his memories anew, renewing their potency and lending them new sites of investment. Gypsy collective memories indicate that forgetting encompasses an essential aspect of memory's production rather than its repression or erosion. Together with Kotre's insights, these examples demonstrate that various gaps in memory and the processes of reconstruction they engender are not exceptions to memory but one of its formative principles.

Is it proper, then, to say that memories *exist?* "Where is the great Cartesian Theater," Kotre asks, "the place where the chemical messengers of memory become actors before our mind's eye?"[40] Memories "exist" in a state of dispersion rather than unity or stability. Depending on the age and significance of a memory, the activation of it will involve several areas of the brain, a host of neuronal firings, and any combination of senses. Whenever we discuss our memories with others, record them in letters, diaries, and other texts, or preserve them with images or sound, we have activated the fickle and nomadic character of memory, ensuring that it will exist in more than one place and form. The memories of Benjy Compson, the first narrator of *The Sound and the Fury,* consist of only a few traumatic fragments, repeatedly invoked by the smell of trees, the voices of golfers teeing up on the course across from his house, or the feel of his sister's worn and dirty slipper. Quentin's recollections, like those of his brother Benjy, do not lie dormant in some fixed cognitive nook but are stimulated by the sound of his father's watch, the smell of honeysuckle, or the sight of his own shadow. Memories, like the Gypsies, lack a proper home—a stable ground or origin. Instead of unity, they connote radical multiplicity. Recall, for instance, how the different narrative perspectives of Faulkner's novel are suffused by the same cluster of incessantly repeated memories, each narrator "traversing the same territory in circling movements," to use Brooks's description. "The families, neighborhoods, and nations that envelop us," Kotre muses, "all have memories of their own that transcend any one individual's. So do the memories in the vast cultures we call Art and Science and Religion. We grow up in the context of collective memory, and over the course of life we breathe it in and breathe it out."[41] Thus, the memories of individuals, collectivities, or even entire cultures evince an inherent capacity to subsist in multiple forms and appearances.

How does this multiplicity influence the formation of *public* memory? Public memories, and the hegemonic ethos they often attain, are engendered by and embodied in the individual recollections of those whose personal memory work contributes to the conglomeration of such communal, religious, or even national memories. According to Young, "A society's memory . . . might be regarded as an aggregate collection of its members' many, often competing memories. If societies remember, it is only insofar as their institutions and rituals organize, shape, even inspire their constituents' memories. For a society's memory cannot exist outside of those people who do the remembering—even if such memory happens to be at the society's bidding, in its name."[42] In this regard, an official site of public memory—a monument, an archive, or sacred ground—represents not the static container of such memory, but the dynamic reference point for the diverse memory work that sustains it, the commemorative nexus formed at the intersection of a public's many mnemonic practices.

Kotre's research, in addition to the examples of memory I have traced throughout this essay, warrants the conclusion that memories are not chosen, possessed, or preserved by individuals or publics, at least not in the conventional senses of those terms. However transparently and intimately they may appear to open an unmediated window onto the past, such memories confirm that, as in Gypsy communities, the fragmentation and discontinuity of memory is not simply coincidental, but elemental, to its formation. Nevertheless, individuals as well as publics derive their sense of identity by attempting to remember with continuity, to symbolically or discursively fashion a meaningful relation between the past and present, precisely by virtue of this mnemonic discontinuity and alterity that forms what Kotre calls "the immense ecosystem" of memory.[43]

From this vantage, Gypsy collective memories do not exhibit commemorative phenomena fundamentally different from conventional Western forms of public commemoration. Kotre and other researchers compel us to acknowledge that the very authenticity and continuity of memory, Gypsy or otherwise, derive from the incorporation of disparate and fragmentary recollections that refer to no certain referent, only discontinuity. Is it possible, then, that even the most traditional forms of public memory serve as disguises of a collective cryptomnesia? Inspired by Robert Musil's conviction that "[t]here is nothing in this world as invisible as a monument,"[44] Young observes that "once we assign monumental form to memory, we have to some degree divested ourselves of the obligation to remember."[45] The abiding expression of Western public memory according to such forms suggests how widely and officially sanctioned this cryptomnesia may be.

To what extent is the study of public memory, which is guided (not exclusively but often enough) by the careful separation of fact from fiction, of vernacular from official, of past from present, prepared to affirm memory's daunting complexity and account for the politics of forgetting intrinsic to processes of remembering? Based on the accounts of memory featured in this essay, I would like to suggest that evaluating public memories according to whether or not they accurately represent the past, or even aspire to a transparent communication of its meanings or lessons, indicates an investment in analytical principles contrary to the formation and perdurance of memory itself. My dispute here is not with the preservationist ethic that motivates a good deal of public memory scholarship; instead, I would like to question the forms of mnemonic enforcement sometimes established in the name of that ethic. Preserving the past by insisting on an essential public memory, on correct and incorrect ways to remember, or even on the representation of a seemingly progressive universal lesson, hinders the production of memory by reducing its inherent susceptibility to the forms of reconstruction—the memory work—by which public memories are adapted to changing needs and desires. Reducing public memory to the repetition of a static, ideal image of the past and domesticating it in a proper home, in other words, elides the fact that even the most hegemonic public memories are engendered by the nomadic and perpetually unfinished memory work of various groups and individuals. Gypsy collective memories most explicitly invoke this feature of public memory in general: without a capacity for variation, such memories would not "exist." Or, more specifically, such memories depend for their relevance and coherence on some principle of modification, perhaps even distortion.

Hence, public memory studies must value the nomadic character of public memory by cultivating its abundant relevance to diverse social interests, not its allegedly essential and unchanging content or meaning. One cultivates the capacity of public memories to accommodate such diverse interests by affirming that collective memory suffuses and continually transforms the temper of social life in the present, by recognizing its aptitude for new sites of application and the establishment of new social relationships—"as a basis for political and social action," in Young's terms.[46] Regarding memory as a repetition of difference rather than a repetition of the same, that is, enables one to value the productive capacities of forgetting and mutation elemental to even the most monumental forms of public memory.

Does an affirmation of the amnesia and reconstruction inherent in public memory legitimate *any* conceivable memory, no matter how contrary to existing memories or the historical record? What ethical and political entailments accompany such an affirmation? Should all public memories be equally valued or be certified as equally authentic? Simply put, does mnemonic reconstruction in the context of public memory amount to irresponsible or even dangerous historical revisionism?

Of course, public memories must be evaluated according to ethical and political criteria. Not any memory will do. I am not advocating a reduction of memory to the category of fiction.[47] I hope to have demonstrated that memories are nomadic, not in the sense of being infinitely unbounded but because they are maintained by a variety of material practices, by a historically determined range of mnemonic conditions. These practices, the ongoing memory work that manifests the social and political relevance or utility of particular memories to a given community, are never invented ex nihilo. They are elicited, rather, by mnemonic conditions that shape what can be publicly remembered and how. Even countermemories, such as those of the Gypsies who trace their heritage to the archetypes of other cultures, derive their social and political significance from existing mnemonic conditions, from established forms of public memory. The erection and maintenance of public memory, therefore, often involves considerable labor, borne of constraint rather than fancy. In this frame, the ethical and political implications of collective or public memories must be measured by the quality of the social relationships established or sustained through their expression rather than the transcendent truth or undiminished authenticity of memory itself. "Instead of stopping at formal questions, or at issues of historical referentiality," Young posits, "we must go on to ask how memorial representations of history may finally weave themselves into the course of ongoing events."[48]

The labor of memory as such, I argue, invokes the repetition of forgetting as much as the repetition of a static memory. Or, rather, every attempt to preserve a static memory, in whatever form, occurs in relation to some form of forgetting. To attest that a memory is engendered and maintained according to an essential unity is to forget the inherent partiality and mutability, the intrinsically nomadic character, of any recollection. Memories are neither forgotten nor preserved: the labor of memory requires forgetting, and the act of forgetting makes possible new memories.

Affirming public memory as such requires an affirmation of public forgetting. Assigning this value to forgetting admittedly runs counter to traditional Western conceptions of memory. Perhaps the familiar injunction that we must not forget the past so as not to repeat it tells only half the story. This injunction treats forgetting as the negative of remembering, as an irretrievable subtraction from a complete and objective apprehension of the past. Memory as such is ideal and original, perfect and unmediated; it is God's memory, not ours. No matter how divine, no matter how constant and immaculate a public memory may appear, there is no such memory without collective memory work, without the material practices that engender the transparent ethos of such memories and sustain their social value and utility. The two forms of mnemonic repetition surveyed in this essay—repetition of a static, uniform memory and repetition of the differences or transformations essential to the evolution of memory itself—are not antithetical. Even those public memories that announce themselves with an apparently homogeneous voice are merely the aggregation of multiple and mercurial recollections.

There is more at stake here than a simple opposition between static or uniform memories and those subject to mutation or fragmentation. Public memories, with their pretensions of permanence and uniformity, are engendered by something distinctly un-public: the disparate memory work of collectivities and even individuals. This is not to say that public memories never attain an ethos of objectivity, uniformity, or permanence; indeed, many do. Instead, I would like to emphasize that such memories derive their monumental ethos from the codification of multiple commemorative practices, from the manifold memory work that sustains it. *In principle,* if not in appearance, public memories attain their sense of objectivity, uniformity, or permanence by virtue of partiality, fragmentation, and forgetting. The question here concerns not a choice between wholly unified and essentially fragmented memories, but an affirmation that public memory is established, even preserved, by virtue of acts of forgetting and that acts of forgetting simultaneously make possible the establishment and preservation of collective and public memories.

To say that even the most monumental memories ultimately lack an essential home or transparent origin is one way of underscoring the fundamental difficulty of defining memory according to fixed categories: as *categorically* public, collective, or private. Far from amounting to a tangential issue, the imbrication of collective and individual memory within public commemoration holds considerable explanatory force for the study of public memory in general. Such study, however, would be concerned not solely with the authenticity of public memory, but with the discursive practices, the diverse memory work, through which public memories attain their rhetoric of authenticity as well as their hegemonic ethos. "Public," "collective," and "private" refer less to essential mnemonic categories and more to the different senses by which memory is distinguished throughout its nomadic life span.

Faulkner's *The Sound and the Fury,* like Gypsy collective memories, suggests that memories are most at home when they travel. Benjy, the handicapped Compson sibling and the novel's first narrator, has erected what might be called a monument, which the novel's other characters refer to as his graveyard. The humble memorial consists of two blue glass bottles containing withered jimsonweed, located in the yard of the Compson house. Curiously, this public memorial symbolizes an impenetrably private meaning: the graveyard undoubtedly anchors Benjy's loosely connected memories of his estranged sister, Caddy, but none of the other members of the household comprehend its exact meaning. Despite the vagueness of their public symbolism, Benjy treats the least disturbance of these markers as a traumatic personal violation.

Vickery observes that this intense effort to preserve the past ideally and originally shapes Benjy's general awareness of the relationship between memory and the present, resulting in "an inflexible pattern which he defends against novelty or change with every bellow in his overgrown body."[49] By treating novelty and change as the antitheses of memory, by insisting on the repeated invocation of an original and unmediated memory, one risks the onset of mnemonic atrophy. "It is not that the bottle has any intrinsic value for Benjy," Vickery continues, "but merely that it forms part of the pattern which must not be disturbed."[50] Like the jimsonweed in Benjy's memorial, the memory itself has withered. Benjy's personal mnemonic dogma has reduced the ductility of such memory to a calcified husk. This unyielding effort to preserve an authentic memory inevitably results in an unwanted act of forgetting, for it sacrifices the robust and suggestive meaning of the memorial to preserve its rigid commemorative form, its pallid and inflexible mnemonic pattern. When this sacrosanct pattern is disturbed, when novelty and change defile Benjy's ideal and original memory, as they always will, he is "momentarily shocked into silence . . . overwhelmed with horror and agony."[51] The fossilization of memory results in an incapacitation, or even dissolution, of the one who remembers. Memory withers and the self is paralyzed when memory's nomadic character, its susceptibility to novelty and change, is denied.

Benjy's trauma over the least disturbance of his memorial suggests the importance of distinguishing between *what* publics remember and *how* they remember it. Dictating how collectivities should remember, uniformly and authentically, amounts to the erection of a public memory whose authority does violence to more than an isolated interpretation of the past. Such commemorative dogma restricts the ability of certain groups and individuals to sustain their communities by virtue of the collective memory work that defines them and according to which they vie for public valuation of their professed heritage. By emphasizing only what is remembered, what is preserved, one risks neglecting the momentous ethical and political implications of *how* such remembrance and preservation occurs or does not occur. By failing to affirm the reciprocity of public remembering and public forgetting, one is condemned to a static commemorative pattern, a petrified memory. A collective allegiance to the bare authenticity of public memory does not lead to deeper communal bonds but to a public potentially incapacitated by the burden of an authoritative or even doctrinal interpretation of the past, unprepared for the vicissitudes of the future. Learning to value the nomadic character of public memory, or to conceive of public memory as the crucible of collective remembering *and* forgetting, presupposes, finally, that we learn to regard the past not as a constraint, but as a condition of ethical and political possibility for the present and future.

Notes

1. Jean-Paul Sartre, "On *The Sound and the Fury:* Time in the Work of Faulkner," in *Literary and Philosophical Essays,* trans. Annette Michelson (London: Rider, 1955), 79.

2. Olga W. Vickery, *The Novels of William Faulkner: A Critical Interpretation* (Baton Rouge: Louisiana State University Press, 1964), 29.

3. Cleanth Brooks, *William Faulkner: The Yoknapatawpha Country* (New Haven: Yale University Press, 1963), 326.

4. Isabel Fonseca, *Bury Me Standing* (New York: Knopf, 1995), 178.

5. See David Crowe and John Koltsi, eds., *The Gypsies of Eastern Europe* (Armonk, NY: M. E. Sharpe, 1991).

6. See Fonseca, *Bury Me Standing,* 83–112; Angus Fraser, *The Gypsies* (Oxford: Blackwell, 1992), 10–22; and Jean-Pierre Liegeois, *Gypsies,* trans. Tony Berrett (London: Al Saqi, 1986), 34–38.

7. Gilles Deleuze, *Difference and Repetition,* trans. Paul Patton (New York: Columbia University Press, 1994), 1.

8. Fraser, *The Gypsies,* 1.

9. Fonseca, *Bury Me Standing,* 243.

10. Michael Stewart, *The Time of the Gypsies* (Boulder, CO: Westview Press, 1997), 246.

11. Fonseca, *Bury Me Standing,* 3.

12. Ibid., 7–9.

13. Ibid., 11.

14. Ibid., 9. For a collection of Gypsy folktales that have nevertheless found their way into print, see Diane Tong, *Gypsy Folktales* (San Diego: Harcourt Brace Jovanovich, 1989).

15. Konrad Bercovici, *The Story of the Gypsies* (New York: Cosmopolitan, 1928), 41–46.

16. Ibid., 46.

17. Stewart, *The Time of the Gypsies,* 58.

18. Fonseca, *Bury Me Standing,* 93–96. See also Fraser, *The Gypsies,* 10–22; Liegeois, *Gypsies,* 17–47.

19. Liegeois, *Gypsies,* 16.

20. Fonseca, *Bury Me Standing,* 88. See also Liegeois, *Gypsies,* 87–141; Ian Hancock, *The Pariah Syndrome* (Ann Arbor: Karoma, 1987).

21. Fonseca, *Bury Me Standing,* 14.

22. Wim Willems, *In Search of the True Gypsy,* trans. Don Bloch (London: Frank Cass, 1997), 3.

23. Young writes, "[O]ne of my aims is to break down the notion of any memorial's 'collective memory' altogether. Instead, I prefer to examine 'collected memory,' the many discrete memories that are gathered into common

memorial spaces and assigned common meaning." See James E. Young, *The Texture of Memory: Holocaust Memorials and Meaning* (New Haven: Yale University Press, 1993), xi.

24. Fonseca, *Bury Me Standing,* 243; Fraser, *The Gypsies,* 269; Hancock, *The Pariah Syndrome,* 61–87. Huttenbach provides the following statistical summary concerning the extent of Gypsy losses during World War II:

> Given present research data, the total number of Gypsies killed by the Nazi genocidal policy can only be estimated, ranging from a conservative low of 250,000 to a possible high of 500,000, out of an estimated population of 885,000 European Gypsies in 1939. One source claims that 75 percent of Europe's Gypsies were killed by the Nazis, while others, using much higher prewar European Gypsy population estimates, have claimed that 1 million to 4 million died in the *Porajmos.* Simon Wiesenthal, among others, has stated that up to 80 percent of all Gypsies in Nazi-occupied Europe were exterminated; some scholars feel 70 percent is more accurate. (45)

See Henry R. Huttenbach, "The Romani Porajmos: The Nazi Genocide of Gypsies in Germany and Eastern Europe," in *The Gypsies of Eastern Europe,* ed. David Crowe and John Kolsti (Armonk, NY: M. E. Sharpe, 1991), 31–49.

25. Fonseca, *Bury Me Standing,* 243.

26. Ibid., 275.

27. Liegeois, *Gypsies,* 54–55.

28. Fonseca, *Bury Me Standing,* 275.

29. See ibid.; Hancock, *The Pariah Syndrome,* 61–87; Ian Hancock, "Gypsy History in Germany and Neighboring Lands: A Chronology Leading to the Holocaust and Beyond," in *The Gypsies of Eastern Europe,* ed. David Crowe and John Kolsti (Armonk, NY: M. E. Sharpe, 1991), 11–30; Tong, *Gypsy Folktales,* 5.

30. Bercovici, *The Story of the Gypsies,* 3.

31. Stewart, *The Time of the Gypsies,* 1.

32. David M. Crowe, *A History of the Gypsies of Eastern Europe and Russia* (New York: St. Martin's, 1994), xi–xvi; Liegeois, *Gypsies,* 44, 56.

33. I have adapted the following treatment of Kotre's work from my previous article, " 'Always a Third Party Who Says Me': Rhetoric and Alterity," *Philosophy and Rhetoric* 34, no. 4 (2001): 343–54.

34. In its Greek root, *cryptomnesia* means "hidden memory." John Kotre,

White Gloves: How We Create Ourselves through Memory (New York: Free Press, 1995), 36.

35. Kotre, *White Gloves,* 36–37.

36. Jean Piaget, *Play, Dreams and Imagination in Childhood,* trans. C. Gattegno and F. M. Hodgson (New York: W. W. Norton, 1962).

37. Kotre, *White Gloves,* 36.

38. Ibid., 37.

39. Ibid.

40. Kotre, *White Gloves,* 25.

41. Ibid., 221. Whether intentionally or not, Kotre's comments recall Maurice Halbwachs's seminal work on the relationship between individual and collective memory. See *On Collective Memory,* trans. Lewis A. Coser (Chicago: University of Chicago Press, 1992).

42. Young, *The Texture of Memory,* xi.

43. Kotre, *White Gloves,* 217.

44. Robert Musil, *Posthumous Papers of a Living Author,* trans. Peter Wortsman (Hygiene, CO: Eridanos Press, 1987), 61.

45. Young, *The Texture of Memory,* 13.

46. Ibid.

47. This is not to deny that some scholars have regarded fiction as an apt genre for the narration of memory.

48. Young, *The Texture of Memory,* 12.

49. Vickery, *The Novels of William Faulkner,* 35.

50. Ibid.

51. Ibid.

9

Renovating the National Imaginary

A Prolegomenon on Contemporary Paregoric Rhetoric

Barbara Biesecker

Particularly when we come upon such aspects of persuasion as are found in "mystification," courtship, and the "magic" of class relationships, the reader will see why the classical notion of clear persuasive intent is not an accurate fit, [*sic*] for describing the ways in which members of a group promote social cohesion by acting rhetorically upon themselves and one another. As W. C. Blum has stated the case deftly, "In identification lies the source of dedications and enslavements, in fact of cooperation."

Kenneth Burke, A Rhetoric of Motives

Paregoric: *n.* an opium derivative used as a mild sedative and to treat diarrhea. [1675–85; <LL *paregoricus* <Gk *paregorikós* soothing = paregor(os) pertaining to consolatory speech (par-PAR + -egoros, adj. Der. of *agorá* public speaking, assembly, AGORA) + ikos—ic]

This essay is about the body, the construction of a corpus, and contemporary U.S. nation building. Specifically, it is an inquiry into the way in which the body is being conscripted and a certain event rescripted so as to newly anchor national life. This is, then, an essay about the politics of the body's and history's (re)inscription in the current conjuncture, of how they are presently being deployed to inspire a new esprit de corps, a new common sense or national sensibility. Another way of putting it is that this is an essay that critically dissects the recent emergence of a paregoric rhetoric, a verbal and visual "opium for the masses" whose dialectically paired and organizing tropes are the pained body of World War II and the contemporary crippled nation, and whose anodynic power is largely an effect of its simultaneous production and exploitation of a growing public intolerance for wounded attachments and so-called victim politics. This is, then, an analysis that tracks how that pained body is being made to trump the historically and socially disenfranchised subject in the national imaginary so as to discern the political work it is doing in/for the patriotic public sphere as we enter what Ronald Takaki has called "the multicultural millennium."[1]

The analysis begins by taking critical notice of one of the most recent and successful attempts to enter the national "given-to-be-seen": the World War II Memorial.[2] First proposed at a time when, according to numerous accounts in the popular press, the National Mall's "satisfying geometry" (that has long served as "an analogue of our society") and "orderly vistas" (which "open receptive minds to the symmetry, balance, proportion and temperateness of our political institutions and the civil society that sustains our common purposes") were being threatened by "irritable factions" vying for national visibility and recognition,[3] the memorial's swift approval for construction in the very heart of the nation's capital is symptomatic of a reconfiguration of the grounds for identification with or belonging to the nation that is now in process. Taking formal leave of the memorial but following the lines drawn by its salient images and motifs, the essay then turns its attention to two of the most widely disseminated and wildly popular of all contemporary paregoric rhetorics—Steven Spielberg's *Saving Private Ryan* and Tom Brokaw's *The Greatest Generation*—and then closes with a studied tour of the less familiar Women in Military Service for America Memorial. By looking closely at these "memory texts"[4] as well as the discourses that circulated about them in the popular press and mass media, I hope to draw out a kind of cultural map of the current conjuncture and identify some of its deeply troubling implications for the politics of contemporary national life.

A functional change in a sign-system is a violent event. Even when it is perceived as "gradual," or "failed," or yet "reversing itself," that change itself can only be operated by the force of a crisis.

Gayatri Chakravorty Spivak, *In Other Worlds*

Oh, get over it, already—and go out and do the right thing.

Dr. Laura

A profound—indeed violent—event is taking place on the National Mall and in the national symbolic: the construction of the World War II Memorial on the sacred ground between the Washington Monument and the Lincoln Memorial. First proposed in December 1987, signed into law by President Clinton on May 25, 1993, and promoted by former senator, disabled veteran, and current Viagra spokesperson Bob Dole as well as the exorbitantly popular cultural icon Tom Hanks (who is not a World War II vet but played one on the big screen), the projected $100 million memorial will be dedicated on Saturday, May 29, 2004. As described on its fund-raising campaign's home page, the memorial's winning neoclassical design, whose latest revision passed the notoriously tough hurdle of approval by the Fine Arts Commission without objection, promises a structure that will at once bestow just tribute to the sixteen million World War II veterans, pay appropriate homage to all Americans who supported the war effort on the home front, and grant due respect to "its magnificent site on the National Mall."[5]

Although first proposed at a time when more than eighty new monuments were warring for position in the nation's capital, approval of the World War II Memorial progressed with relative ease. In this case, unlike so many others, there simply was no debate over whether or not "there are any other existing memorials that pay tribute to like or similar subjects" and no doubt about its "preeminent historical and lasting significance to the nation."[6] Indeed, the only serious reservation aired was that its monumental significance to the nation would seem to necessitate the raising of an edifice whose proper magnitude promised to overwhelm the democratically sublime symmetry of the mall.[7] As John Graves, speaking on behalf of a minority of World War II veterans opposing the initiative, put it on the day the memorial won resounding approval from the commission, "[W]e want a memorial but not on that particular spot."[8] Given that six other sites had been considered for placement of the memorial (the Capitol Reflecting Pool area, the Tidal Basin, West Potomac Park, the Washington Monument grounds, Freedom Plaza, and Henderson Hall), it is no minor detail that nearly five years *previous to* final design selection, the Commission of Fine Arts, the National Capital Planning Commission, and the National Park Service swiftly and unanimously settled on the east end of Constitution Gardens, between Constitution Avenue and the Rainbow Pool, calming opposition by stipulating only that the design "not interrupt the vista between the Capitol, the Washington Monument and the Lincoln Memorial."[9]

Why was priority granted to pride of place? The strong answer came from President Bill Clinton on Veteran's Day 1995 in an oration that officially brought to a close the fiftieth commemoration of World War II:

> [L]et me urge all of us to summon the spirit that joined that generation, that stood together and cared for one another. The ideas they fought for are now ours to sustain. The dreams they defended are now ours to guarantee. In war they crossed racial and religious, sectional and social divisions to become one force for freedom.
>
> Now, in a world where lives are literally being torn apart all over the globe by those very divisions, let us again lead by the power of example. Let us remember their example. Let us live our motto, *E pluribus Unum*—from many, one. Let us grow strong together, not be divided and weakened. Let us find that common ground for which so many have fought and died."[10]

Like that of the memorial's fund-raising campaign, the central theme of Clinton's panegyric to World War II is the urgent need for national reunification today.[11] As he put it again later that afternoon during the site dedication ceremony, the memorial "will be a permanent reminder of just how much we Americans can do when we work together instead of fighting among ourselves."[12]

Like Clinton's, numerous other public statements argued that the projected memorial's capacity to resuscitate a waning sense of the "People" warranted its construction in the very heart of the mall:[13] "There is no other spot. The memorial should be right there, in the center of things, because World War II is central to our history, central to our view of our role in the world, central to our values. A World War II memorial at the foot of the Rainbow Pool would do to our nation's capital just what World War II did to our country. It changed the landscape. It changed the way we look at things. Build it. They will come around."[14] Or, "An event as momentous in American and world history as World War II deserved this prominent site. . . . When it is finally completed, all Americans will be proud of a World War II Memorial that epitomizes what can happen in our country when its citizens mobilize and become united in a just and common cause."[15] In the end, then, a prime piece of property is parceled out for posterity, for the repair of a nation crippled by "division and resentment": a small price to pay for the recognition of what the president, on yet another occasion addressing the matter of "responsible citizenship," referred to as the "common ground" requisite to the forging of a "New [American] Covenant."[16]

Given the memorial's singular location on the mall and the authorizing logic invoked on its behalf, there is obviously a good deal more at stake in this will to display than establishing an eternal repository of the heroic accomplishments of a generation past. Indeed, over the course of this essay I will suggest that the historic decision to place the World War II Memorial at the very center of the Capitol—thereby flanked on one side by the memorial to the veterans of the traumatic Vietnam War and on the other by the memorial to the "forgotten" or Korean War[17]—signals the emergence of World War II as a new national nodal point that promises to secure the national future against the vicissitudes of the multicultural present. Traversing and operating on very different forms and domains of discourse and practice across the national landscape, a certain version or vision of World War II is (re)materializing as the central coordinate of national life, reshaping social relations primarily by way of a reconfiguration of the category of U.S. citizenship. In other words, the privileged positioning of the World War II Memorial on the National Mall is symptomatic of an ongoing effort to rearticulate the relation of the citizen to the nation, thereby newly determining what differently positioned—by class, race, gender, and ethnicity—citizen-subjects can and cannot claim as well as expect from the state.[18] That it will continue to operate in such fashion for the foreseeable future will certainly be one of the effects of—if it is not the intent behind—restrictions drafted in September 1999 by the National Capital Planning Commission, the National Capital Memorial Commission, and the Commission of Fine Arts that would "ban the building of any other memorials in a cross shaped area reaching from the Capitol to the Lincoln Memorial and from the White House to the Jefferson Memorial."[19] Hence, to alter only slightly a phrase taken from the memorial's promotional materials, World War II will have been "the defining event of the [early twenty-first] century in American history."

> It seems possible to me to make fiction work within truth, to induce truth effects within a fictional discourse, and in some way make the discourse of truth arouse, "fabricate" something which does not as yet exist, thus "fiction" something. One "fictions" history starting from a political reality that renders it true, one "fictions" a politics that doesn't as yet exist starting from an historical truth.
>
> Michel Foucault, "Interview"

> I really wanted to tell the stories of these men. . . . I wanted before the end of the century to tell their experience, as opposed to adding one more movie to a long train of World War II films that were filled with excitement and adventure and sacrifice and nobility. Do you sugarcoat it by telling people that dying is easy, and dying is noble? How many movies have said that to us ad nauseam? I would rather show how these boys really died. I really feel that I made this movie as a memorial.
>
> Steven Spielberg, quoted in "Theatre of War"

At the turn of the century, it was beginning to look like the great melting pot was melting down; we were in desperate need of a way to feel national again, and, as always, the mainstream media lent a helping hand. Like clockwork, each evening our national news anchormen would tell us two stories, one on the front end and one on the back: first, a report of yet another instance of acute sexual, racial, ethnic, and religious tension and conflict on our streets or in our schools, at the workplace or in our homespace; last, a so-called human interest story about one or another benevolent corporation, not-for-profit group, neighborhood association, or charitable individual taking up the Good Samaritan challenge to feed the hungry, house the homeless, adopt the abandoned, or retrain the "old economy" workers whose skills had been swiftly outflanked by a high-tech revolution.[20] Out of these narratives, which also became headlines in our newspapers, received prime-time play on our radios, and mutated into "special issues" in our popular periodicals, emerged images of citizenship and incivility as well as a moving moral frame by which we might collectively make sense of them. Indeed, by way of the media whose silences spoke volumes, we were rhetorically induced to believe that the nation was being brought to its proverbial knees by all those "mutually suspicious and antagonistic subgroups" whose over-investment in their own wounded attachments was causing us to lose touch with "our common ground" and lose sight of our most precious national resource—"old values."[21] Never mind that despite unprecedented national prosperity, a stubborn standard-of-living gap between rich and poor was growing ever wider, the nation's social safety net was continuing to unravel (funds for dramatically downsized federal entitlement programs were increasingly being channeled into private, voluntary, and "faith-based" organizations), that anti–affirmative action initiatives were fast becoming common sense and common law, and that fetal rights were slowly but surely upending women's rights. The country, we were encouraged to believe, could be brought back to its feet by little more than a healthy dose of old-fashioned American moral fiber.

With the release of *Saving Private Ryan* in the summer of 1998, the commonweal got a fabulously timely booster shot of homegrown goodness right between the eyes. Set against the backdrop of World War II and the epic invasion of Normandy and delivered from the point of view of the so-called grunts in the trenches, this celluloid fanfare for the common man tells the guardedly triumphant tale of the rescue of "one James Francis Ryan" who, dropped deep behind enemy lines, is discovered to be the last surviving son of a mother of four whose three older boys had recently been felled by enemy fire. Having only narrowly escaped the slaughter on the sands of Omaha Beach, Captain John Miller (played by Tom Hanks) receives new orders from no less a figure than George C. Marshall, the Army's Chief of Staff: Miller is to patch together a small Ranger unit and bring Ryan home to his mother, alive. For the remaining two and a half hours of the film we watch a "public relations" mission for the home front morph into an eight-man moral pilgrimage that leads the "multicultural" squad—Sergeant Horvath (Miller's right-hand man and confidant), Corporal Upham (the bookish, feminized translator), Wade (the merciful medic), Private Reiben (the Brooklyn bad boy), Private Jackson (the Scripture-citing sharpshooter), Private Caparzo (the Italian), and Private Mellish (the Jew)—into greater and greater peril. With them we set out on the journey asking, "Can [anyone] explain the math in this to me? Where's the sense to risk the eight of [them] to save one guy?" And at the end, like the young Ryan, we are left standing on an Allied-held bridge in the fictitious town of Romelle, with Miller's last, barely whispered, command echoing in our ears, "Earn this." Therein lie the simple contours of a story about doing the decent, patriotic thing even when "the whole world has taken a turn for the surreal," even when, on their face, the numbers just don't add up.

Of course the numbers do add up in *Saving Private Ryan* at an astonishing rate. Much of the unbridled enthusiasm for the movie is explicitly attributed to what is typically, albeit mistakenly, referred to by reviewers as its "opening scene," Spielberg's recreation of the U.S. invasion of Normandy. Again and again those twenty-five unrelenting minutes of meticulously chronicled mass slaughter on Omaha Beach are credited with having set new standards for realistic filmmaking. In *Newsweek,* for example, Jon Meacham heralds *Saving Private Ryan* for being the first war film to represent "battle as it really was, in all its bloodshed and brutality, terror and tedium"[22]; Jay Carr of the *Boston Globe* calls it "the war movie to end all war movies"[23]; writing for the *New York Times,* Martin Arnold imputes the film with "introducing a whole new generation to the spilled-guts school of war storytelling."[24] What Norman Mailer's *Naked and the Dead* did for literature, he argues, Stephen Spielberg's *Saving Private Ryan* does for film: it exposes audiences to "the same brutal, sudden, absurd death—but in this case concentrated carnage—that is, the chaos and reality of combat."[25] However tempting it may be to see the film as, in James Wolcott's words, "an overture of pure cinema" that wholly rejects the "ideals of both patriotism and patriarchy"[26] characteristic of nearly all previous Hollywood renditions of World War II, I want to argue that *Saving Private Ryan* functions rhetorically less as a medium for the demystification of the so-called Good War than it works as a vehicle for the production of a new national sensibility that is predicated on the retooling of the category of citizenship.

The first thing that deserves critical attention is the particular manner in which the film deploys the male body in pain. Almost from the start, Spielberg gives moviegoers what he calls an "unblinking look" at the chaos and carnage that is real war. As the Higgins landing craft, crowded with American soldiers, approaches Omaha Beach, the ocean breaking over its sides, orders are issued and raw fear takes its most humble, human form: one GI's hand trembles as it reaches for a canteen and another's vacant eyes look toward the beach; two soldiers vomit and others are barely able to draw in what is certain to be their last breath. Within thirty seconds the ramp is released. Most of the GIs are cut down by merciless rapid German gunfire before they even step off the craft. Those who manage to clamber over the side of the vessel are plunged into a sea of streaming bullets. Some drown from the weight of their gear; others are struck down by what appears to be wandering gunshot. Blood billows. As scores of boys and men scramble to get out of the bloody surf, onto the beach, and over to the seawall, bodies are blown in half, legs and arms are torn off, faces are ripped away. Others die more slowly, clutching their wounds, crying out for their mothers, receiving their last rites as they look with horror upon their own entrails poured out on the sand.

What sets Spielberg's rendition of the human carnage that is war apart from all the others is not merely, as reviewers have noted, the rate at which it confronts us with those pained male bodies. Nor is it simply a matter that for the first time "we [get to] see, thanks to advances in technology, precisely what happens to the soft-shelled human body when it encounters explosives, projectiles, fuel, flame, and sword."[27] The real "sneak punch" of Spielberg's film, as Wolcott correctly points out, "is that it bypasses the usual introductions to its characters" and goes straight into war.[28] What difference does it make that our contact with a battlefield soon to be littered with the pained bodies of war precedes our knowing anything about its many victims and few survivors other than that they are all American? Without a doubt there is more than a touch of artistry in Spielberg's inversion: there is rhetoric. In exposing us to countless trembling bodies, perspiring bodies, gagging bodies, punctured bodies, drowning bodies, bleeding bodies, bodies with missing arms, legs, eyes, and faces before informing us of their individual histories, Spielberg's Omaha Beach scene effectively promotes our patriotic identification with *all* of them while blocking our subjective identification with any *one* of them. In literally bombarding the audience with these not quite empty signifiers, we become witnesses to a mass execution in which the pained male body of war begins to function as a ground for the production of knowledge and judgment. In all its positivity, our collective, albeit mass-mediated experience of mass American slaughter functions as a great leveler of sorts; bearing witness to material, corporal, sensual pain stands in for the pre-ideological, apolitical, universal, and, thus, universalizing experience out of which truth ("what really counts") and prudential wisdom ("what should be done") may emerge.

That bearing witness to the sheer factualness of the American GI in pain—its "realness," "density," and "certainty"—may be the foundation for a new rationality from which can be derived a vision of "the life worth living" is, of course, the story *Saving Private Ryan* finally tells. Having made the trek back to Normandy and standing over Captain John Miller's grave, the aged Ryan with generations in tow closes the film with the following words: "Tell me I have lived a good life. . . . Tell me I'm a good man." If Ryan is positioned *in* the film as someone scripted to gauge the value of his life in relation to those soldiers who, despite differences in age, race, education, class, religion, and ethnicity, collectively sacrificed their own to save it, we are positioned *by* the film to do so as well. Having come "as close to combat as most of us will ever get,"[29] those dead American men, to turn only slightly the well-known phrase from Protagoras, become for us the measure of all things. It is in this way that the moral message of the film bleeds well beyond its diegetic frame and is infused with modern rhetorical force: the pained male body of World War II is made to displace the traumatized psyche as origin, end, and arbitrator of individual and collective national life. As Matt Damon, who played young Ryan in the film, put it for the *Buffalo News,* "You can see us on Sally Jessy Raphael talking about how tough our lives are because we weren't breast-fed long enough. Try taking a *beach*."[30]

The second thing to notice about *Saving Private Ryan* is its heavy reliance on verbal and visual paramnesias, images that, as Lauren Berlant has put it, "organize consciousness, not by way of explicit propaganda, but by replacing and simplifying memories people actually have with image traces of political experience about which people can have political feelings that link them to other citizens and to patriotism."[31] Without a doubt, the pained body of war is one such image; "home" is another. I think it is no accident that the two-and-a-half-hour-long rescue of Ryan is punctuated by real as well as remembered scenes of home. Indeed, when the men in Miller's Ranger unit are not fighting desperately to survive the battles so as to eventually get home, they incessantly talk about it. With them we visit, visually or imaginatively, sanitized and sentimentalized images of "home," from the country kitchen and pristine porch of the Ryan family farm in Iowa, to a dressing room in a small women's shop on a small street in Brooklyn, to a young boy's bedroom visited by a mother who has just returned from the second shift, and to the hammock and rosebushes in Miller's backyard. Decisively juxtaposed against the gritty and grainy chaos of war on foreign territory, "home" is transformed over the course of the movie into a fantastical space that is utterly bereft of the complexities, ambivalences, and incoherence of daily U.S. life both in those war-torn years and today. Such an idealized vision/version of "home" is represented in this film as the nation's humble, homely, utopian aspiration, its version of "the good life."[32]

Having attended critically to these two typically underacknowledged elements of the film, it becomes possible to more fully appreciate the rhetorical import of another: the frame narrative. Contrary to what reviews in the popular press would lead us to believe, *Saving Private Ryan* neither opens on the surf of Normandy Beach nor closes on a bombed-out bridge in the fictitious French town of Romelle; instead it begins and ends with a multigenerational journey to the gravesite of Captain John Miller in a U.S. cemetery in France at which the gray-haired and teary-eyed Ryan delivers his long-awaited soliloquy: "My family is with me today. They wanted to come with me. To be honest with you, I wasn't sure how I would feel coming back here. Every day I think about what you said to me that day on the bridge. I have tried to live my life the best I could. I hope that was enough. I hope at least in your eyes I have earned what all of you have done for me." It is hardly a surprise that nearly all critics fail to mention this scenario that frames the story of Ryan's rescue: the deliberate not noticing of this highly sentimental, even saccharine scene is requisite to saving *Saving Private Ryan* as progenitor to a new generation of American realist cinema. However, something else is at stake as well. In refusing to attend to the truncated narrative that frames the tale of the rescue of young Ryan, critics disavow what may be one of the film's most disturbing consequences for contemporary U.S. collective life: its domestication of civic responsibility.[33]

It almost goes without saying that the drama of the core narrative hinges to a significant degree on the almost infinitely suspended and anxiously anticipated encounter with the real James Francis Ryan. For Miller and his Rangers, progress on this mission is neither steady nor swift. The journey to Ryan is repeatedly interrupted by unexpected and costly encounters with hostile German forces, rerouted because of a mistaken middle name, and nearly aborted by a one-man mutiny. With each calamity and casualty the investment in Ryan goes up, to the point at which even Miller, the captain whose steadfast determination to find Ryan and thus "earn [him] the right to get back to [his] wife," is given pause to question the "mission [that] is a man": "This Ryan better be worth it. He better go home and cure some disease or invent the longer lasting light bulb or something." Of course by the film's end, audiences know that Ryan went home, and they may reasonably surmise on the basis of his mild demeanor and modest dress that he neither developed a vaccine nor "brought new good things to life."

Here the motif of counting that played such a central role in the core narrative of the film makes itself felt in—and beyond—the frame. Did Ryan earn it? Is he a good man? The film ends with the assurance that its audience has learned to count the ways: a wife, a son and daughter-in-law, a grandson and granddaughters. They assure the audience that Ryan has produced a solid body count, has led a fruitful and productive life. All in all, Spielberg leaves us with a portrait of the multigenerational white iconic citizen-subject who embodies the becoming-national of home and the becoming-private of citizenship. For all its blood and guts, *Saving Pri-*

vate Ryan is a paregoric rhetoric that expresses, justifies, and induces nostalgia for a national future in which each individual's debt to the republic may be paid in minor acts of "privatize[d] patriotism."[34]

> Emergence is always produced through a particular stage of forces. The analysis of the *Enstehung* must delineate this interaction, the struggle these forces wage against each other or against adverse circumstances, and the attempt to avoid degeneration and regain strength by dividing these forces against themselves.
>
>   Michel Foucault, "Nietzsche, Genealogy, History"

> It is not enough to say to the citizens, *be good;* they must be taught to be so.
>
>   Rousseau, *The Social Contract and Discourses*

Less than four months after the release of *Saving Private Ryan* and on the eve of the Jasper dragging-death trial, the Center for Individual Rights' anti–affirmative action lawsuit against the University of Washington Law School, and a landmark settlement of $3.1 million to underpaid female employees of the Texaco oil company, Tom Brokaw's *The Greatest Generation* appeared on bookstore shelves across the nation. Within two months this collection of the life stories of forty-seven U.S. men and women whom Brokaw began interviewing on the fortieth anniversary of D-Day and who in one way or another played a part in the Allied war effort was number one on the *New York Times* nonfiction best-seller list. By mid-January of 1999 NBC's *Dateline* had already aired its own prime-time special documentary on Brokaw's book and, owing to its remarkable popularity, *The Greatest Generation* was soon reissued in paperback, large print, and audio editions.[35] On the basis of the substantive and stylistic similarities between Spielberg's and Brokaw's odes to the Americans who came of age during the Great Depression and the World War II years as well as U.S. audiences' obvious appetite for them, columnists proclaimed the emergence of "World War II chic" or "retro patriotism," a new popular culture form whose "purpose . . . is to represent a world where all the tensions of the present are subsumed by the mission and the men."[36]

To read *The Greatest Generation* as inducing readers to escape the social conflicts of the present by imaginatively transporting themselves into the past is to grossly oversimplify the rhetoricity of Brokaw's text. Not only does the book invoke explicitly the domestic social injustices that vexed the country during and immediately after the war as well as commemorate the individual who overcame them, it also persistently calls up the disparities of social power that plague it today and lays all blame for any citizen's failure at her or his own feet. Indeed, by strategically juxtaposing an imperfect past and a troubled present, Brokaw's trip down memory lane doubles as a vicious attack on today's identity politics, using history as an alibi for a civics lesson that instructs its readership to turn a blind eye to the social differences that still make a difference. Indeed, *The Greatest Generation* is a particularly robust contemporary paregoric rhetoric whose war on today's "victim politics" is symbolically subsidized by the "sacrifices" of an entire generation and discursively rationalized by their cumulative homespun wisdom.

Much like Spielberg's cinematic account, Brokaw's treatment of World War II delivers to its readership the World War II of "ordinary" Americans. In the main, it tells the story of the little people's war, of their heretofore unsung struggles and unacknowledged sacrifices: of Lloyd Kilmer who, after spending ten months in German prison camps, returned home to marry, raise a family, sell real estate, and serve as county clerk; of Daphne Cavin, a newlywed who, after learning her twenty-two-year-old husband had been killed by enemy fire in France, made her way as a beautician in Lebanon, Indiana; of Martha Settle Putnea who, as a young black member of the Women's Auxiliary Corps, contended daily with institutional racism but later earned her doctorate and became a professor of history; of Wesley Ko, who, upon his return to the States after serving in the 82nd Airborne, joined forces with a friend and opened a printing business, married, and raised a son and two daughters. As has already been hinted, for all their striking similarities there is something that sets *The Greatest Generation* apart from *Saving Private Ryan*. *The Greatest Generation* has as much to tell us about the lives of these Americans after the war as during it. Indeed, most of the ink in this book is spent on describing, always in meticulous and sometimes tedious detail, the U.S. postwar era, those decades during which "more than twelve million men and women put their uniforms aside," "returned to civilian life,"[37] and, along with those who had worked on behalf of the Allied victory on the home front, "immediately began the task of rebuilding their lives and the world they wanted."[38]

What is the significance of Brokaw's treating our "rendezvous with destiny" as the point of departure for forty-seven tales of personal triumph that take place when all is again relatively quiet on the European and Pacific fronts? It facilitates the transmogrification of World War II from a sign that has the status of an event into what Michel Foucault has called a technology, what rhetoricians have long called *doxa,* and what I, following others, have termed a new esprit de corps that has the status of a structure. In *The Greatest Generation* World War II shifts from being an event in the past about which we make sense to becoming a mode of sense-making in the present. Under Brokaw's pen World War II becomes a shorthand for a retroactive common sense or "matrix of popular reason" through which we are able collectively to comprehend and negotiate the challenges of contemporary life, not the least of which, in his view, is the ideological unity of the U.S. polity itself. As Brokaw opines in the closing pages of the book:

> There is no world war to fight today nor any prospect of one anytime soon, but racial discrimination remains an American cancer. There is no Great Depression, but economic opportunity is an unending challenge, especially in a high-tech world where education is more important than ever. Most of all, there is the need to reinstate the concept of common welfare in America, so that the nation doesn't squander the legacy of this remarkable generation by becoming a collection of well-defined, narrowly cast special-interest fiefdoms, each concerned only with its own place in the mosaic.[39]

As he reports over the course of his sympathetically spun stories, a citizenry that has become ever more heterogeneous and contentious has begun to leave its demoralizing and devastating mark on the nation. Here the anchorman joins with other like-minded statesmen and spokespersons in bemoaning the new "identity" or "victim" politics, holding it accountable for an impending crisis of national character and national culture. Whereas "the women and members of ethnic groups who were the objects of acute discrimination" during and immediately after the war "have not allowed it to cripple them, nor have they invoked it as a claim for special treatment now,"[40] subsequent generations of socially injured Americans are, according to Brokaw, disproportionately invested in their own putative subjection. How, then, might we arrest this attitudinal erosion? How might we reverse the national course, "transcend partisan considerations," and cultivate a sense of oneness? By training, to use Brokaw's words, "a new kind of army"[41] of citizen-subjects schooled in three classic American virtues—self-reliance, self-discipline, and self-sacrifice—that have been retooled to suit the demands of the multicultural and late-capitalist state. Notably, *The Greatest Generation* is that new army's field handbook. Here, what Toby Miller has identified as the call for "the well-tempered self" that first rang out in mid-sixteenth-century Europe with the mass dissemination of Erasmus's *De civilitate morum puerilium* (On civility in children) reaches a new pitch.[42] To have read *The Greatest Generation* is to have completed a tutorial in the kind of radical subjective reformation requisite to national renewal.

It is hard to imagine a popular text more adroit at using history for the purpose of contemporary U.S. nation (re)building. *The Greatest Generation*'s success in doing so lies in the precise manner in which it strategically invokes and foregrounds the social and cultural differences of the past— economic, racial, sexual, and ethnic—to prompt its readers to discount them in the present. That is, *The Greatest Generation* engineers a singular version of the "then" to induce its readers to disavow their own primary and political passionate attachments "now"; allegiance to the nation or interpellation into the national is to be secured by a willed disregard of certain particularities of self that readers, in their reading, will have already begun to enact.

By the book's end readers will be well versed and practiced in the art of personal abstraction that in this book is the sine qua non of national consubstantiality. Brokaw's assemblage of tales, both thematically and formally, is an exercise in disincorporation.[43] Again and again readers encounter yet another variation on the same basic theme: thanks to the qualities of character developed during the war—self-reliance, self-discipline, and self-sacrifice—scores of Americans were able to beat the incredible odds that mitigated against their success, be it physical disability, economic privation, gender oppression, or racial and ethnic discrimination. In each and every case, becoming part of "the greatest generation" is accomplished through the self-conscious dismissal of the particular and potentially disabling material attributes of the body. One representative example is the profile of Sergeant Johnnie Holmes. Indeed, the life story of this black American who, in his early years, served in the 761st Tank Battalion and later in life "specialized" in "low-income rental apartments in buildings in black neighborhoods" supplies Brokaw with an exemplary illustration of how the racially marked and stigmatized person can succeed by re-imagining himself as unmarked:

> For all of his combative ways, Johnnie decided he wouldn't person-ally bow to the inherent frustration of discrimination. As he puts it today, "If I let all of the negatives intervene, I would have never achieved anything. I kept focused on what I wanted to do, which was to make money, provide for my family. . . ." It was as a landlord and as a black man who had overcome so much on his own that he came to hate the welfare system that grew so fast in the fifties, six-ties, and seventies. "It just killed ambition," according to Holmes. "I had all of these [black] tenants who in their late twenties had never worked a day in their life. They just waited around for that govern-ment check. No incentive."[44]

Obviously there is a lot going on here: the unabashed celebration of the individuated self-making liberal subject as well as a bourgeois norm of relative material comfort; the discursive obliteration of the politics—as effects of power—of the asymmetrical distribution of opportunity and resources in the nation; and the privatization of civic responsibility and social virtue.[45] Notably, what underwrites all of the above in this vignette is the persistent self-repudiation of the materiality or particularities of embodiment. Requisite to success and, thus, national belonging is what Sergeant Johnnie Holmes, in his "twilight years," calls keeping one's "focus on what one wants to do."[46]

Second, by virtue of the serial structure of the book, the social and cultural particularities of American bodies—physical ability, class, gender, race, and ethnicity—are rendered merely paratactic. That is, in this assemblage asymmetries of embodiment become differences to which readers learn to be indifferent, markings to which readers are taught to turn a blind eye. It is hardly fortuitous, then, that the first of the forty-seven vignettes recounts the travails and triumphs of Thomas Broderick, who lost his sight to a German bullet in the head. *"What's a handicap?"* asks Brokaw's blind bard in the epigraph that opens the book. *"I don't have a handicap."*[47] Here the pained male body of World War II that in *Saving Private Ryan* was the preideological ground for prudential wisdom and judgment reaches its apogee.

If *The Greatest Generation* is a pedagogy of prosthetic citizenship in the multicultural age that induces readers to enact the fantasy of the undifferentiated "We" of "We the People," what are we to make of the photographs throughout of "those men and women who have given us the lives we have today"?[48] Might these visual displays of the particular block the reader's translation into disincorporated subjectivity? When, in his preface, Brokaw metacritically reflects on his book and declares that he does not understand it to be "the defining history of [the World War II] generation" but "instead, think[s] of [it] as like a family portrait,"[49] he is not speaking only figuratively. Indeed, Brokaw, his research assistants, and his publishers have gone to considerable lengths to recover and reproduce some one hundred thirty amateurish snapshots, stock family photos, and studio portraits that lend the volume the appearance and feel of a family photo album whose images relate a tale that has yet to be determined. As Annete Kuhn has written in *Family Secrets: Acts of Memory and Imagination,* in family photo albums,

> pictures get displayed one after another, their selection and ordering as meaningful as the pictures themselves. The whole, the series, constructs a family story in some respects like a classical narrative: linear, chronological; though its cyclical repetitions of climactic moments—births, christenings, weddings, holidays . . .—is more characteristic of the open-ended narrative form of the soap opera than of the closure of classical narrative. In the process of using—producing, selecting, ordering, displaying—photographs, the family is actually in the process of making itself.[50]

What sort of national family story, then, is being made as we read Brokaw's ensemble of inscriptions of shadow and light?

Contrary to what we might first suspect, the collection of photographs is not a dangerous visual supplement to Brokaw's verbal text. Rather, this visual archive encourages the self-violating interpellation of individuals into abstract citizen-subjects. Significantly, like its verbal counterpart, Brokaw's collection of images is structured as a series of discrete but intimately related vignettes, each of which is composed of at least two photos, a "before the return from the war" shot followed by a "long after the return from the war" shot. Obviously, the strategic sequencing has one primary function—to visually authenticate the verbal text.[51] But if each pair of photos works alone to certify the verisimilitude of the verbal tale told, taken together they produce a different truth effect. When viewed together, "the visual," as Lisa Cartwright has put it, "is anti-visual."[52] As an album or archive, serialization displaces sequence, and the negation of difference is effected through its pluralization. On the visual plane, then, a paratactical logic reduces the asymmetries of embodiment to equivalence, interchangeability, and invisibility. Indeed, by the time readers near the end of Brokaw's tutorial, they will have been trained to disregard that the concluding seventeen vignettes, notably grouped into sections titled "Famous People" and "The Arena," feature the life stories of fourteen white men, two white women, and one "model minority," Daniel Inouye, whose closing words in this context encapsulate, to use Wendy Brown's terms, "liberalism's universal moment" for the multicultural state in late capitalism: "The one time the nation got together was World War II. We stood as one. We spoke as one. We clenched our fists as one, and that was a rare moment for all of us."[53]

All in all, then, *The Greatest Generation* is a particularly robust contemporary paregoric rhetoric. It is also a particularly insidious one: an antipolitical political image text that, in claiming to be merely representing what it is helping to produce and promote, advances a highly normative, indeed exclusionary, notion of the citizen-subject, of the *sensus communitatis,* of the national family.

> Order is, at one and the same time, that which is given in things as their
> inner law, the hidden network that determines the way they confront

one another, and also that which has no existence except in the grid created by a glance, an examination, a language; and it is only in the blank
spaces of this grid that order manifests itself in depth as though already
there, waiting in silence for the moment of its expression.

Michel Foucault, *The Order of Things*

At the groundbreaking in June, what once might have sounded like
radical feminist rhetoric flowed from the mouths of Democrats and
Republicans alike. The idea that bravery and valor are female qualities
was suddenly apple pie and motherhood.

Karrie Jacobs, "A Woman's Place"

With the opening of its doors to the general public in the fall of 1997, the
Women in Military Service for America Memorial (WIMS), a 33,000-
square-foot structure situated at the ceremonial gateway to Arlington National Cemetery, would appear to have dealt a decisive blow to (largely
white) masculine presumption and male privilege on the National Mall
and in the national symbolic. For the first time in our nation's history, the
heretofore unacknowledged accomplishments of the more than two million American women who had served in times of domestic and international crisis since the Revolutionary War were understood to be worth
their symbolic weight if not in gold then in granite, steel, and glass. Thus,
on the eve of the new millennium and in the wake of Tailhook, Aberdeen,
and Citadel investigations, it seemed we were a nation finally prepared to
get our history right. As Mary Rose Oakar, who while serving as a member
of the House of Representatives introduced Resolution 36 to authorize
the establishment of the memorial, put it on dedication day: "This Memorial will change the teaching of American history. . . . We will know that
in every war, contrary to past popular belief, women have been killed,
disabled and injured physically and psychologically. We will know of wom-
en's bravery, courage, their love, dedication and sacrifice for their country
and their strong desire for world peace."[54] But the memorial does much
more than call attention to the systematic exclusion of women from the
annals of U.S. military history and, thus, implicitly call for its revision.
Rather than leave that job to posterity, the memorial takes on itself the
compensatory task. "This memorial," as the mission statement on one of

the central interior walls boldly declares, not only "honors the women who have served in and with the US Armed Forces from the time of the American Revolution to the present. . . . The Education Center within this memorial tells the stories of these forerunners and then focuses on women of the 20th century who have served both in and with the military in ever-expanding roles."

Because of its educative function, WIMS is more akin to a museum than a memorial or monument. To step into the memorial is to leave the minimalist rhetoric and aesthetic of national commemoration and to move into an elaborate system of representation in which a complex assemblage of image texts is strategically engineered for particular pedagogical effect.[55] Upon crossing the memorial's threshold, patrons find themselves in a centrally located exhibit gallery. Various objects—from reproductions of photographs, paintings, drawings, and posters to flight logbooks, dog tags, handmade clothespins, undergarments, and uniforms—are consolidated within exhibit alcoves that track the numerous roles women have played in the nation's military history. With the assistance of explanatory plates and a guidebook as well as a thirteen-minute video presentation, "In Defense of a Nation: The History of Women in the Military," shown at regular intervals in the memorial's state-of-the-art theater, visitors become witnesses to an impressive collection of evidence that points toward one unambiguous and uncontestable truth: from the beginning, women have been *agents* of U.S. history even if they have been excluded from its interested (re)telling.

The memorial's declared pedagogical purpose is advanced in other ways as well. From the renovated hemicycle wall "representing the barriers to greater opportunity and recognition that women have encountered in their efforts to serve our country" to the four new stairways "carved through the existing stone and concrete, symboliz[ing] women's efforts to break through these barriers,"[56] the memorial challenges conventional wisdom and makes visible a national past in which women are seen always to have been vital participants in rather than passive beneficiaries of military engagement, both at home and abroad. Indeed, nowhere is the memorial's repudiation of majoritarian male culture and its biased retelling of U.S. military history made more explicit than on its roof, a literalization—indeed materialization—of the "glass ceiling," this one constructed out of 138 rectangular transparent glass tablets, eleven of which have etched words such as the following:

> From the storm-lashed decks of the Mayflower . . . to the present hour, woman has stood like a rock for the welfare of the history of the country, and one might well add . . . unwritten, unrewarded, and almost unrecognized (Clara Barton, Founder of the American Red Cross, 1911); Let the generations know that women in uniform also guaranteed their freedom. That our resolve was just as great as the brave men who stood among us and with victory our hearts were just as full and beat just as fast—that the tears fell just as hard for those we left behind (Unknown U.S. Army Nurse, WWII); The ground they broke was hard soil indeed. But with great heart and true grit, they plowed right through the prejudice and presumption, cutting a path for their daughters and granddaughters to serve their country in uniform (Secretary of Defense William J. Perry, Ground-breaking, June 22, 1995).

An unguarded, dare we say militant, feminist stance against the received history?

For rhetorical critics poised to appreciate the memorial's contestatory force, an abstract lesson of high theory, that a discontinuous relation always already obtains between origins and ends, may make itself felt as a productive practical caution: to guard vigilantly the question of ideological effects. More specifically, we should refuse to presume that, as Peggy Phelan has put it, "increased visibility equals increased power."[57] Not necessarily, not always, not only, because at this particular conjuncture, it may not.[58] As Lacan once put it, "In this matter of the visible, everything is a trap."[59] Indeed, a critical analysis of the memorial makes it possible to discern the way in which this lesson in revisionary history may be pressed into the service of another ideological agenda.

As noted, the heart or center of the memorial is an exhibit gallery housing sixteen alcoves that by virtue of running the length of the renovated hemicycle may be accessed from double doors on either end. On entering visitors to the memorial inescapably happen upon seven glass-enclosed display cases, four of which house exhibits devoted to women's role in World War II; the other three hold displays documenting women's service in the eighteenth and nineteenth centuries, between 1901 and 1945, and since 1946. Although all of these exhibits visually document the always crucial but expanding role of women in the armed forces through the deployment of reproductions of photographs, drawings, and paintings, the veracity and, thus, force of the World War II displays are enhanced considerably by the incorporation of a massive collection of the paraphernalia of women and war. Indeed, these World War II displays are loaded from floor to ceiling with an array of objects that, notably, do not record the fantastic feats of singular individuals but instead metonymically mark the regular rhythms and daily practices of our nation's servicewomen. Among scores of others are a pair of mosquito boots that protected one army nurse in Africa from contracting malaria, a sample identification card issued to all Women's Army Corps (WAC) recruits, one of the hundreds of summer uniforms issued to Women Accepted for Volunteer Emergency Service (WAVES) inductees, the helmet and calculation instruments used by an unidentified Air Force service pilot, one anonymous student's handwritten notes on how to repair guns and pack parachutes, and another's army-issued underwear and pajamas. From the first installment to the last, what the World War II collection features are ordinary, commonplace objects; typicality rather than rarity subtends the order of things here. The principle of typicality also underwrites the photographs that have been incorporated into the permanent exhibits. Instead of bearing witness to striking moments of uncommon valor, these archived images make visible the collective or cooperative, anonymous and even monotonous or generic, character of servicewomen's daily life: here a sea of telephone operators, there a secretarial pool, here the U.S. Cadet Nurse Corps in formation, there a mass of women working on a factory line so as to "free our men to fight." Although rare, when formal portraits and snapshots of individual women in particular situations do appear, they are reconfigured into a collage, thereby reconstituting them as members of some larger whole and those events as part of a broader-based effort. When amassed, arranged, and placed under or behind glass, then, the artifacts presented in the exhibit alcoves are invested with new significance, are infused with new force, with "representativeness." In this way a seemingly complete, unabridged history of women in the U.S. armed services begins metonymically to be made visible and present.

As noted, all of the objects brought together at WIMS are placed in individual exhibit alcoves that have been clearly labeled and chronologically arranged: "Serving with the Military: 18th and 19th Centuries," "Serving in the Military: 1901–1945," "Women Go to War: World War II," "Servicewomen in World War II: Recruiting, Training and on the Job," "Volunteering on the Homefront: World War II," "Overseas with the Military: World War II," and "Serving in the Military since 1946." Thus, although each individual window into the past is made to represent a distinct period of U.S. military history and women's place in it, the passage from the first to the last reveals, step-by-step, women's *ever-evolving* role in the armed services, their *natural* ascension over time from handmaiden to helicopter pilot, from battlefield nurse to brigadier general. The sequential display of periodized artifacts has been supplemented by two complementary narratives—a relatively elaborate *Self-Guided Tour* manual that visitors may pick up at the entrance to the memorial and a much abbreviated version thereof that appears in installments over the course of the exhibit.

The handheld script is a mechanism to normalize and naturalize women's integration into the armed services by making it appear as the always already determined outcome of a process whose reasonableness has been delivered by and made legible over time. First of all, its repeated deployment of the constative utterance helps conceal the discursive status of the display, thereby leaving patrons with the impression that rather than having been authored by someone, the written supplement has been dictated by the objects and movement of American history itself.[60] The impact of this "exhibition rhetoric" that accentuates the objects as it effaces itself is augmented by two strategic silences that together conceal the artistry at work. Not once does the name of a photographer appear on the legend that accompanies each display case (in every case, however, the collection or archive from which the object has been extracted or donated is clearly identified), and nowhere in the memorial or in any of its public relations literatures are the curators of the exhibits acknowledged.[61] Second, the script's adroit inclusion of directives to patrons on how they are to read crucial elements of the visual text controls to a considerable degree the images' signifying effects. Indeed, when pictures alone may fail, words step in: "The individuals pictured here are representative rather than famous"; "Again, the majority of photos are not of famous women but show the variety of ways in which women have served with the military since WWII"; "The increased number of photographs in this panel reflects the increasing numbers of women in the services during peacetime and times of conflict." Third, the thoroughgoing exclusion from the script of any reference to the asymmetrical social relations, material circumstances, and pyramidal-hierarchical logics that have structured and continue to underwrite the recruitment, incorporation, and containment of women by the armed services makes these processes appear to be the inevitable outcome of a rational historical unfolding, thereby eliding, even as it purports to reveal the historicity of women's enfranchisement. Indeed, this is sensationally demonstrated in the decision to mark and mark off the Women's Armed Services Integration Act of 1948.[62] Presented as a singular, even watershed moment in the exhibit gallery, the memorialization of the act neatly buries gender inequality within U.S. military history as a fait accompli, thereby constituting the present as postfeminist, postpolitical.

To represent history in evolutionary terms is often to privilege a conservative model of social transformation, one that promotes a general tolerance of the status quo predicated on the understanding or belief that change is the consequence of some greater force—capital H History or biology, for example. Nonetheless, the exhibit gallery can be seen to utter an incipient call to a certain kind of collective action, one that is given palpable expression through the memorial's computerized registry and receives dramatic reinforcement from its engraved glass ceiling. Adjacent to the exhibit hall but visible from it is a room that houses twelve computers through which visitors may access "the photographs, military histories and memorable experiences" of "women veterans, active duty, reserve, and guard women, and women who have served in direct support of the military throughout history." Additionally, three larger-than-life screens have been placed above the entrance to the registry; there the name, record of service, and photographic image of every registered servicewoman serially appears by way of a computer-generated around-the-clock roll call. Operating in tandem with the exhibit gallery, the computerized registry deftly deploys the so-called new information technologies, linking the abstract national to the situated local; in their engagement with the official image archive, visitors literally perform acts of national identification that provide them with embodied models of normative national character. Finally, the pilgrimage to the upper terrace caps off the "self-guided tour" of WIMS. For patrons already party to the complex rationalization displayed below, the words etched on the roof not only grant official public voice to the women who have served, but they also function rhetorically as injunctions to serve the national cause:

> You have a debt and a date. A debt to democracy, a date with destiny (Oveta Culp Hobby, Colonel, Director of the Women's Army Corps, World War II); All of us must work at patriotism not just believe in it. For only by our young women offering their services to our country as working patriots in the armed forces can our defense be adequate (Helen Hayes, Defense Advisory Committee on Women in the Services, 1951); The qualities that are most important in all military jobs—things like integrity, moral courage, and determination—have nothing to do with gender (Rhonda Cornum, Major, US Army Medical Corps, Operation Desert Storm).

Hence, in addition to advancing an account of America's military history that for the first time duly acknowledges women's role in it, the Women in Military Service for America Memorial scripts a version of normative U.S. identity in which service to the nation is the *arche* and telos of what it means for any American—man or woman—in the words of the *Self-Guided Tour,* to "exercise full citizenship." Thus, out of a memorial "dedicated to the women who have served" figures forth an abstract category of civic agency that folds feminine subjectivity into universal (masculine) virtues. As Major Marie Rossi, killed in a helicopter crash the day after the close of the Gulf War, stoically noted in a nationally televised interview, a portion of which is woven into the memorial's own video presentation: "It's our jobs. There was nothing peculiar about our being women. We were just the people called upon to do it."

History becomes "effective" to the degree that it introduces discontinuity into our very being—as it divides our emotions, dramatizes our
instincts, multiplies our body and sets it against itself. "Effective" history
deprives the self of the reassuring stability of life and nature, and it will
not permit itself to be transported by a voiceless obstinacy toward a
millennial ending.

> Michel Foucault, "Nietzsche, Genealogy, History"

"My, my. A body does get around."

> William Faulkner, *Light in August*

Between the release of *Patton* and *Tora! Tora! Tora!* and the premier of
Saving Private Ryan, World War II virtually disappeared from the national
popular scene. Indeed, in striking contrast to its popularity during the
postwar era, "by the early 1970s," as Tom Engelhardt notes in his historical
analysis of the "Vietnamization" or "castration" of American culture, "the
'Good War', even in its down and dirty form, had lost its recyclable
quality."[63] Hence, this essay might best be summed up as an effort to take
rhetorical stock of its dramatic uptake almost thirty years later. How exactly, this essay asks, is World War II being given back to us today, and to
what effect?

I have argued that World War II is returning as a paregoric rhetoric,
a distinct rhetorical form whose curative, soothing, and homogenizing
force is predicated on its cultivation of new modes of self-perception
and self-production. Prompted by the unprecedented decision to break
ground between the Washington Monument and the Lincoln Memorial
for a structure commemorating not just the veterans of World War II but
also an exemplary era of "American nation unity," this examination of several contemporary World War II texts argues that the return of World
War II may be understood as a more or less thinly veiled conservative
response to the contemporary crisis of national identity, to our failing
sense of what it means to be an American and to do things the so-called
American way. Indeed, I have tried to demonstrate how *Saving Private Ryan*
and *The Greatest Generation* redefine in highly restrictive and distinctly cen-
trist terms what it means to be a "good American." Although both the film
and book advocate the domestication and privatization of civic responsi-

bility, the latter heightens the effect by coaching readers to an individualist sense of civic self predicated on the imaginative discounting of the marks of structurally and institutionally supported social inequalities that are re-coded in these popular culture texts as *mere* cultural difference. I have also tried to show how the potentially innovative or progressive political force of the Women in Military Service for America Memorial is colonized by its articulation into this broader popular culture frame or formation. Taken together, then, these memory texts assist in the reconsolidation and naturalization of traditional logics and matrices of privilege that today traverse the various arenas of collective life from the political to juridical, the economic to the social. Quite clearly, then, the general lesson to be drawn from this reading of the contemporary World War II formation is unmistakably Foucauldian: "There *is* power, it *is* productive, and it works through the production and dissemination of truth, disciplining the citizen through a pursuit of the popular."[64] But by inflecting the constitutive and not merely mimetic role of these popular culture memory texts, this essay also argues implicitly that it is possible to remember otherwise, that not only what we remember but how we remember it could be different, and that collective memory could be pressed into the service of a very differ-ent politics. Finally, then, this essay urges rhetorical critics and theorists to critically engage a multifaceted and multiplying contemporary U.S. paregoric rhetoric in whose recently renovated narrative of national be-longing "our" future may (not) lie.

Notes

1. Ronald Takaki, *A Different Mirror: A History of Multicultural America* (Boston: Little, Brown, 1993), 92.

2. As Kaja Silverman explains in *The Threshold of the Visible World* (New York: Routledge, 1996), the given-to-be-seen may be defined as "the operation within the field of vision of the system of intelligibility which is synonymous with the dominant fiction." It "depends for its hegemonic effects on the slotting of the eye into a particular spectatorial position—into a metaphoric geometral point. The latter can then be best defined as *the position from which we apprehend and affirm those elements of the screen which are synonymous with the dominant fiction*" (179). Al-though I invoke this phraseology from the Lacanian lexicon to underscore the spectral or visual character of national identification, the ensuing analysis of the

contemporary American cultural and political scene aims to apprehend the rhetorical rather than psychic and—for Silverman—strictly libidinal transactions that seek to secure fidelity to the nation.

3. George F. Will, "The Statue Sweepstakes," *Newsweek,* August 26, 1991, p. 64.

4. Marita Sturken, *Tangled Memories: The Vietnam War, the AIDS Epidemic, and the Politics of Remembering* (Berkeley: University of California Press, 1997).

5. "About the Memorial: World War II Memorial Homepage," http://www.wwiimemorial.com, September 3, 1999.

> The design concept for the memorial is an ensemble of a lowered plaza surrounding the Rainbow Pool, parapet walls surmounted by transparent architectural arms of stone and metal and two monumental memorial arches. The memorial will include iconography, inscriptions and sculpture as part of the final design. . . . Bronze laurel wreaths are suspended from the oculus of each arch . . . [which] overlook the memorial plaza and Rainbow Pool. . . . The floor of the memorial plaza is an orchestrated blend of green spaces and paved surfaces surrounding the Rainbow Pool. A central ceremonial area is placed at the western apex of the memorial plaza. A curvilinear granite wall is embedded into the waterfalls that navigate the vertical transition between the Reflecting Pool and the Rainbow Pool. Inscriptions honoring the fallen and all who served and a flame of freedom will be incorporated into the ceremonial area. . . . In the center of the plaza, the fountains of the reconstructed Rainbow Pool will be restored to their former splendor as part of the memorial."

6. Subcommittee on Libraries and Memorials of the Committee on House Administration, *Guidelines for the Consideration of Memorials under the Commemorative Works Act,* 103rd Cong., 2nd sess., 1994, p. 2. Both substantively and stylistically, public debate (or the relative lack thereof) over the World War II Memorial differs markedly from the lengthy and often heated rhetorical struggles that emerged over other proposals to recognize the nation's fallen heroes by raising a structure on their behalf on the mall, e.g., the Vietnam Veterans Memorial, the Vietnam Women's Memorial, and the Women in Military Service for America Memorial.

7. An interesting exception was delivered by Judy Scott Feldman, chair-

woman of the National Coalition to Save Our Mall, during her testimony before the Commission of Fine Arts. She objected vigorously to the proposed memorial's "imperial and triumphal design" that was "unacceptably reminiscent of Fascist and Nazi regimes." Cited in Irvin Molotsky, "Panel Backs World War II Memorial on Mall in Washington," *New York Times,* July 21, 2001, p. A1.

8. Molotsky, "Panel Backs World War II Memorial." Across the country, forty-three newspapers (including the *New York Times,* the *Washington Post,* and *USA Today*) printed at least one article or editorial opposing the site, many of them, of course, reprints.

9. Rolland Kidder, "War Memorial Will Be in Its Proper Setting," *Buffalo News,* June 6, 1997, p. 3C.

10. "Remarks by President Clinton at the Tomb of the Unknown Soldier, Arlington National Cemetery," *Federal News Service,* November 11, 1995. Online, LEXIS, July 22, 2000.

11. The memorial's statement of purpose is as follows:

The World War II Memorial will be the first national memorial dedicated to all who served in the armed forces and Merchant Marine of the United States during World War II and acknowledging the commitment and achievement of the entire nation. All military veterans of the war, the citizens on the home front, the nation at large, and the high moral purpose and idealism that motivated the nation's call to arms will be honored. Symbolic of the defining event of the twentieth century in American history, the memorial will be a monument to the spirit, sacrifice, and commitment of the American people, to the common defense of the nation and to the broader causes of peace and freedom from tyranny throughout the world. It will inspire future generations of Americans, deepening their appreciation of what the World War II generation accomplished in securing freedom and democracy. Above all, the memorial will stand for all time as an important symbol of American national unity, a timeless reminder of the moral strength and awesome power that can flow when a free people are at once united and bonded together in a common and just cause. ("About the Memorial")

12. "Clinton Salutes Veterans, Dedicates Memorial Site," *Los Angeles Times,* November 12, 1995, p. 4A.

13. These statements contest Arthur Danto's theoretical claim that a clear distinction is to be made between monuments and memorials. He writes: "We erect monuments so that we shall always remember, and build memorials so that we shall never forget. Thus we have the Washington Monument but the Lincoln Memorial. Monuments commemorate the memorable and embody the myths of beginnings. Memorials ritualize remembrance and mark the reality of ends. . . . The memorial is a special precinct, extruded from life, a segregated enclave where we honor the dead. With monuments we honor ourselves" ("The Vietnam Veterans Memorial and the Washington Mall," *Critical Inquiry* 12 [summer 1986]: 153).

14. David Schribman, "Put the Memorial, Like the War, at the Center," *Buffalo News,* April 26, 1997, p. 3C.

15. Kidder, "War Memorial," p. 3C.

16. William Jefferson Clinton, "Remarks on Responsible Citizenship and Common Ground," Georgetown University, July 6, 1995, p. 5, http://www.americanreview.net.

17. Although popular and academic examinations of the National Mall acknowledge the general significance of the whole as a sum of its parts, a stubborn hermeneutic seems to foreclose apprehending the ways in which the piecemeal construction of additional monuments or memorials supplements and alters its rhetorical force.

18. Another way of describing the aim of my analysis would be to say that it seeks to extend Michael McGee's 1975 call for the rhetorical accounting of the discursive production of a <people> by attending not only to the "material forces, events, and themes in history *only as they have already been mediated or filtered by the Leader whose words [we have typically] studied*" ("In Search of 'The People': A Rhetorical Alternative," *Quarterly Journal of Speech* 61 [1975]: 235–49), but also to those other enunciative sites through which national affiliation is today being produced.

19. Wire Reports, "Memorial Moratorium," *Baltimore Sun,* September 9, 1999, p. 2A. Online, LEXIS, September 10, 1999.

20. There is a growing theoretical and critical literature on the relationships among the nation, the media, and the discursive production of the citizen-subject in the late twentieth century. This analysis takes several of its cues from Lauren Berlant's analysis of infantile citizenship in *The Queen of America Goes to Washington City: Essays on Sex and Citizenship* (Durham: Duke University Press, 1997),

Lawrence Grossberg's account of the politically disaffected citizen in *We Gotta Get Out of This Place: Popular Conservatism and Postmodern Culture* (New York: Routledge, 1992), and Toby Miller's treatment of the cultural citizen in *Technologies of Truth: Cultural Citizenship and the Popular Media* (Minneapolis: University of Minnesota Press, 1998).

21. Clinton, "Responsible Citizenship."

22. Jon Meacham, "Caught in the Line of Fire," *Newsweek,* July 13, 1998, p. 50.

23. Jay Carr, cited in Christopher Caldwell, "Spielberg at War," *Commentary* 106 (October 1998): 48.

24. Martin Arnold, " 'Private Ryan' Receives a Genre," *New York Times,* July 30, 1998, p. E3.

25. Ibid.

26. James Wolcott, "Tanks for the Memories," *Vanity Fair* 456 (August 1998): 73.

27. Jean Bethke Elshtain, "Spielberg's America," *Tikkun* 13 (November/December 1998): C73.

28. Wolcott, "Tanks," 75.

29. Meacham, "Caught," 50.

30. Cited in Nick Charles, "Guts and Glory," *People Weekly,* October 12, 1998, p. 162.

31. Berlant, *The Queen of America,* 57.

32. In a book-length analysis of the return of World War II now in progress, I will attend at length to the question of the representation of women and its political entailments. I simply note here the sexism and at times unabashed misogyny at work throughout the film but perhaps most visible in scenes during which combat abates and members of the Ranger unit engage in "intimate" conversation: for example, the Brooklyn bad boy's recounting of Mrs. Rachel Cherbowitz's advice from the dressing room of his mother's shop that "if [he's] ever scared" he "close [his] eyes and remember these" "44EEs" or "massive things"; and Ryan's jovial recollection of "the last night the four [Ryan brothers] were together," memorable for the brothers' thwarted rape of Alice Jardine, "a girl who just took a nose dive from the ugly tree and hit every branch coming down." Furthermore, although there are no fantasy rape scenarios in Tom Brokaw's *The Greatest Generation* (New York: Random House, 1998), I will argue that certain women fare no better there. I will suggest that the subtle but crucial shift from a neoconservative rhetoric of "family values" to a rhetoric of the "national family"

that I analyze in the following section of this essay is effected in part by the strategic re-membering and repositioning of female bodies and desire. Out of this re-membering emerges a newly determined abject feminine, the "feminist," who refuses to submit her agency to the will of the national family.

33. It is not without consequence that *Saving Private Ryan* structurally elides the sixties and seventies—those socially and politically tumultuous decades in U.S. history during which citizens literally took to the streets.

34. Edward Rothstein, "Rescuing the War Hero from 1990s Skepticism," *New York Times,* August 3, 1998, p. E2.

35. Brokaw has since edited and published several other best-selling books for which World War II serves as the central reference, organizing theme, or point of departure. See, for example, *An Album of Memories: Personal Histories from the Greatest Generation* (New York: Random House, 2001), and *The Greatest Generation Speaks: Letters and Reflections* (New York: Random House, 1999), all reissued in audio format.

36. Richard Goldstein, "World War II Chic," *Village Voice,* January 19, 1999, p. 47.

37. Brokaw, *The Greatest Generation,* 15.

38. Ibid., xx.

39. Ibid., 388–89.

40. Ibid., 388.

41. Ibid., xx.

42. Toby Miller, *The Well-Tempered Self: Citizenship, Culture, and the Postmodern Subject* (Baltimore: Johns Hopkins University Press, 1993).

43. My discussion of disincorporation is indebted to Michael Warner's theorization in "The Mass Public and the Mass Subject," in *The Phantom Public Sphere,* ed. Bruce Robbins (Minneapolis: University of Minnesota Press), 234–56.

44. Brokaw, *The Greatest Generation,* 200–201.

45. Again and again the dismantling of the welfare state and privatization of social responsibility is sometimes boldly and other times more subtly encouraged. See, for example, the story of James and Dorothy Dowling in the midst of which Brokaw writes: "James Dowling was orphaned soon after he was born. His mother died when he was only six months old and his father was unable to care for this baby and his four brothers and sisters. *In those simpler times, when much of social welfare was a matter of good-hearted people,* the plight of James and his siblings was made known in the church. The minister announced that someone had

to take in these children. James and two of his brothers were taken home by the Conklins, Clarence and Anna" (*The Greatest Generation,* 46, emphasis added). Or Brokaw's closing words to "The Dumbos," a vignette recounting the postwar trials and tribulations of four couples "in the small South Dakota city of Yankton": "Outside of our own families, to those of us growing up in Yankton at the time, these World War II couples were emblematic of the values that shaped our lives. In many respects, *their marriages and the way they conducted them were a form of community service*" (249, emphasis added).

46. Brokaw, *The Greatest Generation,* 200.

47. Ibid., 17.

48. Ibid., xxx.

49. Ibid.

50. Annete Kuhn, *Family Secrets: Acts of Memory and Imagination* (New York: Verso, 1995), 17.

51. The literature on the relation of the visual image or the photograph and the verbal text is extensive. Some key works are: Roland Barthes, *Mythologies* (London: Cape, 1972); Roland Barthes, "The Rhetoric of the Image," *Image-Music-Text* (New York: Noonday, 1977), 32–37; John Berger, *Ways of Seeing* (New York: Viking Penguin, 1997); W. J. T. Mitchell, *Picture Theory: Essays on Verbal and Visual Representation* (Chicago: University of Chicago Press, 1994); Susan Sontag, *On Photography* (New York: Doubleday, 1977); and John Tagg, *The Burden of Representation: Essays on Photographies and Histories* (Minneapolis: University of Minnesota Press, 1993).

52. See Lisa Cartwright, *Screening the Body: Tracing Medicine's Visual Culture* (Minneapolis: University of Minnesota Press, 1995).

53. Wendy Brown, *States of Injury: Power and Freedom in Late Modernity* (Princeton: Princeton University Press, 1995), 57.

54. Linda Witt, *The Day the Nation Said "Thanks!" A History and Dedication of the Women in Military Service for America Memorial* (Washington, DC: Military Women's Press, 1999), 96.

55. On the minimalist aesthetic (and I would add rhetoric) of monumental material culture, see, for example: Carole Blair, Marsha S. Jeppeson, and Enrico Pucci Jr., "Public Memorializing in Postmodernity: The Vietnam Veterans Memorial as Prototype," *Quarterly Journal of Speech* 77 (1991): 263–88; John Bodnar, *Remaking America: Public Memory Commemoration, and Patriotism in the Twentieth Century* (Princeton: Princeton University Press, 1992); John R. Gillis, ed., *Commemo-*

rations: *The Politics of National Identity* (Princeton: Princeton University Press, 1994); Kirk Savage, *Standing Soldiers, Kneeling Slaves: Race, War, and Monument in Nineteenth Century America* (Princeton: Princeton University Press, 1997); and Sturken, *Tangled Memories.*

56. Witt, *The Day the Nation Said "Thanks!"* 94.

57. Peggy Phelan, *Unmarked: The Politics of Performance* (New York: Routledge, 1993), 7.

58. The argument I am advancing here is not that WIMS never could perform a radical, interruptive politics. What I am claiming is that at this particular time-place, in the context of the cultural formation of which it is a part, it is not doing so. It may be worthwhile to note here that one of the implications of this analysis for thinking about rhetoric more generally is that the popular "polysemy thesis" oftentimes begs rather than answers the question, "What rhetorical work is being done by or through this text?" Although grasping the polysemic nature of all discourse and practice is an important first step, a rigorous rhetorical analysis proceeds to discern those forces that operate provisionally to secure—through processes of articulation, disarticulation, and rearticulation—the effectivity of the text, utterance, or practice. For a cogent review of the literature in the field and a call to sharpen our theoretical assumptions and critical practice, see Leah Ceccarelli, "Polysemy: Multiple Meanings in Rhetorical Criticism," *Quarterly Journal of Speech* 84 (1998): 395–415.

59. Jacques Lacan, *Four Fundamental Concepts of Psychoanalysis,* ed. Jacques-Alain Miller, trans. Alan Sheridan (New York: Norton, 1979), 93.

60. Indeed, the exhibit's hand-held script is replete with various gestures of pointing: "See the uniform of Navy nurse Doris Yetter"; "Notice the hand-made clothespin used by Madeline Ullom"; "Also in the exhibit is a pair of custom-made mosquito boots, worn by Army nurses in Africa"; "Notice the photograph of a woman packing a parachute"; etc. For an extensive analysis of the deployment of the constative utterance in museums of natural history and fine art, see Mieke Bal, *Double Exposures: The Subject of Cultural Analysis* (New York: Routledge, 1996).

61. I borrow the term "exhibition rhetoric" from Bruce Ferguson, "Exhibition Rhetorics: Material Speech and Utter Sense," in *Thinking about Exhibitions,* ed. Reesa Greenberg, Bruce W. Ferguson, and Sandy Nairne (New York: Routledge, 1996), 175–90. There he tethers together Enzensberger's expanded concept of the "cultural industries" ("to include advertising, education, and any in-

stitutional use of media techniques intended for vast audiences or what is now often referred to cynically as 'infotainment' " [176]) and a classical conception of rhetoric ("a strategic system of representation" [176]) in order to argue that "[t]he will to influence is at the core of any exhibition" (179).

62. It should be noted that the integration act exhibit, originally placed next to a wholly separate exhibit documenting the history of the memorial's emergence, will soon be moved to a display case situated between the World War II and new Korean War exhibits (Brigadier General Wilma L. Vaught, Ret. [President, Women in Military Service for America Memorial Foundation, Inc.], interview by author, Washington, DC, June 6, 2000).

63. Tom Engelhardt, *The End of Victory Culture: Cold War America and the Disillusioning of a Generation* (New York: Basic Books, 1995), 236.

64. Miller, *Technologies,* 265.

10

Framing Memory through Eulogy

Ronald Reagan's Long Good-bye

Amos Kiewe

On August 12, 1996, Nancy Reagan, the former First Lady, gave tribute to her husband during the Republican National Convention in San Diego. Mrs. Reagan spoke briefly but poignantly following a videotape viewing dedicated to the former president. Her short tribute brought tears to many in the convention hall. At the conclusion of her presentation she repeated a line Ronald Reagan had spoken during the 1992 Republican National Convention: "When I'm gone, I hope it will be recorded that I appealed to your best hopes, not your worst fears." The tears and emotional displays at the convention were indicative of Reagan's cherished memory and heroic standing among Republicans. The tribute was also a testament to Reagan's rhetorical efforts in conditioning memories of his presidency. But above all else, the tribute given by Mrs. Reagan to her husband (quoting her husband's own words) was situated within the context of death. As such, the tribute took on a eulogistic form—a eulogy before death. Why would a living former president be given a tribute that borders on a eulogy? This tribute and other speeches, I contend, were consistent with a strategic effort on the part of Ronald Reagan and those entrusted with the construction of his historical place to frame the public memory of his role in renewing the American dream.

All leaders are concerned with their heritage and consequently are eager to secure their place in history. Presidents, in particular, are prone to the practice of conditioning memories. These efforts are often understood in terms of the recognized genre of the farewell addresses. My purpose in the present paper, however, is to set aside these generic qualities and instead attend to these efforts in terms of the rhetorical construction of public memory.[1] While presidents seek to leave a legacy of their achievements in office, the construction of public memory requires additional rhetorical efforts that aim at mythologizing a president's time and space in the nation's collective memory.[2]

Like other recent presidents Reagan was concerned with his place in history, but unlike other presidents he pursued numerous opportunities to fuse eulogistic references to suggest his preferred memories. Late in his second term and on several occasions thereafter, Ronald Reagan used his speeches and public statements to condition memories in a unique way—by crafting his own eulogy. Reagan's efforts, I contend, are different from mere wishes of a leader for a good historical account of one's public life. Reagan, I submit, consciously sought rhetorical opportunities to condition his own legacy by crafting the very words he hoped others would utter after his ultimate departure. I arrive at this contention by analyzing Reagan's efforts at incorporating eulogistic elements in several of his late speeches and his efforts at framing the discourse of his public memory.

Ronald Reagan understood better than most recent presidents the power of rhetoric and mastered its practices throughout his political life. He would often suggest the narratives that would one day reflect on his presidency and his political life. At the zenith of his many years in politics he began to write his final chapter and to project a historical account of his political role and significance. Eulogistic elements would thus fuse themselves into several of Reagan's late public orations, such as his 1989 farewell address and his 1992 Republican Convention address.

I ground my discussion in the functions of the Greek funeral orations. I supplement this discussion with the notion of time and timing and the conversion of time into space.[3] The connecting thought here is the view that eulogies are temporal discourses meant to construct timeless memories and consequently seek to construct future space for such memories.

The eulogy seeks an enduring presence located in an audience member's memory. Likewise, eulogies to prominent individuals seek presence in a community's myth and narrative.

I stipulate here that similar to the Greek *epitaphioi* that established Athens through myths and sacred values attributed to its past heroes, in departing and eulogizing the polis, Reagan eulogized himself to secure historical memories. I argue that in fusing eulogistic elements in his late speeches, Reagan sought to offer an account of his presidency that he hoped would be accepted and repeated after his ultimate departure. In other words, he hoped to condition a preferred account of his presidency that would be installed in the polity's public memory. Reagan developed his persona mythically by converting the temporal into timeless and hence into memory.[4] The framing of public memory was constructed by turning the temporal into sacred and moral text via eulogistic references.[5] Thus, the temporal Reagan sought to become a mythically enduring Reagan by constructing space for his time in the polity's story. In so doing, Reagan hoped to invest his political persona with moral imperatives whose very endurance could guarantee memory.

The connection between rhetoric and public memory has ancient origins. The ancient Athenians recognized the importance of public address in crafting stable and stabilizing public memories. Contemporary students of public memory would do well to attend to classical rhetorical notions of the construction of public memories.

Epitaphioi and *Encomium* in the Service of Political Memory

In addition to serving ceremonial discourses to memorialize the dead and console the grieved, eulogies have been used throughout history as political tools. Likewise, the *encomium* is more than tribute as it, too, functions to instill more than just a lasting memory. The *encomium* has political objectives embedded in the intersection between character and ideology and between the temporal and the mythic. Both *epitaphioi* and *encomium* are more than what they appear to be as the ceremonial wrapping can camouflage political objectives.

As epideictic speech, funeral orations are performative, as they rely on noble acts and thoughts and their ritual function is to create "a sense of community among its participants."[6] Memory, in this sense, is a function of the ritual of eulogies. Epideictic speech, Farrell argues, closely resembles the genre of *Poetics,* and in a eulogy the literary form functions "to praise or exalt the virtues of a human life before an audience that Aristotle described as 'spectators'."[7] Referencing Loraux, Farrell contends that she "has grasped perfectly how aesthetic pain can prepare us for the invention of public rhetorical meaning."[8] Eulogy, then, "creates and evokes emotions (pathos) not so much as a vehicle of proper audience cognition, but rather as an affiliative bond between perfected action and human response."[9] Eulogies can thus function beyond commemorating the deeds of the dead. The emotional state of loss and the memories of the deceased can be harnessed to rhetorically instruct, educate, guide, and motivate.

Similarly, Hauser presents the case for the epideictic as carrying a much more significant role in public life than mere commemoration.[10] Seeking to resurrect ceremonial address from mere praise or blame, Hauser links epideictic and *phronesis* to show how rhetoric can "overcome the emotion of prejudice in framing public issues."[11] In this sense, epideictic functions to educate and not just commemorate. "In this respect," writes Hauser, "epideictic occupies a unique place in celebrating the deeds of exemplars who set the tone for civic community and the encomiast serves an equally unique role as a teacher of civic virtues." Aristotle, who understood well the role of the epideictic, assigned "its practitioners the responsibility for telling the story of lived virtue." Thus, "by valorizing heroes who are emblematic of a society's best qualities, encomia provide concrete guidance on how to live in harmony with noble ideals." Virtues are "proven" through the narration of the hero's deeds, not through the factional judgments of deliberative and forensic speeches.[12] The user of the epideictic, then, can advance political objectives without necessarily resorting to overt partisan advocacy. Persuasion, in this sense, can succeed when generated by an appealing narrative as distinct of an overt advocacy.

Just as the Greek *epitaphioi* invented Athens, political discourse, especially presidential discourse, has functioned to invent the American myth.[13] Presidential speech is often not about historical truth but about rhetorical truth or myth (one can argue that historical truth is indeed rhetorical). Hope, vision, and optimism, the ingredients of political and social continuity and stability, and the bridge between the cherished past and an unknown future, can make sense only through the rhetorical. Similar to funeral orations, several aspects are present in the rhetoric of memorializing: the marking of time, the dialectic between past and future, praising the dead and lamenting their departure, preservation of the polis, and the empowerment of the polity and its citizens.[14]

In the presidential farewell address, Campbell and Jamieson tell us, the president engages in the "ritual of departure."[15] Reagan, however, used his late addresses to achieve more than a mere "ritual of departure." He suggested his own eulogy. Similar to famous Greek funeral orations, Reagan's late addresses extolled the nation and its myths. These eulogistic-like narratives can and do invent a persona and a myth and thus can condition future discourses and accounts. Though the myth is usually created through eulogies to a deceased, most intriguing is the notion that eulogies can also be delivered by a departing yet living individual. In the case of Ronald Reagan, the rhetoric of departure, his 1989 farewell address, his 1989 last radio address, his 1992 Republican Convention address, and even his 1994 "Alzheimer Letter," can collectively be read also as eulogy narratives. Though most if not all presidents are concerned with two kinds of audiences, "the living citizens and the future historians,"[16] Reagan, in my view, distinctly sought to condition historical memories.[17] I go even further. I can detect the very suggestion of specific words Reagan hoped others would use in establishing his public memory.

Reagan's January 11, 1989, Farewell Address

This (almost) final speech in office (three days later Reagan would give his final radio address) reads like the final chapter in a long and unfolding story. In fact, Reagan would use the very word—chapter—as a metaphor for political life depicted as a story whose final chapters were drawing to a close. The address was distinctly nostalgic and personal, and the use of first-person references was extensive.

The address was about the marking of time: "This is the 34th time I'll speak to you from the Oval Office and the last. We've been together 8 years now, and soon it'll be time for me to go." Reagan was parting with mixed emotions: "[P]arting is such sweet sorrow."[18] One can easily read this statement in two ways: the physical departure from the office as well as the spiritual departure from the living. Such a reading is not out of place given the association Reagan made among "departing," "time," and "soon." In a poetic sense, the phrase "soon it'll be time for me to go" can be read as a hint of ultimate departure.

Writing himself into the Capitol's political scene, Reagan also recalled moments of solitude when viewing the scenery from a window in the family quarters of the White House. As he described the view he incorporated in the scene the monuments to the nation's great leaders: Washington, Jefferson, and Lincoln. The very viewing of a cherished scene for the last time enhanced the double meaning of Reagan's departure. One can read in Reagan's narrative the subtle inclusion of his character with these men.

Reagan described his term in office as a journey whose end has come: "[W]e are reaching our destination."[19] Again, the emphasis was on the "end" and the reaching of one's destination. The journey, though, was at times rough, sometimes exhilarating, he said. Reagan highlighted two achievements he was most proud of and which he wanted to be remembered for: the economic recovery and the recovery of the nation's morale. At the end of the journey he was proud of the respect the United States enjoyed throughout the world. His mission, he stated, was rather simple: to rediscover America's strength. His job was simple because the task was simple. Implied in Reagan's observation was his surprise that such a simple truism was not rediscovered earlier and that it had fallen on him to show the way. Reagan also implied that his greatness lay in his ability to use common sense in the service of the country.[20]

Reagan set out to prove in his farewell address the rightness of his political agenda. In so doing he provided a narrative wrapped in time metaphor: "Well, back in 1980, when I was running for President, it was all so different. Some pundits said our programs would result in catastrophe." The result was the opposite—"The longest peacetime expansion in our history." This achievement he attributed not to his being "The Great Communicator" as some had suggested but his communicating ideas and principles grounded in two centuries of wisdom and experience.[21] In other words, Reagan humbly rejected his authorship of the economic success and attributed the success to implementing principles established long ago by others but largely forgotten. Such humility defined his character as a great but humble president.

The successes, stated Reagan, were greater than anticipated: "We meant to change a nation, and instead, we changed the world."[22] Reagan shifted to "we," thus sharing the successes of his administration with those who believed in him and supported him. But the proceeding statement was unmistakably designed to leave a legacy. Reflecting on earlier years, Reagan told of the fork in the river "right in the middle of my life. I never meant to go into politics. It wasn't my intention when I was young . . . I was happy with my career in the entertainment world, but I ultimately went into politics because I wanted to protect something precious." Thus, out of pure and innocent conviction arose a politician with a purpose who ended up ushering a revolution, "the first [revolution] . . . in the history of mankind that truly reversed the course of government, and with three little words: 'We the People.' . . . This belief has been the underlying basis for everything I've tried to do these past 8 years."[23]

Reagan merged the generic lesson of presidential farewell address with the recounting of his achievements. The lesson that he advocated not be forgotten was the need for "informed patriotism." Against the background of ambiguity and ambivalence regarding America's heritage and tradition, Reagan warned "of an eradication of the American memory that could result, ultimately, in an erosion of the American spirit. Let's start with some basics: more attention to American history and a greater emphasis on civic ritual."[24] The historical lessons Reagan asked be taught again and with renewed purpose were the same lessons that guided his political life, especially his presidency. The teaching of this history would fit well the patriotic spirit Reagan brought to the country since 1981 and would thus fit perfectly with the narratives of his many speeches. An "informed patriotism" would include, no doubt, Reagan's role in restoring patriotism to America.

The phrase that came to identify his presidency—a "shining city upon a hill"—captured the essence of the memories Reagan sought to secure: his time and his vision. Reagan explained its origin in John Winthrop's vision of America and throughout his life his vision as well—"a tall proud city built on rocks stronger than oceans, windswept, God-blessed, and teeming with people of all kinds living in harmony and peace." Reagan continued: "And how stands the city on this winter night? More prosperous, more secure, and happier than it was 8 years ago . . . after 200 years, two centuries, she still stands strong and true on the granite ridge, and her glow has held steady no matter what storm. And she's still a beacon, still a magnet for all who must have freedom, for all the pilgrims from all the lost places who are hurtling through the darkness, toward home." The final line climaxed the mythical moment: "We've done our part."[25] "We"—Reagan and "the men and women of the Reagan revolution"—brought America back from the abyss and made the city upon the hill shine and beacon *again*.[26] Humbly and subtly Reagan wrote himself into his unfolding saga—he restored precious and timeless principles and values that helped put America back on its feet. Reagan wrote himself into history as a leader assigned with the mission to restore America's spirit and to make the country stronger and sounder for the world to witness.

Final Radio Address: January 14, 1989

Officially, this very short speech was Reagan's final presidential address. The marking of time was the address's main thrust, but the tone differed from the address given only three days earlier. If the farewell address was personal, the final radio address was intimate, bordering on self-disclosure. The eight years in office were surprisingly described as "tumultuous . . . in perspective." Quick to balance this statement, Reagan suggested that his years as president are "best left to the impartial judgment of history." Yet, recounting America's accomplishments under his leadership and the country's renewed strength and respect throughout the world, Reagan stated that "the story of these last 8 years and this Presidency goes far beyond any personal concern. It is a continuation really of a far larger story, a story of a people and a cause—a cause that from our earliest beginning has defined us as a nation and given purpose to our national existence."[27] Reagan sought to project his leadership as unique and wanted his successes to be appreciated in the context of tumultuous years.

History for Reagan was a *story,* an apt metaphor for his preferred narrative mode, as it allowed him to write himself into his narrative and thus project his preferred interpretation. Though Reagan claimed that his was only part of a continuous story/history, reminding the people of America's story and his role in it amplified the very character he so humbly portrayed. Reagan's very attempt to let history be the judge functioned to promote the opposite strategy—to condition a favorable version of his role through the passivity of his approach.

Republican Convention Speech: August 17, 1992

In 1992 former president Ronald Reagan was invited to speak to the Republican National Convention. Reagan delivered his familiar ode to the party, to conservatism, and to his presidency and heritage. Though Reagan sought to rally people behind the candidacy of George Bush, Reagan's speech contains distinct references to his role in history, to final good-byes, to eulogy to self, and to posterity.

Addressing the party at the formal and official start of a new presidential campaign was one more opportunity for Reagan to say farewell. But the differences between this address and a presidential farewell address are worth noting. For one, the address of a former president at a convention is not invested with the symbolic and ceremonial attributes of a presidential speech. The status of a former president is not the same as that of a sitting president though a former president can be held in great esteem. Yet the opportunity to influence is present, especially the opportunity to appear wiser and more reflective. The appearance itself could be construed as the last hurrah and the final opportunity of an elder politician to write oneself into history.

Former presidents, especially successful and loved ones, can offer the party convention the discourse of unity and a metaphorical transition from a cherished past to an optimistic future. The former president can influence the electability of the presidential candidate and instill confidence in the party's future, its agenda, and its elected candidate. For Reagan, the convention also afforded another opportunity to depart, to talk about the end of his journey, and to shape the historical account of his presidency—in short, to eulogize himself.

The address is distinctly about time: the passing of time, the marking of time, and Reagan's role in constructing America's time. The address is about Reagan and his time and about the age-youth polarity. The beginning of the speech signaled the theme: "Over the years, I've addressed this convention as a private citizen, as a Governor, as a presidential candidate, as a President and now, once again tonight, as private citizen Ronald Reagan." Reagan noted his advanced age and the life journey he enjoyed thereof. In sign-posting his political life cycle, Reagan noted that he had seen the range of technological marvels from the Model-T to landing on the moon, two world wars, and the rise and fall of communism. The recounting of these momentous events was set to establish Reagan's age-related wisdom. The detailing of events over a century's span was also meant to signal that Reagan approached the end of his journey, but not before he would spend a few minutes to "talk about a country that is forever young."[28]

"I have not only seen, but lived the marvels of what historians have called the 'American Century,' "he said. According to Reagan, his wonderful journey paralleled America's greatest period—the twentieth century. He enjoyed his journey because he knew that his future was inspired by America's past, and with this simple formula he said he implemented throughout his political life, the country had been kept forever young. In his view, America's uniqueness was found in its ideals, as distinct from an empire of landmass, subjugated peoples, or military might.[29] The faith in the ideals of democracy and "the creativity and entrepreneurial drive of the American people" were the attributes that made America a special country.[30] These ideals were Reagan's ideals. With the teacher-student polarity, Reagan implied that he was taught a lesson by the founder-teachers, and now it was he who was teaching others the successful lesson.

His optimism, Reagan stated, and his rejection of those who considered America as weakening were the foundations of his presidency. Reagan interjected himself as an agent in the perpetuation of America's idealistic scene. He rejected the malaise of his predecessor, the high interest rates, and the double-digit inflation rate. With his inherent optimism, implied Reagan, he set a different course for America.[31] He reminded the audience of his long fight against Soviet communism and that despite ridicule from the other party his course proved to be the correct one.[32] Reagan also spoke of the simplicity in changing the domestic course. Here, too, with a simple truism, he reversed the course of the government, helping those who should help themselves. Reagan attributed to himself the success of conservative ideology. The life cycle Reagan outlined functioned to write himself into a successful century, replete with achievements, progress, and optimism. The proximity of Reagan to the various times of his narrative served to elevate him from mere observer to an experienced and wise elder statesman whose own achievements were driven by the nation's growth and vision.

His task now was to ensure the continuation of his idealism after his departure from the scene, repeating his famous rhetorical aphorism: "America's best days are yet to come. Our proudest moments are yet to be. Our most glorious achievements are just ahead." The essence of his political views was summed up by quoting Emerson, who proclaimed America "The country of tomorrow." "And yet tomorrow might never have happened had we lacked the courage in the 1980's to chart a course of strength and honor."[33] In Reagan's account of his time, it was his courage and the people's courage that brought the required change. He returned briefly to his earlier apocalyptic rhetoric, suggesting the dire fate America would have suffered had he not intervened and changed the nation's erroneous course.

The qualities required of the president were enormous, he stated, adding, "The presidency is a serious business. We cannot afford to take a chance."[34] Though Reagan seeded doubt in the Democratic candidate, his endorsement of George Bush was less than enthusiastic, and it, too, revealed much about Reagan himself. Though Reagan called Bush "a trustworthy and level-headed leader," the metaphor he used indicates otherwise. Reagan had often fashioned himself as the "captain" or the "skipper" of the nation, the one who navigated "the nation to safe waters and a secure harbor." Yet, relative to Reagan's sense of direction and mission, Bush was only "a steady hand on the tiller through the choppy waters of the 90's."[35] Reagan implied that Bush lacked the sense of direction and that supporting the Bush candidacy was important only to the extent of ensuring Reagan's legacy.

Reagan portrayed the crucial nature of the 1992 presidential election by an allusion to his first prominent national address twenty-eight years earlier: a "time for choosing."[36] As in 1964, the country had now reached a crossroad. Stated Reagan: "There is widespread doubt about our public institutions and profound concern, not merely about the economy but about the overall direction of this great country."[37] Reagan often used the road, crossroad, or fork in the road/river metaphors as the vehicle for portraying the correct choices he made. The correct direction for the country was clearly Reagan's, reminding the nation not to stray from the course he had charted.

Implied in Reagan's narrative was his hope that Bush would keep the Reagan course. It was for the rest of the nation to do the same. Stated Reagan: "[N]othing could be more tragic, after having come all this way on the journey of renewal we began 12 years ago, than if America herself forgot the lessons of individual liberty that she has taught to a grateful world."[38] By personifying America, Reagan could only imply his role in the nation's history—precisely his objective since any direct attribution of heroism to self would backfire.

The proof for his successful course could be found in the emulation of America's democratic experience by the new democracies springing up around the world. With the proof of the successful course at hand, Reagan requested that his lessons continue to be taught. Reagan projected a future beyond his life, stating that America "remains on a voyage of discovery, a land that has never become, but is always in the act of becoming," and "A decade after we summoned America to a new beginning, we are beginning still."[39] The metaphors of continuity woven into famous phrases from past addresses were designed not only to ensure the polity's future but also to ground the future in Reagan's political compass.

Though the country's journey was described as continuing, Reagan's personal journey, he said, had reached "the latest chapter in a story that began a quarter of a century ago." His political life, he indicated, was a continuous story with identifiable chapters. Now he had completed the latest chapter. Though his phrasing left open the door for yet another fare-well, his following statement revealed that the end was nearing: "And whatever else history may say about me when I'm gone, I hope it will record that I appealed to your best hopes, not your worst fears, to your confidence rather than your doubts." With death hovering above the spec-ter of hope and fear, confidence and doubt, Reagan eulogized himself for posterity, hoping for a favorable account. Unhesitatingly, he talked about "when I'm gone" and the historical record of his time. Projecting be-yond his lifetime, Reagan added: "My dream is that you will travel the road ahead with liberty's lamp guiding your steps and opportunity's arm steadying your way."[40] His legacy was based on two overlapping values: optimism and confidence in the future. All Reagan could hope to achieve now was to secure these very values as metonomical of his political persona.

Like a parent or grandparent on the deathbed, offering blessings to surrounding family members, Reagan's departing words were telling:

> My fondest hope for each one of you—and especially for the young people here—is that you will love your country, not for her power or wealth, but for her selflessness and her idealism. May each of you have the heart to conceive, the understanding to direct, and the hand to execute works that will make the world a little better for you having been here.
>
> May all of you as Americans never forget your heroic origins, never fail to seek divine guidance, and never lose your natural, God-given optimism.
>
> And finally, my fellow Americans, may every dawn be a great new beginning for America, and every evening bring us closer to that shining city upon a hill.[41]

The departing message to the next generation included words of wisdom couched in the familiar "city on a hill" metaphors of Reagan's polity. In his final thoughts, Reagan condensed his lifelong political perspective— America's heroic past as the vehicle for inspiring future generations, divine guidance in America's civil religion, and an inborn American optimism. Now, Reagan was ready to depart, but "Before I go," with its literal and metaphoric meaning co-joined, he asked his beloved wife and ultimately his partner in his "life's journey" to join him.[42] The final departure with its double meaning ended Reagan's journey.

Reagan's Alzheimer Letter: November 1, 1994

In a brief but touching letter, Ronald Reagan informed the nation of his affliction with Alzheimer's Disease. The letter confirmed earlier rumors that the former president was ill. Now in a formal and official way, the disease was disclosed. The letter sought to disengage Reagan from the public, resorting to sentimentality as the primary strategy of remembrance. The letter signaled that Reagan would speak in public no more.

Yet, in one brief but distinct paragraph, Reagan departed (again) from the nation, fusing eulogistic reference:

> Whenever the Lord calls me home, whenever that may be, I will leave with the greatest love for this country of ours and eternal optimism for its future.
>
> I now begin the journey that will lead me into the sunset of my life. I know that for America there will always be a bright dawn ahead.[43]

Reagan's lifelong pursuit—projecting optimism and confidence in America's future—did not fail him even as he prepared for the ultimate departure. The journey metaphor, an apt one for politicians who wish to claim that they have been happy because they did good deeds, was nearing its end. Though the journey for our hero is nearing its end, the nation's journey is forever ongoing. Life-death, continuity-end—these are the implied themes of this narrative.

With the juxtaposition of life and death, self and country, pessimism and optimism, sunrise and sunset, Reagan artfully fused eulogistic elements into his final good-bye. Reagan put the nation above all while his own life was now in the Lord's hands. Time is the master metaphor here, whereby Reagan's time is fast approaching while the nation's time is forever secured. The underlying message is that while the hero is departing, his deeds will live forever.

Reagan's Epilogue as Eulogy

The perspective taken here is that of recasting public address in terms of the construction of public memory and the usefulness of classical rhetorical principles in understanding modern political discourse. The case of Ronald Reagan illustrates an ancient rhetorical practice and explains the construction of an enduring legacy of a president.

Funeral orations are about the passing of time, preserving a heritage, and empowering the living. Such were Reagan's most recent addresses. Toward the end of his political career and as a former president, Reagan would look back and claim to have come full circle—a circle that began many years earlier also at a Republican convention. Reagan's time/story served to elucidate the virtues he implemented and now he asked that they be continued. He did not elaborate on his political time for his sake but for the country's sake. This strategy allowed Reagan to project humility and to imply his lifelong vision of a better tomorrow for the nation. With this narrative, Reagan hoped he would be remembered as the humble and selfless hero.

Time is the distinct mark of these discourses and the metaphor for the life-death polarity. With the aid of age-youth polarity, the nearing of death is hovering above his rhetoric. Indeed, funeral orations generate "extraordinary knowledge . . . by taking its hearers out of ordinary time," and thus make time sacred." The occasion asks "participants to embrace past, present, and future," and thus creates "a strong sense of immortality . . . of time beyond time, of life beyond life."[44] Ultimately, the funeral oration works through "a transcendent principle that makes . . . otherwise chaotic and brutal history intelligible and even worthy of celebration."[45]

The passing of time intuitively means that the aging process is underway. But in Reagan's narrative only he was aging, not the nation. Reagan made references to his advanced age and experience but rejected the aging process of the nation or its glory. On the contrary, his addresses projected optimism in a distinct contrast with his dawn of life. The strategy is striking. By downplaying his fate and extolling the nation's, Reagan humbly but successfully narrated his departure, hoping for a space in the nation's public memory. The temporal, Reagan hoped, would become timeless.

In this timeless, sacred moment Reagan sought to create a permanent space for his legacy within the broader narrative of America. These late addresses function to both create this sacred space and craft the shape of Reagan's legacy within American public memory. While time moves onward, Reagan's rhetoric constructs America as fixed and stable, enduring and unassailable. It is in this enduring, sacred American space that Reagan seeks to fashion his own memorial and, thereby, craft his own eulogy.

The addresses are not devoid of ideological trappings, however. Republican ideology, artfully and subtly dispersed under the cluster of time and journey metaphors, is central to Reagan's addresses. With the simplicity of repetition, Reagan romanticized his role in America's history, resorting to his favored themes and his best-known rhetorical staples: "the time for choosing," "evil empire," "new beginning," and "a shining city upon a hill."

In all of these addresses, Reagan was very much the hero of his own narrative. Like the speaker in a eulogy, the recounting of the past centered on familiar and cherished memories—the kind that could easily secure identification with the people through mythical presence.

Reagan's addresses are about *his* account of America's history; they are not about conveying truths but about accepting ideals. Like the Athenian *epitaphioi* that purposefully blurred the distinctions between life and death, reality and fantasy, in order to invent a utopic Athens, so are Reagan's addresses. Indeed, the addresses are about an American utopia that remains constant—"a shining city on a hill" very much like the mythic city the Athenians invented.[46]

Just as funeral orations place symbols in opposition to function rhetorically on the audience,[47] Reagan's addresses are about contrasting symbols. He spoke about his advanced age relative the nation's youthfulness (age-youth), his successful presidential time in contrast with his predecessor's time of despair (light-dark), his party's ideals in contrast with those of the opposition (light-dark, words-deeds), and the American century of successes in a world replete with wars and subjugation (America/Freedom-others/subjugation).[48] In all these polarities, Reagan stated that America was always "set apart by our faith in the ideals of Democracy."[49] As he narrated America's successes, Reagan elucidated a historical account of the nation that was stable, idealistic, and visionary. The successful course had been charted already. What was required now was to continue the safe course.

Reagan's addresses of departure are not about projecting an argument but about accepting premises, which were foundational to his ideology. He attributed America's successes to its core values of individualism, optimism, simplicity, democratic ideals, divine guidance, free markets, and the rejection of a powerful government. Though the addresses collectively supply ample examples to prove the rightness of these premises, the addresses are not about proving but about accepting these values. This strategy works when fantasy and vision are constructed as long enduring, thus they appear traditional and mythical. They are not presented as propositions, nor are they open to counterarguments. Finally, as Ochs suggests, the funeral address is not an argument but a story, not reasons with proofs but a dramatic form capable of containing a plot, characters, and action—Reagan's addresses are inherently stories with a plot, characters, and action.[50] The Reagan story/plot is about belief in a better future, about moral lessons, and about succeeding despite insurmountable odds and doomsayers. Reagan is the unstated hero of his plot against a government that thought it knew better. He acted on his faith, relied on the nation's moral character, and got results. He was now ready to depart knowing he did good deeds. His last request was for America to "travel the road ahead with liberty's lamp guiding your steps."[51]

Throughout these addresses, Reagan projected virtues to be continued after he is gone. A lament is implied in case his work did not continue. As the predominant feature of his address was the success of his presidency and the restoration of American values, the addresses maintain an undertone of lament for a future devoid of his legacy. The lament functions as both a subtle persuasive strategy and a eulogy. As a strategy, the lament focuses attention on action and his character, which should be admired after death. As a eulogy, the lament adds the sadness and sorrow appropriate for the occasion of a beloved person departing from the scene and the contemplation of life without the deceased.

Ever conscious of what history would say about him and his role in America's polity, Reagan ended his political life with a series of addresses that suggest a preferred historical accounting. His rhetorical strategy is intriguing as he sought to influence those who would look back at him after his ultimate departure. The Great Communicator was concerned about communicating his version of America's story. The addresses that feature eulogistic elements were on the surface deliberative and ceremonial addresses, designated as farewell addresses, meant to rally the nation or the party behind a presidential candidate or designed to promote awareness of a debilitating disease. These addresses share a subtle strategy to secure the memory of a leader by resorting to eulogistic elements of and by a departing leader.

Notes

1. See Karlyn K. Campbell and Kathleen Hall Jamieson, *Deeds Done in Words* (Chicago: University of Chicago Press, 1990).

2. It is one thing to remember President Eisenhower's warning about the

military industrial complex, but it is at an entirely different level to remember President Reagan as the one who renewed the nation's values.

3. Michael Leff, "Textual Criticism: The Legacy of G. P. Mohrmann," *Quarterly Journal of Speech* 72 (1986): 377–89.

4. Robert Hariman, "Time and the Reconstitution of Gradualism in King's Address: Response to Cox," in *Text in Context: Critical Dialogues on Significant Episodes in American Political Rhetoric,* ed. Michael C. Leff and Fred J. Kaouffeld (Davis, CA: Hermagoras Press, 1989), 205–17.

5. Michael Leff, "Dimensions of Temporality in Lincoln's Second Inaugural," *Communication Reports* 1 (1988): 26–31.

6. M. F. Carter, "The Ritual Functions of Epideictic Rhetoric: The Case of Socrates' Funeral Oration," *Rhetorica* 9 (1991): 209–32.

7. Thomas B. Farrell, *Norms of Rhetorical Culture* (New Haven: Yale University Press, 1993), 118.

8. Ibid., 119.

9. Ibid., 137.

10. Gerard A. Hauser, "Aristotle on Epideictic: The Formation of Public Morality," *Rhetoric Society Quarterly* 29 (1999): 5.

11. Ibid., 6.

12. Ibid., 14, 15.

13. N. Loraux, *The Invention of Athens: Funeral Orations in the Classical City,* trans. Alan Sheridan (Cambridge, MA: Harvard University Press, 1986), 1–2.

14. See ibid., 19; Donovan Ochs, *Consolatory Rhetoric: Grief, Symbol and Ritual in the Greco-Roman Era* (Columbia: University of South Carolina Press, 1993), xi, 1.

15. Campbell and Jamieson, *Deeds Done in Words,* 191.

16. E. J. Hughes, *The Living Presidency* (New York: Penguin, 1972), 26.

17. Walter Fisher, "Romantic Democracy, Ronald Reagan, and Presidential Heroes," *Western Journal of Speech Communication* 46 (1982): 299–310.

18. *Weekly Compilation of Presidential Documents* (Washington, DC: GPO, 1989), 53.

19. Ibid.

20. W. F. Lewis, "Telling America's Story: Narrative Form and the Reagan Presidency," *Quarterly Journal of Speech* 73 (1987): 280–302.

21. *Weekly Compilation,* 54.

22. Ibid.

23. *Weekly Compilation,* 55.

24. Ibid., 56.

25. Ibid., 56–57.

26. Ibid., 57, emphasis added.

27. Ibid., 71, 72.

28. Davis W. Houck and Amos Kiewe, eds., *Actor, Ideologue, Politician: The Public Speeches of Ronald Reagan* (Westport, CT: Greenwood Press, 1993), 330.

29. Ibid.

30. Houck and Kiewe, *Actor, Ideologue, Politician,* 331.

31. See Lewis, "Telling America's Story."

32. Houck and Kiewe, *Actor, Ideologue, Politician,* 332.

33. Ibid.

34. Ibid.

35. Houck and Kiewe, *Actor, Ideologue, Politician,* 333.

36. Kurt W. Ritter, "Ronald Reagan and 'The Speech': The Rhetoric of Public Relations Politics," *Western Speech* 32 (1968): 50–58.

37. Houck and Kiewe, *Actor, Ideologue, Politician,* 333.

38. Ibid., 334.

39. Ibid.

40. Houck and Kiewe, *Actor, Ideologue, Politician,* 335.

41. Ibid.

42. Ibid.

43. Ronald Reagan, "Alzheimer's Letter," *New York Times,* November 1, 1994.

44. Carter, "The Ritual Functions of Epideictic Rhetoric," 223.

45. Ibid., 221.

46. Gary Wills contends that "America as second Athens" was an idea that became prominent in the mid-nineteenth century. See his *Lincoln at Gettysburg: The Words That Remade America* (New York: Simon and Schuster, 1992).

47. Ochs, *Consolatory Rhetoric,* 1.

48. Wills, *Lincoln at Gettysburg,* 56–57.

49. Houck and Kiewe, *Actor, Ideologue, Politician,* 331.

50. Ochs, *Consolatory Rhetoric,* 109.

51. Houck and Kiewe, *Actor, Ideologue, Politician,* 335.

Contributors

Barbara Biesecker (Ph.D., University of Pittsburgh) is associate professor of communication studies at the University of Iowa and author of *Addressing Postmodernity: Kenneth Burke, Rhetoric, and a Theory of Social Change* (University of Alabama Press). Her work has also appeared in *Philosophy and Rhetoric* and the *Quarterly Journal of Speech*.

Stephen Howard Browne (Ph.D., University of Wisconsin) is professor of speech communication at Pennsylvania State University and the author of *Angelina Grimké: Rhetoric, Identity and the Radical Imagination* (Michigan State University Press), *Edmund Burke and the Discourse of Virtue* (University of Alabama Press), and coeditor of *Readings on the Rhetoric of Social Protest* (Strata). He is also editor of the journal *Philosophy and Rhetoric*.

Edward S. Casey (Ph.D., Northwestern University) is professor of philosophy at the State University of New York, Stony Brook. He is the author of *Remembering: A Phenomenological Study* (Indiana University Press), *Getting Back into Place* (Indiana University Press), and *The Fate of Place: A Philosophical History* (University of California Press).

Rosa A. Eberly (Ph.D., Pennsylvania State University) is associate professor in the departments of Communication Arts and Sciences and of English at Pennsylvania State University. She is the author of *Citizen Critics: Literary Public Spheres* (University of Illinois Press) and coauthor of *Elements of Reasoning* (Allyn and Bacon).

Horst-Alfred Heinrich (Ph.D. and Habilitation, Justus-Liebig University) is senior lecturer at Justus-Liebig-Universitaet, Giessen, Germany, and writes on fascism, the politics of memory, national identity, and collective stereotyping. His recent book, *Collective Memories of the Germans,* is based on survey data testing the relationship between remembrances on the micro and macro levels among different German subgroups.

Amos Kiewe (Ph.D., Ohio University) is chair and associate professor of speech communication at Syracuse University. He is the coauthor of *A Shining City on a Hill* (Praeger), coeditor of *Actor, Ideologue, Politician: The Public Speeches of Ronald Reagan* (Greenwood), and editor of *The Modern Presidency and Crisis Rhetoric* (Praeger).

Charles E. Morris III (Ph.D., Pennsylvania State University) is assistant professor of communication studies at Vanderbilt University. His work has been published in *Quarterly Journal of Speech* and *Women's Studies in Communication,* and he is the coeditor of *Readings on the Rhetoric of Social Protest* (Strata).

Kendall R. Phillips (Ph.D., Pennsylvania State University) is associate professor of speech communication at Syracuse University. His previous publications include *Testing Controversy: A Rhetoric of Educational Reform* (Hampton Press) and essays in such journals as *Philosophy and Rhetoric, Literature / Film Quarterly,* and *Communication Monographs.*

Barry Schwartz (Ph.D., University of Pennsylvania) is professor of sociology at the University of Georgia. His recent work on collective memory includes *Abraham Lincoln and the Forge of National Memory* (University of Chicago Press). He is working on a second volume about Lincoln, tracing his place in American memory from 1930 to the present. His research on American and German judgments of the past is part of a broader series of studies involving Korea, Japan, China, and Israel.

Charles E. Scott (Ph.D., Yale University) is Edwin Erle Sparks Professor of Philosophy at Pennsylvania State University and the author of *The Time of Memory* (SUNY Press), *On the Advantages and Disadvantages of Ethics and*

Politics (Indiana University Press), and *The Question of Ethics: Nietzsche, Heidegger, Foucault* (Indiana University Press).

Bradford Vivian (Ph.D., Pennsylvania State University) is assistant professor of communication studies at Vanderbilt University. His work has appeared in *Philosophy and Rhetoric* and *Western Journal of Communication*.

Barbie Zelizer (Ph.D., University of Pennsylvania) is Raymond Williams Term Chair and associate professor of communications at the Annenberg School of Communications, University of Pennsylvania, and the author of *Covering the Body: The Kennedy Assassination, the Media, and the Shaping of Collective Memory* (University of Chicago Press) and *Remembering to Forget: Holocaust Memory through the Camera's Eye* (University of Chicago Press). She also edited *Visual Culture and the Holocaust* (Rutgers University Press).